THE FLAME REKINDLED-NEW HOPES FOR INTERNATIONAL ARBITRATION

This is the commercial edition of the Special Issue
of the Leiden Journal of International Law 1993.

Leiden Journal of International Law

The Flame Rekindled

New Hopes for International Arbitration

Edited by

Sam Muller (editor in chief)
Wim Mijs

MARTINUS NIJHOFF PUBLISHERS
DORDRECHT / BOSTON / LONDON

Library of Congress Cataloging-in-Publication Data

The Flame rekindled : new hopes for international arbitration / edited
  by Sam Muller, Wim Mijs.
       p.   cm.
   Special issue of the Leiden journal of international law.
   Includes index.
   ISBN 0-7923-2659-8 (hb : acid-free paper)
   1. Arbitration and award, International. 2. International courts.
I. Muller, Sam (A. Sam), 1964-   . II. Mijs, Wim. III. Leiden
journal of international law. Special number.
K2400.F57   1994
341.5'22--dc20   93-44432

ISBN 0-7923-2659-8

Published by Martinus Nijhoff Publishers,
P.O. Box 163, 3300 AD Dordrecht, The Netherlands.

Sold and distributed in the U.S.A. and Canada
by Kluwer Academic Publishers,
101 Philip Drive, Norwell, MA 02061, U.S.A.

In all other countries, sold and distributed
by Kluwer Academic Publishers Group,
P.O. Box 322, 3300 AH Dordrecht, The Netherlands.

Printed on acid-free paper

Printed in the Netherlands

Table of Contents

IN MEMORIAM MANFRED LACHS

When Manfred Lachs died I lost more than a friend.

Vividly I remember the day -now nearly twenty years ago- he stepped into my room at the Foreign Office. He was announced as "His Excellency Judge Lachs, President of the International Court of Justice". According to the strict rules of protocol I think he should not have come to me but instead have asked me to come to his office, he being the President of the highest judicial organ of the international community, me a mere State Secretary of one of the member-states, be it the host-state. But if a problem was bothering him, he was willing to go to the ends of the earth to solve it and at that time something was seriously bothering him.

The World Court was considering the possibility of moving out of The Hague as a number of its members were dissatisfied with the conditions under which they had to carry out their function; relations between the Court and the host-Government had been strained for some years and the possible transfer of the Court's seat had been placed on the agenda of the General Assembly. Those who know Manfred Lachs also know that strained relations were not much to his liking. But -and that is even more important- he was of the opinion that moving the Court from its long-established base would ultimately damage the Court. It should not be forgotten that the Court had barely recovered from the profound loss of esteem it had suffered as the result of its decision in the *South West Africa case* of July 18, 1966. This esteem had been regained to a certain extent by the famous *obiter dictum* in the *Barcelona Traction case* on obligations *erga omnes* and by the advisory opinion on *Namibia* but, nevertheless, the Court's reputation was still vulnerable. Moving the Court away from The Hague could entail various risks for the Court, which he all discussed with me. If there was one thing which mattered in this world for Manfred Lachs, professionally speaking, it was the Court and at that moment he was President of that Court and that gave an extra dimension to his concern.

Together with the then foreign Minister we were able to solve all problems and the Court stayed at The Hague. But as the present Minister of Foreign Affairs of the Netherlands, I wish to say that it is to a great extent due to Manfred Lachs that these problems could be solved and that the item of the seat of the World Court could be removed from the General Assembly's agenda. His straightforwardness, his openness, his integrity and his fairness were of great help. Although he loved The Hague and the Netherlands, it was not his love for this country but his deep love for the Court which prompted him to try to keep the Court in The Hague.

This common experience made us friends. But Judge Lachs came to see me more often than was necessary for consultations on the issue of the Court's seat in those days. There was another problem which troubled him deeply and again it was love for the Court which moved him. The *Nuclear Tests cases* were pending before the Court; by applying the law strictly and basing itself faithfully on the closed categories of formal sources of law, the Court could easily -and from a legal point of view not incorrectly- have come to the conclusion that there was no legal impediment for France to continue to carry out its nuclear atmospheric tests. But maybe more than anybody else, Manfred Lachs was aware of the devastating effects such a decision could have for the reputation of the Court, as the General Assembly had pleaded in numerous resolutions for a discontinuance of such tests. Esteem for the Court in the international community could plummet to a new low. He realised that a repetition of 1966 could be fatal for the Court and as the Court's President he hoped to avoid such an outcome. So he looked for other venues but he wanted to try them out first. He needed a sounding board and because of the friendship which had grown between us, I happened to be that sounding board. During numerous get-to-gethers, luncheons etc. he argued and asked for my reactions and, although I never was sure which outcome he really wanted, during these conversations my admiration and respect grew; I had not only found a friend, but -even more important- a tutor, a guru. During these conversations I looked with new eyes at law as a social phenomenon. I learned to understand the function of law not only as a conservating element but also as a vehicle for change.

The final decision of the Court has been severely criticized; nevertheless I think that Mc Whinney is right when he says that it was historically correct and necessary. And, in a tribute for Manfred Lachs, he adds:

> The Judgment is recognisably from Judge Lachs' pen and stands as an exercise in judicial pragmatism by a Court President trying carefully to build a majority among judges, who were then even more cautious then today, as to venturing on the avant-garde in doctrinal-legal terms (into law making through jurisprudence).

During these conversations I learned to recognize judicial wisdom. Years later I gave a course on judicial wisdom and legal reasoning in international adjudication for the Hague Academy. Then I said:

> Legal reasoning unaccompanied by judicial wisdom may lead to a decision that is legally correct but in actual life is an application of the maxim "let justice be done though the sky falls". Judicial wisdom without accurate and sound legal reasoning is judicial folly, for it will impair the confidence in the legal system and in the judicial system as such. Judicial wisdom, therefore, is nothing more or less than making the socially correct choice between various applications of legal rules on a concrete case.

After the first lecture a student came to me and asked me whether I could give a definition of judicial wisdom. Judge Lachs was standing in a corner of the room, talking, as usual, with students as he liked to do. I told the student that I could not give him a definition, that I hoped that he would be able to recognize judicial wisdom after the last lecture but that I could show him its personification and I pointed to Judge Lachs.

Because that is how I will remember him most; as the personification of judicial wisdom, permanently driven by his love for the Court, his love for justice and, therefore mostly striking the right balance; a legal scholar through and through but at the same time aware of the demands and the needs of society. "More perhaps than any other Member of the Court", Mc Whinney says,

> Judge Lachs is seen as personifying the new judicial thinking, with its renouncing of the 'dead-hand control' of old doctrines and old jurisprudence developed in other, earlier times, in favour of rational contemporary solutions to contemporary problems of the world community.

We are used to think of world leaders in terms of politicians and the high and the mighty. Manfred Lachs was a world leader in his own right. When he died we lost more than a friend.

Prof. P.H. Kooijmans[*]

[*] Minister for Foreign Affairs of The Netherlands

PREFACE

Nearly three decades ago, in 1964, I directed a seminar entitled 'Comparative Study of Existing International Tribunals and their Competence' at the Centre for Studies and Research of the Hague Academy of International Law. One of the main themes which animated discussions at the seminar was international arbitration. Some of the papers delivered there were later published in a book entitled *The Prospects of International Arbitration* to which I contributed the Preface.[1] This is an indication of my continuing interest in the subject. I am therefore delighted to provide an introduction to a publication dealing with this subject.

The choice of international arbitration as the focus of discussion on this second issue of the Journal, devoted to reflections on international dispute settlement, provides a timely opportunity for an in-depth analysis and assessment of the various issues relating to the specific peaceful means of settlement of disputes between states, mentioned in Article 33, Paragraph 1 of the Charter of the United Nations. The choice further demonstrates the commendable efforts of the *Leiden Journal of International Law* to continue making concrete contributions towards the achievement of some of the aims of the United Nations Decade of International Law (1989-1999), proclaimed in General Assembly Resolution 44/23 of November 17, 1989.

It may be recalled, in this connection, that among the aims of the Decade, as described in the said resolution, is the promotion of the means and methods for the peaceful settlement of disputes between states. The programme of activities which was subsequently adopted by the General Assembly for the first term of the decade thus called upon, *inter alia*, national associations and institutions such as the *Leiden Journal*, to make suggestions towards the fulfilment of this objective, which specifically called for the promotion of resort to and full respect for the International Court of Justice, as discussed in the first *Special Issue*.

In the present second *Special Issue*, the *Leiden Journal* turns its attention to another third-party compulsory procedure -the international arbitration- in its widest sense. It explores the roles of institutions such as the Permanent Court of Arbitration, and the prospects for pre-constituted, non-*ad hoc* arbitral institutions which may be considered in the general framework of peaceful settlement of disputes between states, as well as between states and other actors (commercial arbitration) in the present day international system, through the process of international adjudication.

The discussions on international arbitration in this volume will inevitably touch upon issues of the role of this institution in comparison especially with an international court such as the ICJ. In this connection, it is worth noting that, the 1899 and 1907 Hague Conventions for the Pacific Settlement of International Disputes described the object of international arbitration as the settlement of disputes between states by judges chosen by the parties themselves and on the basis of respect for law. The Hague Conventions further provided that recourse to the arbitral procedure implied submission in good faith to the award of the tribunal. Accordingly, one of the basic characteristics

---

1. See M.A. Chaudhri (ed.), The Prospects of International Arbitration (1966). *See also* my analysis of the work of the Center, The Hague Academy of International Law, *Jubilee Book, 1923-1973*, 139-157, at 151.

of international arbitration is that it is a procedure which results in binding decisions upon the parties to the dispute.

The power to render binding decisions is therefore a characteristic which arbitration shares with the method of judicial settlement by international courts, the judgments of which are not only binding but also, as in the case of the International Court of Justice, final and without appeal, as indicated in Article 60 of the Statute of the ICJ. For this reason, arbitration and judicial settlement are both usually referred to as compulsory means of settlement of disputes.

However, while both arbitration and judicial settlement are similar in that respect, the two methods of settlement are nevertheless structurally different from each other. Arbitration, in general, is constituted by mutual consent of the states parties to a specific dispute where such parties retain considerable control of the process through the power of appointing arbitrators of their own choice. By contrast, judicial settlement relies upon pre-constituted international courts or tribunals, the composition of which is not to the same extent subject to control by the parties to the dispute.

Apart from the 1899 and 1907 Hague Conventions, arbitration, as a means of peaceful settlement of disputes between states, is provided in a number of multilateral treaties of global or regional character and also in a number of bilateral treaties and has thus emerged as one of the third-party procedures most frequently chosen for the settling of a number of disputes.

The publication of this volume dealing with some of these issues, will thus, in a general sense, also contribute towards the promotion of the study, teaching, dissemination and wider appreciation of international law; and towards the acceptance of principles of international law; and towards its progressive development and codification, all of which are among the specific aims of the United Nations Decade of International Law.

Once again, I wish to congratulate the *Leiden Journal of International Law* for the commendable dedication to the task of promoting the Decade.

Dr. Boutros Boutros-Ghali[*]

[*] Secretary-General of the United Nations

ACKNOWLEDGEMENTS

Before you lies the *Special Issue on International Arbitration* of the *Leiden Journal of International Law* (LJIL) devoted to the Decade of International Law so solemnly proclaimed by the United Nations General Assembly in 1989. It is published at a time when LJIL is half a decade old. Within its five years of existence, this is the second time that LJIL has focused its attention on the Decade and contributed in a very practical way to the realization of its aims.

To begin with, we would like to thank the Secretary-General of the Bureau of the Permanent Court of Arbitration (PCA), Mr. P.J.H. Jonkman and Mr. G. Tanja of the Dutch Ministry of Foreign Affairs with whom we first discussed our ideas for the book, one and a half years ago. For us, their support at that time was crucial; as was their continuing support along the way.

To show our deep appreciation for the inspiring and enlightening meetings we subsequently had with the late Judge Manfred Lachs, we have dedicated this book to his memory.

We would also like to thank Mr. J. Jansen for helping us to tackle the bureaucracy. We are grateful to the Dutch Ministry of Foreign Affairs, the Bureau of the PCA and the *Legatum Visserianum Foundation* for their financial support.

In addition, we would like to thank our language editor, Steven Mirmina, and Mieke Jacobs, Ingrid de Caluwé and Corinne de Keuning for their unrelenting support.

Finally, we would like to reserve a word of special thanks to Roeland van Schaik, the copy editor of the LJIL. Without his enthusiasm and his hard work, we would never have made it to the presses. Although he joined our team near the end of the project, he is in many ways one of the editors of the work.

Leiden, June 1993

Sam Muller
Wim Mijs

INTRODUCTION BY THE SECRETARY-GENERAL OF THE PERMANENT COURT OF ARBITRATION

The founders of the Permanent Court of Arbitration (PCA) in 1899 had a vision: to create an institution, accessible at all times, competent to deal with all disputes between states which could not be resolved by diplomatic means. They were aware of the necessity to offer states a choice between settlement methods representing different degrees of third party involvement: fact finding, good offices, mediation and arbitration. Later, in 1937, conciliation was added to these methods. It was an ambitious undertaking. The PCA was the first global mechanism for the settlement of inter-state disputes.

The Court was responsible for most of the inter-state arbitrations and some important fact finding commissions during the first 15 years of its existence. After the First World War recourse to the PCA became less frequent. An effort to give fresh impetus to the Court in 1962 through authorizing the use of its facilities for the arbitration and conciliation of international disputes between two parties of which only one is a state -thus making it available for resolving commercial disputes- met with little success. Absence of awareness of the PCA's facilities and services, and failure to adapt the functioning of the PCA to the changing needs of states and of private companies were probably the reasons for the PCA's decline. New institutions appearing on the arbitration scene seemed more responsive to those needs, and became more popular.

During the nineteen-eighties interest in the PCA revived. The Iran-United States Claims Tribunal, probably the most important arbitral tribunal to date, was established with the cooperation of the Court's International Bureau. The first and fourth Presidents of the Tribunal were Members of the PCA. During the period 1980-1992 the Bureau placed its offices and staff at the disposal of some 17 tribunals, set up *ad hoc* or under the auspices of other arbitration institutions. The International Bureau assisted in providing premises and registry services for the *US/UK arbitration concerning Heathrow Airport user charges* (1989-1993).

The Arbitration Rules prepared by the United Nations Commission on International Trade Law (UNCITRAL) in 1976 contributed to the revival of interest in the PCA, as they entrusted to the Secretary-General of the PCA a function vital to the maintenance of the integrity of the arbitral process, that of 'appointing authority' in the circumstances specified in Articles 6-12 of the Rules. Pursuant to arbitration clauses prescribing application of these Rules, some 33 requests for the designation of an 'appointing authority' have been submitted to the Secretary-General, nine in the course of 1992 alone. Six similar requests were made to the Secretary-General pursuant to other arbitration clauses.

The PCA, however, remained far from realizing its founders' vision, and its potential as a dispute settlement mechanism. In May 1991 a Working Group of 22 international lawyers, chaired by Judge Manfred Lachs, was invited to analyse the causes of the relative indifference to the PCA displayed by states and international organisations, and to propose remedial measures. Inspired by the views expressed by the members of the Working Group -published in a booklet entitled *The Permanent Court of Arbitration - New Directions*- the International Bureau endeavoured by

1

S. Muller and W. Mijs (eds.), The Flame Rekindled, 1–3.
© 1994 *Leiden Journal of International Law. Printed in the Netherlands.*

various means to make the potential and the flexibility of the PCA dispute settlement system better known. The administrative Council (composed of the diplomatic representatives of the parties to the Conventions accredited in The Hague), finding that the procedural rules in the Hague Conventions had important *lacunae*, in October 1992 authorized the Secretary-General to establish a new set of procedural rules, to be known as the "Permanent Court of Arbitration Optional Rules for Arbitrating Disputes between Two States", taking into account the views of international experts on the subject. These Optional Rules have now been distributed to the states parties to the Hague Conventions. New rules for arbitrating disputes between two parties of which only one is a state will be issued separately, in order to replace the 1962 Arbitration Rules on that subject which were considered to be out of date. Meanwhile, The Netherlands, depositary of the Hague Conventions of 1899 and 1907 for the Pacific Settlement of International Disputes, have continued to encourage states that were not yet parties to these Conventions to accede to them.

The Administrative Council also authorized the Secretary-General of the Court to seek observer status for the PCA with the General Assembly of the United Nations, thus creating an institutional link between the two organisations. It is hoped by this means to increase awareness of the PCA's dispute settlement potential among the membership of the organisation, enabling the PCA system in due course to undertake a more active role in implementing Article 33 of the Charter of the United Nations and to supplement more effectively the functions of the International Court of Justice. The International Bureau, which has already made a contribution to the programme for the UN Decade of International Law, expects to continue its participation in the Decade's activities.

Remarking the end of the 'Cold War' that had subsisted between two powerful ideological blocs for 45 years, the first paragraph in the Annual Report of the PCA's Administrative Council for 1990 reads:

> Recent radical changes in relationships among states give rise to the hope that they may indeed be moving toward the establishment of a genuine world community wherein the aspirations of its individual members will take account of the interests of the community as a whole. Such a trend may be expected to presage new respect for the rule of law among nations. The last decade of this century seems to offer statesmen the opportunity to lay firm political and institutional foundations on which to build an international order for a new millennium of freedom and justice under law. International dispute settlement mechanisms to which parties could have recourse, with confidence, form an essential part of such an international order.

Regrettably, instead of the emergence of a stable legal order, the world has seen the eruption in violence of problems which until recently had been smouldering under the surface of superpower-control. The world community and regional organisations remained hesitant to intervene and to impose solutions they considered just, because of the complexity of the problems and the substantial risks that would attend such action. Peaceful settlement mechanisms such as those offered by the PCA could have been utilised, but the political will to do so was often lacking.

Although these circumstances appear daunting, institutions concerned with the peaceful settlement of disputes should ensure that the functioning of the mechanisms they administer remains optimal, against the time when their application may be sought. This could happen at any time, since the yearning for an end to violence must eventually prevail, and the efficacy of methods of peaceful settlement be recognised. In this spirit, it is the intention of the Administrative Council and the International Bureau of the PCA to maintain and, where necessary refine, its several methods for dispute settlement enabling states and other parties, should they wish to do so, to choose the method best suited for a particular type of dispute.

The strength of the PCA settlement system lies in the fact that it can serve as a valuable complement to judicial settlement by the International Court of Justice, as the principal judicial organ of the United Nations, for resolving certain types of inter-state disputes. These could include disputes that contain complex political elements; disputes comprised of a considerable number of claims (such as those before the Iran United States Claims Tribunal); and disputes that involve essentially questions of a highly technical nature (such as the *US/UK Tribunal concerning Heathrow Airport User Charges*). Its facilities can also be resorted to for resolving certain disputes which might fall outside the jurisdiction of the International Court of Justice, e.g., certain adversarial proceedings between states and international organisations, or between states and private companies.

Settlement services available under the PCA system include fact-finding, good offices, mediation and conciliation, as well as assistance in the selection of qualified candidates for the application of these mechanisms. If efforts to resolve a dispute by these means fail, the parties may agree to submit their case to a final and binding decision through arbitration. The PCA system would not be complete if such an option would imply that, once parties have chosen for an arbitral decision, the process would still be dependent on their readiness to cooperate in the procedure or to agree with the award. For this reason the new procedural rules referred to above provide -if parties agree to use them- a procedure that leaves as little room as possible for frustration of proceedings through non-cooperation by a party or by a member of a tribunal appointed by it.

The new rules are based on the conception that fact-finding, good offices, mediation and conciliation are essentially means of settlement, that allow parties to retain control of the process and its outcome, while arbitration is in principle a means of settling disputes whereby parties accept beforehand the decision of a third party (the arbitral tribunal) as final and binding.

The PCA aims at making settlement procedures more cost-effective and speedy. It is well equipped for the purpose, being an independent non profit institution, and maintaining only a small permanent staff. The Court's International Bureau is able to offer spacious and convenient facilities, as well as a range of services which could facilitate the settlement process, including in particular the Carnegie Library, a unique collection of works on international law. Upon request, the Bureau would provide advice and assistance in resolving difficulties that could arise in the course of proceedings.

Nearly a century has passed since the vision of its founders brought into existence the Permanent Court of Arbitration and the associated dispute settlement mechanisms. Today, some 250 Members of the Court, the Administrative Council and the International Bureau, faithful to that vision, are no less resolved "to use their best efforts to ensure the pacific settlement of international differences".

P.J.H. Jonkman, Secretary-General of the Permanent Court of Arbitration

THE FLAME REKINDLED

Sam Muller and Wim Mijs*

> [...] risks and conflicts of interest can be overcome by rules of conduct adequate to the challenges of life if a conscious effort is made to foresee and counter the problems likely to emerge.[1]

1. INTRODUCTION

It is clear to any regular reader of newspapers that we have not yet succeeded -as was so solemnly declared in the preamble of the UN Charter- in saving "succeeding generations from the scourge of war" or establishing "conditions under which justice and respect for the obligations arising from treaties and other sources of international law can be maintained".[2]

With regard to the settlement of international disputes as a way to achieve these goals, two thoughts come to mind. Either it has not yet been possible to develop a foolproof system to settle international disputes peacefully and correctly. Or, we are in the possession of a good system but are not able to utilize it properly. With such fundamental issues in mind, it is not surprising that the UN General Assembly has proclaimed a Decade of International Law, with the promotion and development of the peaceful settlement of disputes as one of its principal aims.[3] It is the second time that the *Leiden Journal of International Law* has devoted special attention to this important proclamation.[4] This time, its contribution to the Decade will not be directed

---

* Sam Muller is research fellow at the Department of Public International Law of Leiden University. Wim Mijs is legal officer at the legal service of the ABNAMRO Bank in The Netherlands. Both have studied public international law in Leiden.

1. Manfred Lachs, *Thoughts on Science, Technology and World Law*, 86 AJIL 689 (1992).
2. Paragraph 1 and 3 of the preamble of the Charter of the United Nations.
3. General Assembly Resolution 44/23 of December 17, 1989.
4. *See* 3 LJIL (1990).

S. Muller and W. Mijs (eds.), The Flame Rekindled, 5–16.
© 1994 *Leiden Journal of International Law. Printed in the Netherlands.*

at international dispute settlement in general, but at a more specific mode: international arbitration. The specific choice of subject was inspired by the recent initiatives of the Secretary-General of the International Bureau of the Permanent Court of Arbitration (PCA), to revive the "sleeping beauty of the Peace Palace", as Professor Sanders has so eloquently called it.

2.   MOVING FROM 1899 TO 1993

In his book *The Peace Palace*, Arthur Eyffinger[5] captures the atmosphere of the first day of the Hague Peace Conference brilliantly:

> The opening of the International Peace Conference on 18 May 1899 was welcomed by a perfect spring day; The Hague presented a stirring and picturesque spectacle. The flags of many nations were flying in the wind from public buildings, hotels and embassies and from many private houses. At 10 a.m. the members of the Russian delegation, in full uniform and with a splendid escort, attended mass in the tiny Orthodox Chapel near Scheveningen to pray in honour of the Czar's birthday. Interestingly enough, this chapel was situated on the very spot where, eight years afterwards, the founding stone of the Peace Palace was to be laid.
>
> The opening ceremony of the Conference was set for 2 p.m. From noon onwards, shining varnished open carriages drawn by four in hands could be seen traversing the two miles from the city centre. They passed by the drillfield of the Malieveld, then through the woods, skirting the ponds, up to the simple, but striking beauty of the tiny summer palace. The brilliant caparisons of the horses and the colourful ceremonial dress of the delegates were a sight to see in the beaming sun.

It was in this atmosphere that delegates from many nations met to try and halt the arms race and it was this conference that almost accidentally conceived the Permanent Court of Arbitration (PCA). Of course the idea did not come out of the blue, but the issue of arbitration was included as an additional point on the agenda. In retrospect, it can be said that the Convention for the Peaceful Settlement of International Disputes was the greatest achievement of the first Peace Conference in the Hague.

Interest for means of peacefully settling disputes between states, and more in particular arbitration, was on the rise during the nineteenth century. In most cases resort to arbitration depended on an *ad hoc* agreement; the tribunal to which the dispute was referred was created *per* dispute and it ceased to function after the case had been settled. It was only after the middle of the century that parties began to agree in advance -that is, before the emmergence of an actual dispute- to resort to arbitration. Bipartite arbitration treaties were very rare before 1850. After the turn of the century there were an increasing number of multilateral conventions in which

---

5. Arthur Eyffinger, The Peace Palace (1988).

provisions for arbitration were included. At the end of the nineteenth century the time seemed to be ripe for the creation of a permanent agency for inter-state arbitration. The Convention for the Peaceful Settlement of International Disputes created this institution: the Permanent Court of Arbitration, although, as one of the delegates to the second Hague Peace Conference jokingly remarked, it was neither a court, nor permanent. A Bureau, headed by a Secretary-General was the permanent component of the organization. The other element -the 'Court'- was but a list of individuals from which the parties in dispute could choose their arbitrators.

In the period before the outbreak of the war in 1914, the Court had its most notable moments of glory. The convention which created it was revised in 1907 and the 15 cases conducted up to that time were brought to a satisfying end for all the parties involved. The moral authority of the PCA rose and it was clear from the number of bilateral arbitration *compromis* concluded that arbitration was now firmly rooted in the minds of the leading politicians.

With the outbreak of the First World War much of the international political system collapsed and this cast a shadow over the Court as well; no cases were referred to it. In the interbellum new optimism led to the foundation of the League of Nations and to a new lettee in the Peace Palace: the Permanent Court of International Justice (PCIJ). The international community now had recourse to two mechanisms to settle their differences. Nevertheless, the installation of the famous roommate did not help the PCA, and little or no use was made of its facilities. The number of cases which were referred to it went down to almost zero. Perhaps part of this can be explained by the fact that, with the creation of the PCIJ, the world finally had what idealistic minds had always craved for: a real world court. At that time, the more flexible and *ad hoc* mode of dispute settlement 'arbitration' was generally seen as the best viable way to settle disputes states could agree upon; judicial settlement of disputes, however, was the dream. For the PCA it was clear that new fields had to be found in which the Court could play its part. As early as the 1930s, the Administrative Council of the PCA discussed the option to create a facility for arbitration between state and non-state entities. Although work started on the exploration of this new field, war broke out again in Europe and it was only in 1962 that optional rules for these kinds of disputes became available.[6]

The Second World War shook the world thoroughly. The turmoil proved to be a rich breeding ground from which new institutions grew. The United Nations were founded and the PCA found itself with a new neighbour: the International Court of Justice. Sadly the PCA was unable to play an important role within the framework of the United Nations and the state of affairs generally stayed the same as before the Second World War.

6. These rules did not have the succesful effect they were hoped to have. One of the reasons for this is that they came too late. By the early sixties there were already a number of other institutions operating in this field.

It is said that a Secretary-General after the Second World War told his colleges that the Permanent Court was a majestic, traditional institution and that it could not be expected to take part in a fight for 'market share', the way an enterprise or another entity would. Although the Permanent Court of Arbitration is indeed a traditional institution, it is strongly felt by many that this lack of 'market orientation' is one of the factors that led to the lack of referral of cases to the Court after 1945; a time when new opportunities arose in the international community.

In the 1980s a new interest in arbitration became apparent. The first sign of such a changing atmosfere, was the succes of the continuing Iran-United States Claims Tribunal. This institution was set up under the special PCA facility for so-called special tribunals under Article 47 of the Convention for the Peaceful Settlement of Disputes of 1907. In this set-up the International Bureau of the PCA and its offices are placed at the disposal of the contracting powers. It was this service that was rendered to the Claims Tribunal when it began its work in 1981. All parties involved were very satisfied with the services before the Tribunal moved to its own premises in 1983. It is believed that there is an important role to be played by the PCA in disputes between states and non-state entities. At this moment the rules of 1962 are being revised and a prominent place in this work has been reserved for the work of the Expert Group on the Revision of Some Aspects of the Permanent Court of Arbitration.[7]

In 1991, the Secretary-General of the PCA called together an Expert Group to seek new directions for the PCA. Its recommendations are published in this work. Finally, attention should be drawn to the interesting French-German Proposal for a European Court for arbitration and conciliation within the framework of the CSCE. The swift development of this proposal, which originated from Robert Badinter in the spring of 1991, proves that there is a new market for arbitration. Within the CSCE it was felt that many of the foreseeable disputes in Europe[8] would go beyond the possibilities of the existing 'Valetta Mechanism' and that a new body was necessary. As we are writing, the new convention (also known as the Stockholm Convention) has been signed by almost all of the participants of the CSCE and the financial protocol is in its final draft. When examining the Stockholm Convention some similarities with the PCA are noted. The Court is to establish a bureau that keeps two lists: one of possible conciliators and one of possible arbitrators. The system of the lists is striking, because the PCA's experience with its list are not altogether succesful. Many of the contracting parties regard the lists as an unnecessary restriction. In addition to this, it has been voiced that the lists do not always provide a sufficient guarantee for the quality of the arbitrators. This is a result of the different methods in appointing arbitrators, used by the contracting parties. Hopefully the new

7. *See* the contribution by Jeff Bleich in this *Special Issue*, 17.
8. One only has to think of minority-, economic-, commercial- and environmental issues.

court will not face these same problems and hopefully the lists will be seen as a helpful instrument, rather than a burden. Another factor that has to be noted is that the PCA runs an extremely cost-efficient organisation. Looking at the financial estimations for the CSCE Court, it is estimated that the annual cost of the new court will be at least four times higher that that of the present PCA. One of the arguments Robert Badinter used to discharge the PCA in his initial proposal, was that it lacked a backing body. In view of the similarities with the proposed court it could be interesting for the CSCE to examine a possible cooperation with the PCA. Though the work on the new European Court for Arbitration and Conciliation is, without a doubt, of great importance, it would absolutely be of value to learn from the PCA's experiences and to avoid the 'reinvention of the wheel'.

It is apparent from the above, that as the world approaches the magic date of 1999, there is a lot of movement going on in the field of arbitration, albeit not directly in the PCA. After two centuries of inter-state arbitration (since the Jay treaty, 1794) and one century of presence of the PCA, it is clear that arbitration is still a valuable mechanism to settle international disputes. It would be exciting to be around in 2099 and to describe the delegations to a possible Hague Peace Conference of 1999 in the same colourful way that Arthur Eyffinger described the one of 1899. Certainly arbitration should have a prominent place on the agenda of this conference.

3.   INTERNATIONAL ARBITRATION IN A CONTEXT

Moving from 1899 to now, the setting of arbitration as a way of settling international disputes has changed. To begin with, international arbitration has been institutionalized considerably. In addition to this, arbitration has gradually been encapsulated in an international system of dispute settlement.

Article 33 of the UN Charter is an elaborate codification of ways in which international disputes can be solved,[9] and has a number of specific features. To begin with, it was designed for disputes between states only. In the second place, this provision was drafted in accordance with the axiom "free choice for the parties". It is up to the parties to choose the means best suited for their particular dispute, leaving the parties "*la possibilité d'adaptation des procédés de règlement aux particularités de chaque litige*".[10]

Although the listing of Article 33 may give a different impression, the distinction

---

9. With the weight of the universal UN organization behind it, this article sums up the following methods states should resort to: "[...] negotiation, enquiry, mediation, conciliation, arbitration, judicial settlement, resort to regional agencies or arrangements, or other peaceful means of their [the parties] own choice". It is interesting to note that Article 12 and 13 of the Covenant of the League of Nations only mentioned arbitration, diplomatic negotiations and recourse to the Council of the League of Nations.
10. J.P. Quéneudec, *Règlement Pacifique des Differends*, *in* J.P. Cot, A. Pellet (ed.), *La Chartre des Nations Unies* 570 (1985).

between the modes of settlement is not always a clear one. Two parties may start by attempting to settle their dispute by negotiation but may find themselves slowly drifting off into conciliation through the good offices of a third party.[11] This in turn may result into an agreement to arbitrate in an *ad hoc* manner, or in an institutionalized form. It may lead to requesting the International Court of Justice to form a chamber to deal with the case. By then a mechanism containing elements of both arbitration and litigation will be in use.[12]

Efforts to tackle the conflict in and around the former Yugoslavia involve intergovernmental negotiations, good offices, mediation by the European Community and the United Nations, conciliation, a possible *ad hoc* arbitration over the question of the name of Macedonia, and a more institutionalized form of arbitration within the context of the CSCE. For one particular aspect of the dispute -human rights- a fact finding commission to investigate war crimes has been established,[13] which, in turn was followed up by a decision to start work on the establishment of an international war crimes tribunal.[14] In addition to this, the Secretary-General of the United Nations has propagated the use of so-called preventive diplomacy to prevent the dispute from spreading to other areas.

Thus we see that arbitration, as laid down in Article 33, features as only *one* of many ways of solving a dispute. It can no longer be seen as it was regarded by some at the beginning of this century: a more or less isolated conflict resolution mechanism second best to the dream of judicial settlement.[15]

International arbitration not only features within the UN Charter mechanism for dispute settlement. Because of its large measure of party autonomy, its flexibility and its detachment from national legal orders, arbitration has also grown to be the most widely used dispute resolver in international commercial relations.[16] Most of the disputes involved here are however fundamentally different from many inter-states disputes: in commercial relations, rapid solution of a dispute is desirable. In political

11. Good offices is not mentioned seperately in Article 33. It is however added to the listing of Article 33 in the Declaration of Manilla (U.N. Doc. A/Res/37/10).

12. On the issue of the difference between arbitration and adjudication, *see* S. Rosenne, *Reflections on International Arbitration and Litigation in the International Court of Justice*, 9 Forum Internationale 1-21 (1987); S. Schwebel, *Chambers of the International Court of Justice Formed for Particular Cases,in* International Law at a Time of Perplexity - Essays in Honour of Shabtai Rosenne 739-770; E. Lauterpacht, Aspects of the Administration of International Justice 85-98 (1991) and the dissenting opinion of Judges Shahabuddeen and Tarassov in the El Salvador/Hunduras case, 1990 I.C.J. Rep. 3, at 92.

13. The Commission of Experts established pursuant to Security Council Resolution 780(1992), also known under the name of its president, as 'the Kalshoven Commission'.

14. *See* Security Council Resolution 808 of February 22, 1993.

15. *See* for a description of the role of the PCA in its first decade of existence: Manley O. Hudson, *The Permanent Court of Arbitration*, 27 AJIL 440-460 (1933). *See also* Pinto's contribution to this *Special Issue, 43.*

16. *See* A. Redfern & M. Hunter, Law and Practice of International Arbitration 22 *et seq.* (1991).

relations, this is not always the case.

If a Third Peace Conference were to be held in The Hague in 1999, it is unlikely that the delegates would spend as much time as they did in 1899 and 1907 on attempting to define the exact nature of arbitration. Essentially, they would most likely agree that arbitration as it functions today, is what the parties want it to be. Considerable party autonomy distinguishes it from judicial dispute settlement and the binding character of the arbitral award differentiates it from conciliation and mediation. Within these two extremes, the parties can mould it into anything they require to suit their needs. They can opt for the more rigid formula's of the 1899 and 1907 Conventions and the ILC Draft of 1958,[17] use the widely acclaimed UNCITRAL Arbitration Rules, or set up their own more flexible rules. They can use existing institutional structures for arbitration, such as the International Chamber of Commerce (ICC), the American Arbitration Association (AAA) and the International Centre for the Settlement of Investment Disputes (ICSID), or they can set up their own. They can combine arbitration with other methods of conflict resolution such as enquiry, conciliation and mediation. This applies to all variety of parties mentioned in the previous paragraph: states, international organizations, private parties and any combination of these.

Thus, on the face of it international arbitration *as such* is no longer an issue. It has become a widely utilized way of dispute settlement, taking on many forms. Dispute settlement is however an issue, and, if seen in that wider context, international arbitration -as one of the ways of solving international disputes- is as well. In their respective contributions to this study, Judge Lachs, Asante, Brus and Pinto stress that in finding remedies for legal imperfections, one must go beyond merely studying existing rules and procedures -in this case arbitral rules and procedures- and endeavour to locate the reality or part of the reality at which the rules and procedures are directed. This is always a tedious undertaking, which requires looking behind closed doors, reading between lines and listening to what is not said.

4.   THE DISPUTES OF TODAY

What international, cross-border disputes do we see today? At the risk of being labelled pretentious and without claiming to be exhaustive, an attempt will be made at an inventory. An overview of the kinds of conflicts in the international arena, however limitative, may provide an insight (again; however, limitative) into some of the requirements international dispute settlement should meet if it is to be effective.

For a lawyer working in the field of public international law, the most obvious disputes are those between states. This determination is however not precise enough,

---

17. 1958 Report of the ILC (tenth session), at 2-10 (U.N. Doc. A/3859).

because states have a wide range of subjects over which they may be in disagreement. A survey of the international media reveals *inter alia*, disputes over borders (both land and sea), the application of treaties, trade, human rights, terrorism, drug trafficking and environmental issues. Many conflicts are made up of combinations of these subjects, and each specific dispute carries with it its own political connotation having its influence on the interest of the parties to solve the dispute rapidly. Thus, the 1991-1992 Gulf War carried in it elements of border delimitation, human rights and (oil)trade. Each of these elements were clothed in a veil of immense political prestige. The Hungary-Slowenia dispute over the hydroelectric dam in the Danube involves border and environmental issues, although it is legally brought down to a conflict over the application of a treaty. A completely different situation is the conflict (currently being arbitrated) between the USA and the UK over user charges for Heathrow Airport. This is a mainly commercial dispute, largly devoid of political prestige and involving highly technical matters.

There are also conflicts which involve a state and a non-state entity, such as an international organization, a multinational corporation or an individual. These disputes mostly concern trade and economic issues and/or the application of a treaty or a private law contract. The United Nations differed with its host country in the interpretation of the UN-US headquarters agreement.[18] With its continuing growth of competencies, it is not implausible that the European Community could one day be held internationally accountable before an international forum for acts committed *vis à vis* a third, non EC State.[19] A state and a multinational corporation or other commercial company could differ in their understanding of the terms of a private law contract. States can also be involved in a dispute with an individual or a group of individuals within its territory. Most of these conflicts would deal with the application of internationally recognized human rights standards in their widest sense, but they could also concern commercial matters. More often than not political factors are contained in these disputes.

Finally, we see cross-border disputes between two non-state entities: intergovernmental organizations, legal persons in private law and individuals. Most of these conflicts centre around commercial issues and are seldom of a political nature, although this is by no means always the case, for through their member states, intergovernmental organizations can become political tools. As already pointed out however, the adagium "time is money" provides the parties with a direct interest to settle their differences swiftly.

This brief survey discloses that there is a wide variety of disputes or potential disputes, each with its own specific features, a finding which should be placed against

18. Ultimately resulting in the Advisory Opinion on the Applicability of the Obligation to Arbitrate under Section 21 of the United Nations Headquarters Agreement of June 26, 1947, 1988 I.C.J. Rep. 12.
19. Article 34 of the Statute of the International Court of Justice only grants states *ius standi* before the Court.

the background of the ever-increasing role of international law since World War II. The fundamental changes that the world has gone through in the last eight years do not suggest that the role of international law will diminish, on the contrary, there is reason enough to expect the process to increase.

Any mechanism created to settle international disputes must take this reality into account. From the pile of rubble containing all the different kinds of disputes -be they concerned with trade, human rights, environmental or a combination of these issues; be they entwined with high political stakes or very technical- such a mechanism must be able to make the right matches between the mode of dispute settlement and the situation at hand. It is with this in mind, that the work on this *Special Issue* started out.

5. THE CHOSEN APPROACH

"What new can you come up with in international arbitration?" was the provocative question Judge Lachs confronted us with when we presented him our ideas for a special issue on the subject. What followed was silence, the shredding of our initial plans, and subsequently this work.

A number of eminent experts in the field of international arbitration and international dispute settlement have been asked to contribute an essay -each from their own specific background- enquiring into the definition of international arbitration, the place of arbitration amongst the other modes of international dispute settlement and the possibilities for its application. The PCA, its newly revised rules, and the coming centenary of the 1899 Hague Peace Conference have served as general background. The emphasis has been on new ideas and what Judge Lachs called "creative thinking". Three scholars have been asked to complete the work by writing a conclusion, based on the various specific contributions.

Jeff Bleich examines the work of the Working Group and the subsequent Expert Group which were convened by the International Bureau of the Permanent Court of Arbitration to revaluate and improve the Court. Similar to the Working Group consisting of leading minds on international arbitration, *Bleich* reaches the conclusion that there is still a role for the PCA in the wide range of arbitral and non-arbitral dispute resolution mechanisms available today. This conclusion is however reached at a cost: the PCA must improve its working methods and expand its services drastically. He subsequently goes on to discuss these improvements by looking at the new optional rules for arbitration -based on the UNCITRAL Rules- with which the PCA hopes to make a comeback on the stage of international arbitration.

In his contribution, *Mr. M.C.W. Pinto* embarks upon the difficult task of defining the 'essence' of international arbitration. Rightly so, he contends that international arbitration must reflect the views of *all* states of the international community for it to be truly international. His thoughts on arbitration suggest a move towards more flexibility in international arbitration rules. He opposes views which result in casting international arbitration in what he calls the 'judicial mould'. For him, the essence of international arbitration is its voluntary and flexible nature.

Judge H.M. Holtzmann has provided ten concise reflections upon the nature of arbitration. His considerations are primarily aimed at various aspects of party autonomy as the most fundamental feature of this mode of conflict resolution and the convergence of arbitration law in the field of public international law and private law.

Professor E. McWhinney examines reasons for the decline of the use of the PCA, first from the perspective as a member of the national group for the selection of PCA arbitrators. In this connection he discusses the Courts' function in the election of judges for the International Court of Justice (ICJ). Subsequently, *McWhinney* looks at the relationship between the PCA and the ICJ, in particular the World Courts' chamber system, which blurs the traditional doctrinal distinction between arbitration and adjudication.

Dr. Shabtai Rosenne's contribution, entitled "The International Court of Justice and International Arbitration", also deals with the relationship between arbitration and adjudication. He establishes the constructive contribution that the jurisprudence of the ICJ has had on international arbitration, and pushes aside all assertions that arbitration and judicial dispute settlement are in competition with each other.

Judge Manfred Lachs, in what is probably one of his last publications, examines the concept of equity as it is used in international arbitration and the judicial settlement of international disputes. In doing so, he also dwells upon arbitration in relation to that other mode of dispute settlement in which he was so active: adjudication. He does not deem it useful to dwell for too long upon the differences between disputes suitable for arbitration and those which can be settled judicially. In his view, the will of the parties should be decisive here. *Lachs* lifts the subject of this study out of its limited context, and places it in a wider setting, encompassing dispute settlement in general. Equity, as he sees it, functions as a regulator of the laws which in their turn regulate international behaviour.

With Sub-Saharan African countries as a main point of reference, *Mr. S.K.B. Asante* poses similar questions as *Pinto*, albeit in another field. He calls for reforms in the substantive law applied in international commercial arbitration to fit the problems, needs and viewpoints of a particular group of states. According to *Asante*, the PCA may offer developing states a forum more open to their particular perspectives than many of the prevailing institutions.

Professor P. Sanders also looks into the specific advantages of the PCA over other arbitral institutions and dispute settlement mechanisms. He suggests that the PCA include a provision containing an explicit waiver of immunity of execution in the current drafts of the new Special Rules of the PCA for Arbitration between a State and Private Parties. Such a provision would make the services offered by the PCA unique. That this would be in full conformity with international law as it has developed recently, is illustrated by the contribution by *Mr. A. van Blankenstein*.

As already stated, the study is completed by three conclusions. They will not be discussed here for fear of appearing to want to "conclude upon a conclusion". A short remark however, on the choice of the authors. *Judge Stephen Schwebel*, the highly experienced arbitrator and Judge of the International Court of Justice, writes as practitioner of public international law. *Professor A.J. van den Berg*, also a highly experienced arbitrator and a practitioner of law, discusses from the viewpoint of a commercial arbitration lawyer. *Marcel Brus*, the co-author of the previous *Special Issue* of the *Leiden Journal of International Law* who is in the final phase of completing his PhD thesis on international dispute settlement, represents the academic perspective.

6.   AN OUTLOOK

Generally speaking, the authors conclude that there is a future for international arbitration as a way of solving international disputes and a role for the PCA. However, as *Brus* rightly points out, it is doubtful whether the isolated improvement and enhancement of one of the mechanisms codified in Article 33 of the UN Charter will greatly contribute to a decrease in the worlds' conflicts. In the words of Ramcharan:

> piece-meal approaches and strategies will no longer suffice and [...] we shall have to devise, in the future, broad and integrated strategies of management and of governance.[20]

Given this state of affairs, we firmly believe that a next step forward *would* be a Third (Hague) Peace conference, organised along more or less the same lines as the United Nations Conference on Environment and Development (UNCED) and the World Conference on Human Rights (to be held this summer in Vienna). Such a conference could consider the establishment of a UN Dispute Resolution Council, operating next to the Security Council. Ideally, its membership should be made up of independent, highly qualified international lawyers with sufficient political 'clout' behind them. This organ would not involve itself in the actual solving of disputes but would serve as a kind of hallway through which states and international organizations could pass on their way to the dispute resolution mechanism best suited for their particular case. The council could advise the parties on the method and forum most suited, leaving it up to the forum - be it the ICJ, the PCA, *ad hoc* arbitration, mediation, conciliation or a mixture of these- to pronounce itself on the actual dispute. Through a compromisory clause contained in the legal document establishing the council (or a special agreement), states and international organizations could bind themselves to bring

20. B.G. Ramcharan, The International Law and Practice of Early-Warning and Preventive Diplomacy: The Emerging Global Watch at 33 (1991).

their disputes before the council. The Security Council and the Secretary-General of the UN could function as the councils' antenna's, bringing to its attention, at the earliest possible stage, situations which could benefit from the mechanisms of Article 33 of the UN Charter. They could also provide the political backing the council would need in difficult situations.

This would perhaps be a more structural way of enhancing international arbitration, which takes the current, and the foreseeable state of the international community more into account.

A NEW DIRECTION FOR THE PCA: THE WORK OF THE EXPERT GROUP

J.L. BLEICH[*]

1. INTRODUCTION

Until recently, the Permanent Court of Arbitration has been an institution that one reads about, if at all, principally in the background sections of international law casebooks. This article suggests, and indeed this issue of the *Leiden Journal of International Law* confirms, that the level of scholarly attention to the Court is changing due to recent developments in the work of the PCA. The purpose of this article is to report and reflect on an emerging effort in the international community to restore the PCA to a prominent place in international arbitration. This article describes the impetus for this effort and the actions taken to re-establish the PCA, as well as the challenges that lie ahead in that effort.

Specifically, this article describes the work of two bodies of international arbitration experts assembled by the International Bureau of the PCA to re-evaluate the work of the Court. Section 2 describes the findings of the Working Group of the PCA, which was convened in May of 1991 as a 'think tank' to assist the PCA in improving its performance. That Group asked basic questions that had long gone unconsidered: Is the PCA still necessary in the post-War era? Why have parties generally refrained from presenting their claims to the PCA? And what changes must be made in the organization and operation of the PCA system for it to attract parties and effectively to serve their interests? In particular, Section 2 relates the Working Group's conclusion that the PCA, although a potentially valuable arbitral institution, has failed to fulfill its role in world affairs by not maintaining a sufficiently high profile, and by retaining out-dated or undesirable features. Section 2 concludes by recounting the Working Group's specific recommendations for expanding and adapting the PCA's range of services to meet the needs of parties seeking international arbitral assistance.

[*] B.A. Amherst College, 1983; M.P.P. Harvard University, 1986; J.D. University of California at Berkeley, 1989. Mr. Bleich served as a law clerk to the Chief Justice of the United States Supreme Court from 1990-91, and as a legal assistant at the Iran-United States Claims Tribunal from 1991-92. The opinions expressed in this article do not necessarily reflect the opinions of the International Bureau of the Permanent Court of Arbitration.

17

S. Muller and W. Mijs (eds.), The Flame Rekindled, 17–42.
© 1994 *Leiden Journal of International Law. Printed in the Netherlands.*

Section 3 summarizes the second phase of the PCA staff's (i.e., the International Bureau's) effort to improve the functioning of the PCA: the convening of an 'Expert Group' to help implement the recommendations of the Working Group. The Expert Group, which is composed of arbitration experts from 22 countries, serves as an advisory body. It met for the first time in February of 1992 to discuss the first of several proposed improvements in the PCA system. Because the work of the Expert Group is still in progress at the time of this writing, this part evaluates only its principal effort thus far: namely, to modernize the procedural rules of the PCA in disputes arising between states. This Section describes in detail the optional rules presently being promulgated by the Expert Group. In doing so, it attempts to describe both the advantages offered by these new rules and to serve as a resource to parties applying those rules in the future.

Section 4 attempts to place the work of the Working Group and Expert Group in perspective. It evaluates the function of the groups in assisting the work of the PCA, and makes some general observations about their effectiveness thus far. It concludes by identifying several challenges that remain for these bodies and for the PCA.

2.   THE WORKING GROUP

2.1   Background

The Permanent Court of Arbitration was responsible for most of the inter-state arbitrations in the beginning of the 20th Century,[1] yet it has been largely underutilized since 1932. For the past 60 years, the Court has played only a modest role in international dispute resolution: making its staff and facilities available for *ad hoc* arbitrations, or assisting in the establishment of other arbitral bodies.[2] Its role as the preeminent institution for resolving international disputes involving states has been steadily eclipsed by institutions such as the International Court of Justice (ICJ) (which resolves state-to-state claims), the International Chamber of Commerce (ICC), and the World Bank's International Centre for the Settlement of Investment Disputes (ICSID) (both of which handle, *inter alia,* disputes between states and private parties). Until recently, even the 76 member nations that formally participate in the activities and maintenance of the Court, appeared generally to have overlooked it as a resource for peaceful dispute settlement.[3]

---

1. *See* International Law 239 (1986); between 1910 and 1930, the PCA arbitrated 22 inter-state disputes, including the highly influential Island of Palmas Case, 2 U.N.R.I.A.A. 829 (1928).
2. International Bureau of the PCA, *Permanent Court of Arbitration: 91st Annual Report 1991* 13-17 (1992) [hereinafter *Annual Report*].
3. International Bureau of the Permanent Court of Arbitration, *The Permanent Court of Arbitration - New Directions* 21 (1992) [hereinafter *New Directions*].

In 1990, the staff of the PCA (the International Bureau), concerned by the general lack of recourse to the PCA's services, enlisted an outside group of consultants -the Working Group- to advise it on improving the performance of the PCA. The Working Group was convened in May 1991 to evaluate the effectiveness of the Court, and to suggest measures for improving the Court's functioning. The International Bureau intended for the Working Group to serve several functions. First, it hoped that the Working Group could help to identify the reason for the PCA's underutilization, based upon the members' own experiences with international arbitration. Second, the Working Group could serve as a 'think tank', to recommend ways to cure any perceived shortcomings in the PCA system. And third, the act of assembling international scholars and arbitration experts to think about the PCA, and discuss it as a forum for the arbitration of disputes, could in itself help reintroduce the PCA into the international community's consciousness.

To accomplish these purposes, the International Bureau invited individuals with experience in international arbitration, reputations for creativity in problem solving, and general influence in the international legal community. Judge Manfred Lachs of the International Court of Justice served as chairman of the group, which included 22 leading figures from 18 countries.[4]

2.2.   Findings of the Working Group

The Working Group reached three principal conclusions at its May 1991 meeting. First, the PCA could serve a valuable role in the world community by complementing existing services and by improving upon the quality of available services. Second, the principal reasons for lack of recourse to the PCA are a general lack of awareness of

4. The Working Group consisted of: Mr. Andres Aguilar Mawdsley, Judge of the ICJ (Venezuela); Mr. Koorosh-Hossein Ameli, Member of the Iran-United States Claims Tribunal (Iran); Mr. Carlos Arguello Gomez, Agent of Nicaragua to the International Court of Justice (Nicaragua); Mr. Mohammed Bedjaoui, Judge of the ICJ (Algeria); Mr. Borut Bohte, Ambassador of Yugoslavia to the Netherlands (Yugoslavia); Mr. Bengt Broms, Member of the Iran-United States Claims Tribunal (Finland); Mr. Achol Deng, Ambassador of the Sudan to the Netherlands (Sudan); Mr. C. Flinterman, Professor of International Law at the University of Limburg (Netherlands); Mr. V.K. Grover, Ambassador of India to the Netherlands (India); Mr. Gilbert Guillaume, Judge of the ICJ (France); Mr. W.A. Hamel, General Director of the Carnegie Foundation (Netherlands); Mr. Howard Holtzmann, Member of the Iran-United States Claims Tribunal (U.S.A.); Sir Robert Jennings, President of the ICJ (U.K.); Mr. Manfred Lachs, Judge of the ICJ (Poland); Mr. F.X. Njenga, Secretary-General of the Asian-African Legal Consultative Committee, New Delhi (India); Mr. S.A. Ordzhonikidze, Deputy Director of the International Law Dept., Ministry of Foreign Affairs, Moscow (C.I.S.); Mr. Christopher Pinto, Secretary-General of the Iran-United States Claims Tribunal (Sri Lanka); Mr. G.J. Tanja, Assistant Legal Adviser, Ministry of Foreign Affairs (Netherlands); Mr. Jorge Antonio Tapia-Valdes, Ambassador of Chile to the Netherlands (Chile); Mr. Nikolai Tarassov, Judge of the ICJ (C.I.S.); Mr. C.C.A. Voskuil, Director of the T.M.C. Asser Instituut (Netherlands); Mr. N. Wuhler, Deputy Secretary-General of the Iran-United States Claims Tribunal (Germany).

the PCA, and the perception among those who are aware of the PCA that its operations are out-dated, inflexible, or unresponsive to modern demands of states. Third, in order to reclaim its role as a principal institution in world affairs, the PCA must begin a systematic effort to modernize its procedures and to demonstrate to the international community its ability to respond flexibly to the concerns of potential parties.[5]

2.2.1. *Viability of the PCA*

Prior to the convening of the Working Group, there was serious debate within the International Bureau over whether the PCA's services were still needed. At the time that the PCA was created, there were no other comparable bodies for the resolution of international disputes, and thus the PCA served an indispensable role. In the years that followed, however, the Permanent Court of International Justice was established (and then succeeded by the ICJ) to resolve cases arising between states, and, as noted, other important institutions were created to arbitrate disputes between state and non-state parties.[6] The first question posed to the Working Group was whether, in the light of the existence of these other institutions capable of resolving commercial and non-commercial disputes among states and non-states parties, the PCA was still necessary.

There were two schools of thought on the value of the PCA at the Working Group meeting, but both schools agreed that the PCA was necessary. The first group concluded that, despite the existence of many other competent institutions for peaceful dispute settlement, significant gaps in arbitral resources remained. In particular, these experts noted that some potential parties were unable to obtain proper arbitral assistance because of limitations on the jurisdiction, procedures, or expertise of active institutions. Most state/non-state arbitral bodies have some restriction on their jurisdiction. For example, ICSID is competent only to hear disputes related to investment matters.

---

5. *New Directions, supra* note 3, at 8-17.
6. *See, e.g.,* International Centre for the Settlement of Investment Disputes (ICSID) (founded in 1965 to resolve disputes between states and nationals of other states arising in connection with investments between the national and the contracting state); the International Chamber of Commerce (ICC) (founded in 1923 to supervise commercial arbitrations, deals principally in claims between nationals of different states); the London Court of International Arbitration (LCIA) (founded in 1892, internationalized in 1985 to resolve disputes between nationals of different states); the American Arbitration Association (AAA) (founded in 1926, international arbitral component established in 1985 to resolve commercial disputes, principally among nationals of different states); the Stockholm Chamber of Commerce (founded in 1917, reorganized in 1949 to assist in the settlement of domestic and international disputes); the Asian-African Legal Consultative Committee (AALCC) (founded in 1978 to resolve disputes arising out of economic and commercial transactions in the Asian-African region); and the Chamber of Commerce and Industry of Geneva (CCIG) (created in 1875, but restructured in 1980 to resolve disputes arising from commercial dealings, focusing principally on disputes between nationals of different states).

In the state-to-state context, the PCA could offer a complementary alternative to the ICJ by offering the resources of the Peace Palace, but allowing parties to choose their finder-of-fact, to select the law which will govern their dispute, and to elect to make the proceedings and award in their case confidential. Moreover, none of the existing institutions mentioned have committed themselves to establishing specialized competence in emerging areas of international disputes such as environmental issues, claims by and against international organizations, and disputes involving the newly reorganized Eastern European nations. The PCA could provide an invaluable service by developing special expertise in these areas, and by offering efficient and cost-effective services.

Other members of the Working Group deemed the existence *vel non* of gaps in the arbitral landscape as irrelevant to whether the PCA could serve a useful role. These members noted that regardless of the character of other institutions, the PCA could serve the international community by expanding the range of options available to disputing parties, and thereby increasing the likelihood that parties will be able to find an institution that matches their preferences. In this sense, the institutions do not 'compete' with one another, but merely provide alternatives to suit the tastes of disputing parties. These Working Group members concluded that the unique characteristics of the PCA, such as the advantages of the Peace Palace resources, broad membership, and professional staff, alone were sufficient to attract claimants in state/non-state cases, once the PCA remedied other aspects of its organization that had heretofore discouraged potential parties.

The Working Group thus concluded that an important role still exists for the PCA. A modernized PCA could fill perceived gaps in the field and also allow parties to satisfy their institutional preferences more precisely.

2.2.2. *Reasons for lack of recourse to the PCA*

Having found that the PCA could still provide a valuable service to the international community, the Working Group turned to the question of how the PCA could fulfill that potential. The key to improving the PCA's performance was to identify why parties had not turned to the PCA in the past. The Working Group identified two sets of reasons. First, the Group found that certain political factors inhibited parties with arbitrable disputes from submitting these disputes to any institution, not just the PCA.[7] Second, the Group concluded that, among parties who *were* willing to submit their claims to arbitration, shortcomings in the PCA caused these parties to select a different forum for arbitrating their disputes.[8] The Working Group thus analyzed the

7. *New Directions, supra* note 3, at 9-11.
8. *Id.*, at 9.

reasons why parties do not arbitrate disputes at all or do not arbitrate with the PCA, in order to identify a way of changing those decisions, and encouraging recourse to the PCA.

i.   *Why some cases are not arbitrated*

Several members of the Working Group concluded that part of the reason why cases are not presented to the PCA is that many states are not comfortable bringing their disputes to arbitral institutions generally. Developing nations, it was noted, may be particularly reluctant to seek the services of established international institutions because these institutions were often created without their participation.[9] An international body such as the PCA which was created in 1899 may be perceived as representing a different set of interests and a different conception of international law than those held by the third-world parties requiring arbitral services. In addition, developing countries may suffer from a lack of financial and human resources to put their case forward effectively in an adversary proceeding. Thus, one basis for the small caseload of the PCA is that it has not enlisted sufficient participation among developing countries in its operations to allay third-world mistrust or otherwise developed programs for assisting developing countries in bringing their claims to arbitration.

ii.   *Why cases are submitted to other institutions*

The Working Group identified several reasons why parties choosing to arbitrate their disputes might pick a forum other than the PCA. The principal reason, the Group found, was that potential parties generally were not aware of the PCA's resources or lacked confidence in the PCA in the light of the Court's recent inactivity.[10] The other main reason for nonrecourse to the Court was that parties perceived certain constitutional, procedural, or organizational shortcomings in the PCA system relative to other institutions.[11] I will discuss each of these perceived defects in turn.

---

9. *See generally*, Anand, *Role of International Adjudication, in* Gross, II The Future of the International Court of Justice 4 (1976), noting "the vast expansion of the international society from the old 'Hague Community' with little or no connection left with the so-called tradition of the Hague system [...]". There are, however, some indications that this apprehension towards so-called Western institutions is abating. Recently, in fact the International Court of Justice has attracted several cases brought by developing nations. *See, e.g.*, Frontier Dispute (Burkino Faso *v.* Mali) case, 1986 I.C.J. Rep., at 554; case Concerning Military and Paramilitary Activities in and against Nicaragua, 1986 I.C.J. Rep., at 14; Border and Transborder Armed Actions (Nicaragua *v.* Honduras) case, The Frontier Dispute (El Salvador *v.* Honduras) case, the Phosphate Lands (Nauru *v.* Australia) case, and the Arbitration Award of July 31, 1989 (Guinea/Bissau *v.* Senegal) case.
10. *New Directions, supra* note 3, at 9-10.
11. *Id.*, at 10-11.

Lack of awareness. As a practical matter, post-War generations of international lawyers are largely unfamiliar with the PCA. As noted, several new arbitral institutions were created after the First World War, as part of an international effort to resolve disputes through peaceful means. International lawyers (in the case of state/non-state claims) and diplomats (in state-to-state disputes) were understandably anxious to see these fledgling institutions succeed, and thus routinely directed cases away from the already-established PCA in order to strengthen and expand the operations of the new arbitral bodies. By the 1950s, these institutions possessed the vast majority of experience in arbitrating post-War disputes, and had become virtually the exclusive mechanism for resolving claims through arbitration. Lawyers were thus trained to refer their cases to institutions other than the PCA as a matter of routine. Eventually, the superior experience of these institutions came to justify such a decision, and over time many international lawyers, quite frankly, forgot about the PCA as an option. International law courses generally do not discuss the PCA or refer to it only as a precursor to more modern arbitral bodies. Similarly, practical and scholarly literature rarely refers to the PCA due to the recent lack of cases. Thus, without some mechanism for generating interest in the PCA, it is no surprise that the Court has generally fallen into disuse.[12]

The Working Group thus concluded that, as a general matter, the international community is unaware of the work of the PCA.

Reduced confidence. Just as the Court's inactivity has reduced awareness of the PCA, it has also reduced confidence in the Court even among those who know of its services. Potential parties considering where to bring a case are more likely to select an institution with an established record over an institution with no recent record or one whose performance is difficult to predict. In particular, parties may not be able to evaluate the quality or efficiency of the PCA's administration, the relative cost of

12. It should be noted that, recently, there have been some indications by international legal institutions of a renewed awareness of the PCA. For example, the Sixth Committee's Working Group on the Decade of International Law has recommended that nations take greater advantage of the PCA in resolving their international disputes. *See Comprehensive List of Suggestions with Respect to the Programme for the United Nations Decade of International Law Proposed by States and International Organizations.* Similarly, the Conference on Security and Cooperation in Europe (CSCE), suggested broadening the administrative role of the PCA's Secretary-General and International Bureau. *Report on the Meeting of Experts on the Peaceful Settlement of Disputes* (Valletta, 1991). In addition, the PCA or its offices have been selected to assist in disputes arising from the European Energy Conference, the Antarctic Treaty Conference (*Annual Report, supra* note 2, at 9), and the recently concluded Treaty between The Netherlands and Surinam. The PCA has already assisted in the conduct of the arbitrations between the US and the UK concerning user fees at Heathrow Airport (*Annual Report, supra* note 2, at 15), the Iran-US Claims Tribunal (*Annual Report, supra* note 2, at 13), and all arbitrations employing Arts. 6 and 7 of the UNCITRAL Arbitration Rules. These developments, although promising, offer only a glimpse of the PCA's full promise.

bringing a case before the PCA, or the predilections of the Court generally. As a result, concern over predictability has caused many parties to bring cases before other, more tested, institutions.

Inactivity has also led to secondary structural problems in the Court which have further eroded confidence. For example, as the caseload of the PCA has diminished, the principal function of members of the Court has been, not arbitration, but helping to nominate candidates to the ICJ as members of national groups. As a result, some pragmatic states parties to The Hague Conventions have appointed as members of the Court persons more suited to the quasi-political function of nominating ICJ judges than to the arbitration of disputes. Potential parties may thus be concerned that not all members of the Court are committed to or familiar with prevailing arbitral practice or would not be properly disposed to perform their duties as arbitrators in certain cases.

Outmoded procedures. The Working Group also noted that, due to their age and their lack of modern testing, the procedural rules of the PCA had become outmoded and unattractive to parties.[13] As examples, the then-existing rules for both state-to-state and state/non-state disputes failed to make any provision for such common matters as the disclosure of documents, the challenge of arbitrators, and standard procedures designed to prevent delay and frustration in proceedings. The Working Group concluded that the PCA would be more attractive to potential parties if its rules were revised along the lines of those used by other modern arbitral institutions.

Organizational defects. Finally, the Working Group concluded that the PCA had become somewhat unresponsive as an institution due to its many years of relative inactivity. In recent years, the Administrative Council, which is responsible for policy- and decision-making at the PCA, has met only once a year to consider questions of policy and administration. Similarly, the International Bureau, which manages the daily operations of the PCA, has operated on a relatively low budget and a skeleton staff for several years. The Working Group noted that before the PCA could hope to attract parties, it would need to make provisions for actively engaging the Administrative Council and for increasing the personnel and financial resources of the International Bureau.

2.2.3.   Recommendations for improving the performance of the PCA

The Working Group offered three general groups of recommendations for improving the performance of the PCA.[14] First, it suggested that the PCA begin an organized

---

13. *New Directions, supra* note 3, at 15.
14. *Id.,* at 11-17.

campaign to generate greater awareness of the Court and its resources. Second, it recommended a variety of procedural and organizational changes to increase the attractiveness of the PCA as a forum for resolving disputes. In particular, it recommended that changes be implemented to permit the PCA to resolve a wider range of cases in a more flexible manner and to broaden the autonomy of parties that choose to bring their cases to the PCA. Third, the Working Group suggested that the PCA investigate the possibility of developing expertise in important areas of international conflict and explore means of increasing the participation of developing countries.

i. Publicity

The Working Group recommended that the Secretary-General begin a systemic effort to publicize the services of the PCA.

General publications. As a first step, the Group recommended that the Secretary-General distribute a range of informational materials to both state representatives and arbitration practitioners. The Working Group encouraged plans to publish a brochure describing the work and the organization of the PCA in non-technical terms, and explaining the advantages of recourse to the PCA.[15] The Group also encouraged members of the PCA and other interested members of the arbitration community to publish journal articles about the Court. Finally, the Group recommended publication of a pamphlet describing the present efforts of the PCA.[16]

Direct contact with states. The Working Group urged the PCA to provide direct assistance to member states and other potential states parties. The Group recommended that PCA members be encouraged to include arbitration clauses in their bilateral and multilateral agreements designating the PCA as the arbitrating body. The Group also suggested that the Secretary-General offer similar services to the non-aligned states (including those who were not parties to the Conventions) as the initiators of the UN Decade of International Law, and to solicit the views of states in an effort to identify particular areas of controversy.

Participation in UN activities. The Working Group recommended that the Secretary-General make direct appeals to prominent international organizations. It suggested that he attend, for example, meetings of the Sixth Committee of the United Nations to publicize the availability of the PCA and to seek formal recognition as a

---

15. This brochure was published in October 1991 by the T.M.C. Asser Institute as *The Permanent Court of Arbitration: What It Is, What It Does.*
16. Such a book was in fact published in December 1991 by the T.M.C. Asser Institute, *see supra* note 3, *The Permanent Court of Arbitration - New Directions.*

mechanism for peaceful dispute settlement. The Group also suggested that the PCA attempt to gain observer status for the International Bureau at future Sixth Committee meetings.[17] Along these lines, the Working Group encouraged the Secretary-General to explore the possibility of involving the PCA more directly in on-going UN events. One member of the Working Group suggested that the Secretary-General seek to have The Hague designated as a center for planning the UN Decade of International Law, so that the Court could assist the UN Secretariat in coordinating events. As an alternative, the Secretary-General was urged to consider co-sponsoring a general international conference with the UN at which the role of the PCA might be discussed.

Educational programs. The Working Group recommended that the PCA disseminate materials to law school faculty, in order to encourage teachers of international law to discuss the PCA in their general courses and scholarly works. The Working Group noted that the annual courses at The Hague Academy provide a particularly convenient opportunity for the Secretary-General to reach a large number of legal experts and students and thereby increase awareness of the PCA in younger generations of international lawyers.

ii. Procedural and organizational change
The Working Group recommended several structural changes in the present operation of the PCA.

Improved procedural rules. The Working Group noted that the existing procedural rules were inadequate in the light of modern arbitral practice, and needed to be updated. The Working Group promptly identified a relatively simple means of modernizing the tribunal's procedures, which did not require any formal amendment of The Hague Conventions. Articles 21 and 31 of the 1899 Convention, and Articles 41 and 51 of the 1907 Convention, already provide that parties to the respective Conventions are free to adopt alternative rules of procedure.[18] The Working Group concluded that although this option has always been available under the Conventions, an individual state contemplating arbitration is unlikely to take on the considerable task of drafting new procedural rules simply to arbitrate its case before the PCA. The Working Group reasoned, therefore, that a panel of experts should be assembled to draft a model set of arbitration rules that could be made available to prospective

17. The Secretary-General did, in fact, pursue the Working Group's recommendation that he attend Sixth Committee sessions, and he has proposed that the PCA receive observer status at Sixth Committee Sessions. U.N. Doc. A/C6/46/SR37 1991.
18. *See* Convention for the Pacific Settlement of International Disputes of 1899 [hereinafter Hague Convention of 1899], and Convention for the Pacific Settlement of International Disputes concluded at The Hague on October 18, 1907 [hereinafter Hague Convention of 1907].

parties.[19] The parties would then have the option of adopting those up-to-date rules to govern their arbitration, and to make additional modifications to those rules as provided for in The Hague Conventions.

The Working Group recommended that the expert panel (later, the Expert Group) draft the model optional rules along the lines of the UNCITRAL Arbitration Rules, which it deemed to be the most recent, tested, and comprehensive rules of practice.[20] The Working Group further recommended that the Expert Group keep the values of party autonomy and flexibility in mind when drafting, and accommodate the sovereign status of states parties. Finally, the Working Group suggested that the Expert Group draft a model arbitration clause, similar to that employed by UNCITRAL, to assist parties wishing to take advantage of these alternative procedures.[21]

Expanding list of arbitrators. The Working Group noted that the attractiveness of the PCA had been limited by restrictions on who may be appointed as an arbitrator. Article 24 of the 1899 Convention and Article 45 of the 1907 Convention provide that all arbitrators "must be chosen from the list of members of the Court".[22] Under the Hague Conventions, the membership of the Court is restricted to 304 members (four members nominated by each of the 76 signatory states). It was noted, however, that parties may desire the services of other experienced arbitrators, not on the list, in the specific circumstances of their case. The Working Group observed that, notwithstanding the Articles 24 and 45, the Conventions grant parties the option to

19. *New Directions, supra* note 3, at 17.
20. Formally titled the Arbitration Rules of the United Nations Commission on International Trade Law. These rules were developed by the United Nations Commission on International Trade Law to assist in the arbitration of international commercial disputes. The Rules were first adopted by UNCITRAL at its ninth session. U.N. GAOR, Thirty-First Session, Supplement No. 17 (A/31/17), Chap. V, Sect. C. The Rules were subsequently recommended for use by the General Assembly by virtue of U.N. Res. 31/98 adopted December 15, 1976. Although the Rules were originally developed to assist in the arbitration of international commercial disputes, they have proved to be readily adaptable for governing arbitrations involving states. They have, for example, been employed successfully by the Iran-U.S. Claims Tribunal in The Hague since its inception in 1983. Because of the wide acceptance of the UNCITRAL Rules by states and their adaptability, the Working Group concluded that these Rules would be an appropriate starting point for drafting the PCA's Optional Rules.
21. *New Directions, supra* note 3, at 17.
22. One member of the Expert Group pointed out that the strictness of this provision is open to debate. He noted that the English text of the Hague Conventions uses the term 'must', which suggests that reference to the list is mandatory. By contrast the French text uses the term '*doit*' which would indicate that reference to the list is permissive. For present purposes, it is not necessary to determine here which text is controlling, because the Working Group and the Expert Groups do not rely upon this provision to support their recommendation that parties be allowed to draw arbitrators from outside of the list. However, it is worth noting that at the time the 1899 and 1907 Conventions were ratified, the official text of both Treaties was in French. Accordingly, under customary international law (as codified in The Vienna Convention on the Law of Treaties, Arts. 31 and 32), it appears that the, less restrictive, French definition would apply.

draw upon outside arbitrators by providing for ˙special' arbitration tribunals,[23] or by allowing parties in the *compromis*, or in some other agreement, to choose arbitrators who are not listed as Court members.[24] The Working Group recommended that the Administrative Council take measures to publicize the fact that the Hague Conventions also permit parties to establish ˙special tribunals' composed of arbitrators drawn from outside the list as well. The Working Group thus recommended that the Expert Group consider incorporating such special agreements in the model arbitration clause or model optional rules.[25]

Organizational changes. The Working Group suggested numerous structural changes in the operation of the Administrative Council and the International Bureau to increase their respective levels of responsiveness. The Group recommended that the Administrative Council establish small standing committees, which, because of their manageable size, would permit the Council to respond more quickly and directly to issues that may arise as the PCA's caseload increases. As for the International Bureau, the Working Group recommended that it diversify its personnel to represent more closely the membership of the Court. In recent years, the International Bureau has been staffed principally by Dutch nationals. It was recognized that drawing personnel from other nations, in particular developing countries, would improve world confidence in the PCA as a representative institution.[26]

Membership of the Court. As part of the general effort to encourage applications to the Court, the Working Group recommended that the Administrative Council take measures to improve confidence in the ability of the membership of the Court to arbitrate complex disputes. The Group recommended that the Council promulgate additional criteria for selecting Court members to strengthen the membership of the Court, and thereby to enhance its international reputation. These criteria would be designed to ensure that members are available to serve within a reasonable time, and can be relied upon to exercise independent judgement when appointed to an arbitral tribunal. The states would be urged to withdraw members who do not satisfy these criteria and replace them with members whose principal qualification is the capacity and willingness to serve as an independent arbitrator.[27]

23. *See* 1899 Hague Convention, *supra* note 18, Art. 21; 1907 Hague Convention, *supra* note 18, Art. 42.
24. *See* 1899 Convention, *supra* note 18, Arts. 31 and 32; 1907 Convention, *supra* note 18, Arts. 52 and 55.
25. *New Directions*, *supra* note 3, at 14.
26. *Id.*, at 15.
27. This initiative was largely abandoned in response to a later development by the Expert Group. *See infra* note 33 and accompanying text. As noted therein, Art. 8 of the Expert Group's Draft of the Optional Rules provides that parties may draw arbitrators from outside of the PCA list. Accordingly, the Expert Group concluded that it was not necessary to alter the criteria for the selection of PCA members, as parties would be free to select members from the PCA or non-members as they see fit.

Funding. The Working Group's final institutional recommendation was for the Administrative Council to reconsider the present funding structure of the PCA. The Working Group suggested that the Council request a modest increase in the regular contribution of members to support both the proposed informational and outreach programs. It also recommended that the PCA publish a schedule of tariffs and charges. Finally, it suggested establishment of a fund to enable qualifying developing countries to meet the costs of arbitration.

iii.   Expansion and specialization
The final set of recommendations from the Working Group encouraged the PCA to be forward-thinking in its plans by increasing the range of cases presented to the Court, by coordinating efforts with other arbitration institutions, and by identifying areas for specialization.

Recruiting new member states and non-state parties. The Working Group recommended that the PCA begin efforts to extend its services by recruiting new states to the Conventions, and by offering services to both non-member and non-state parties. Article 47, Paragraph 2 of the Convention of 1907, and Article 26, Paragraph 2 of the Convention of 1899, permit the extension of services and facilities to disputes involving non-contracting powers. The Working Group, recognizing that many international disputes involve states not parties to the Conventions, or arise between state and non-state parties, advised the Administrative Council to make efforts to encourage non-member states or non-states to arrange to have their cases presented to the PCA.

Cooperation with other organizations. The Working Group next urged the International Bureau to expand its existing set of cooperative arrangements to other organizations, including the International Chamber of Commerce and the Asian-African Legal Consultative Committee. The Group noted that, in this way, the PCA would still be able to conduct its own cases outside of The Hague by sharing other institutions' facilities, and it could provide reciprocal assistance to those other institutions in The Hague.

Database and specialization. The International Bureau was encouraged to maintain a database on international and regional specialized dispute-settlement centers, and on the particular expertise of potential arbitrators, which it could furnish to prospective parties. In the process of accumulating this database, the International Bureau could also investigate possible areas of specialization by which it could meet presently unfulfilled needs. In particular, it was suggested that the PCA might take the initiative in developing a resource library and a list of experts in the fields of environmental law, disputes between international organizations, and issues uniquely affecting developing nations.

2.3.   Conclusions of the Working Group

The Working Group recommended extensive changes in the structure, organization, services, and operations of the PCA. As conceived by the Working Group, the PCA would expand its membership, its source of arbitrators, its areas of competence, its available rules and procedures, and its involvement with other institutions. To accomplish these reforms, the PCA would require more than simply the efforts of the Administrative Council and the International Bureau, although their actions would of course be indispensable. To assist the PCA organs, the Working Group recommended that the PCA enlist an expert body of consultants to help it in accomplishing these reforms.

3.   THE EXPERT GROUP

Pursuant to the Working Group's recommendations, the International Bureau convened an Expert Group on the Revision of Some Aspects of the Permanent Court of Arbitration in February 1992.[28] Once again it was chaired by Judge Manfred Lachs, and drew prominent international legal figures from all over the world. The Expert Group was charged with refining and implementing the recommendations of the Working Group.

The Expert Group selected as its first task to modernize the procedures of the PCA in order to facilitate more frequent use of the Court's resources. It concluded that

---

28. The Expert Group is composed of 25 members representing 22 countries. The Expert Group's membership is as follows: Mr. Ion M. Anghel, Ambassador of Romania (Romania); Mr. Andres Aguilar Mawdsley, Judge of the ICJ (Venezuela); Mr. Abdel Meguid, Counsellor of the Embassy of Egypt (Egypt); Mr. Koorosh-Hossein Ameli, Member of the Iran-United States Claims Tribunal (Iran); Mr. Carlos Arguello Gomez, Agent of Nicaragua to the ICJ (Nicaragua); Mr. Mohammed Bedjaoui, Judge of the ICJ (Algeria); Mr. A. Bos, Dutch Ministry of Foreign Affairs (Netherlands); Mr. Bengt Broms, Member of the Iran-United States Claims Tribunal (Finland); Mr. Hans Corell, Under-Secretary for Legal and Consular Affairs, Ministry of Foreign Affairs, Stockholm (Sweden); Mr. Achol Deng, Ambassador of the Sudan (Sudan); Dr. Luigi Ferrari-Bravo, Chef du Service du Contentieux Diplomatique des Traites et des Affaires Legislatives, Ministry of Foreign Affairs, Rome (Italy); Mr. L. Hardenberg, Lawyer (Netherlands); Mr. Reinhard Hilger, Head of Section on General International Law of the Ministry of Foreign Affairs, Bonn (Germany); Mr. Howard Holtzmann, Member of the Iran-United States Claims Tribunal (U.S.A.); Mr. Manfred Lachs, Judge of the ICJ (Poland); M. Jean-Pierre Puissochet, Le Directeur Des Affaires Juridiques, Ministry of Foreign Affairs, Paris (France); Mr. Shigeru Oda, Vice-President of the ICJ (Japan); Professor Pierre Pescatore, Former Judge at the Court of Justice of the European Community (Luxembourg); Mr. Christopher Pinto, Secretary-General of the Iran-United States Claims Tribunal (Sri Lanka); Mr. P.M.A.L. Plompen, Legal Adviser of Philips, Inc. (Netherlands); Dr. P.S. Rao, Ministry of External Affairs, New Delhi (India); Mr. Jacques H. Schraven, Legal Adviser of Shell Oil Company (Netherlands); Mr. Stephen Schwebel, Judge of the ICJ (U.S.A.); Mr. L. Skotnikov, Legal Adviser, Ministry of Foreign Affairs, Moscow (C.I.S.); Mr. Jorge Antonio Tapia-Valdes, Ambassador of Chile (Chile); Mr. C.A. Whomersley, Foreign Office, London (U.K.).→

revising the Rules would advance all aspects of the program to promote the PCA, by making the Court a more attractive forum to arbitrate state-to-state disputes. In addition, the Group decided that it was best to construct these new state-to-state rules immediately to avoid a situation in which the PCA received cases as a result of the Secretary-General's efforts, but was not capable of arbitrating these claims effectively due to inadequacies in its procedural rules. The Group agreed that upon completion of these state-to-state rules, the PCA would be better situated to draft new rules for state/non-state disputes.

The Expert Group used the Working Group's recommendations as a starting point. Thus it decided to adopt the UNCITRAL Arbitration Rules as a model for bringing the PCA's procedures up-to-date.[29] The Expert Group also adopted the suggestion that it draft model arbitration clauses to assist parties who wish to take advantage of these optional Rules.[30] The Working Group noted that these Rules and clauses could later serve as a basis for drafting alternative procedural rules for disputes involving state and non-state parties.

3.1. Constitutional authority

As noted, The Hague Conventions permit parties to adopt their own rules of procedure to govern disputes.[31] Although parties have thus been free to substitute their own rules for the outdated procedures described in The Hague Conventions, states parties have been understandably reluctant to draft an entire new set of rules for each arbitration. Thus, the Expert Group determined to construct a set of optional rules that would be available to parties to consult or adopt in fashioning an alternative to The Hague Convention procedures. The parties would of course be free to deviate from the model rules, but at the very least they could have confidence that these up-to-date procedures had been endorsed by leaders in the field of arbitration. To assure public acceptance, the Expert Group determined to pay particular attention to improving the flexibility and responsiveness of PCA procedures, in accordance with modern arbitral practice.

In addition, the Secretary General contacted the following eminent international law figures and consulted them on the Rules before transmitting those Rules to the Administrative Council for final approval. Mr. Bola Ajibola, Judge of the ICJ (Nigeria); Mr. Eduardo Valencia-Ospina, Registrar of the ICJ (Columbia); Mr. Kenneth Keith, President of the International Law Commission of New Zealand (New Zealand).
29. *New Directions, supra* note 3, at 15.
30. *Id.*.
31. *See supra* note 18 and accompanying text.

3.2. Procedure of the Expert Group

Beginning in 1991, the International Bureau, assisted by a drafting committee from the Expert Group, prepared a set of optional rules for disputes between states parties. The Expert Group formally reviewed and commented upon this draft set of optional rules and model clauses at its first meeting on February 27, 1992. The Rules were subsequently redrafted in light of the group members' comments, and resubmitted for comments on April 15, 1992. The Experts commented upon these Rules once again, and the drafting committee prepared a third draft which represented the predominant view of the Expert Group. That draft was distributed to the Administrative Council on May 27, 1992. The Administrative Council subsequently authorized the distribution of these Rules on October 20, 1992.

3.3. Draft Rules of the PCA

Rather than describing each provision of the approved Rules and thereby inflicting serious fatigue on the reader, it appears advisable merely to note the basic structure of the Rules and identify when and how they deviate from the UNCITRAL Arbitration Rules.

3.3.1. Structure of the Rules

As noted, the Expert Group determined that in order to produce a set of rules that was more consistent with modern state practice, the PCA should pattern such procedures on the UNCITRAL Arbitration Rules, making modifications as necessary to adapt those rules to the particular circumstances of the PCA and public law practice.[32] In particular, modifications were made in order (i) to reflect the public international law character of disputes between states and diplomatic practice appropriate in such disputes; (ii) to indicate the functions of the Secretary-General and the International Bureau, and the relationship of the proposed new rules to the 1899 and 1907 Hague Conventions; and (iii) to give parties the flexibility and autonomy to fashion a process that suits their particular needs. The participants generally agreed that they should avoid tinkering with the UNCITRAL Rules, but should modify those Rules only as necessary to keep faith with the three preceding principles.[33]

3.3.2. Deviations from the UNCITRAL Rules

Most of the changes made to adapt the UNCITRAL Rules to suit claims between

---

32. *See supra* note 20 and accompanying text.

33. The Experts agreed that it was best to publish a full set of rules rather than merely adopt the UNCITRAL Rules with modification by renvoi. The Experts decided that the Court, as an independent institution, must publish a free-standing set of rules. However, noting that some States might be reluctant to adopt what appear to be untested rules, the Expert Group agreed that the PCA would be aided by a document that revealed at a glance the fundamental similarity between the PCA Rules and the UNCITRAL Rules.

states are of a purely technical nature, and thus require no explanation.[34] The remaining changes are less ministerial and thus warrant a brief discussion.

Article 1: Scope of application

The application of the Optional Rules is, of course, limited by the terms of The Hague Conventions. Thus, UNCITRAL's Scope of Application section was modified to reflect that the 1899 and the 1907 Conventions continue to apply to arbitrations where both parties are signatories to the same Convention. These Optional Rules, however, would, to the extent that they are adopted by the parties to an arbitration, supplant any *rules of procedure* in the relevant Convention respecting that arbitration, as provided by Articles 21 and 31 of the 1899 Convention and Articles 41 and 51 of the 1907 Convention.

The Article has also been redrafted slightly to clarify that principal responsibility for administration of the dispute remains with the International Bureau.

Article 3: Notice of arbitration

This Article was redrafted to streamline the requirements for filing a notice of arbitration. The modifications avoid redundancy by relieving parties of the duty to include matters in the notice of arbitration which will already be contained in the arbitration clause. Accordingly, the Rules do not require parties automatically to identify the appointing authority (or the process by which an appointing authority will be selected), because such information would likely be contained in the arbitration clause.

Article 5: Number of arbitrators

The Expert Group concluded that, in the interest of party autonomy, it would be preferable to give parties increased freedom in structuring the arbitral tribunal. Thus, Article 5 of the UNCITRAL Rules was modified to give parties the option of having five arbitrators (the UNCITRAL Rules provide only the option of one or three). This necessitated corresponding technical changes in Articles 7, 13, 31, and 32 as well.

34. Specifically, the following changes were made throughout: (1) all references to parties as 'he' or 'his' were changed to 'it' or 'its', respectively, to reflect that these Rules relate solely to disputes between state parties (*see* Arts. 6, 7, 11, 18, 19, 20, 24, 25, 28, and 30); (2) the term 'contract' was replaced by the term 'treaty or other agreement', to reflect that only public law disputes are subject to these Rules (*see* Arts. 1, 3, 8, 18, 19, and 21); (3) all time limits placed upon parties were doubled, in deference to the parties' sovereign status (*see* Arts. 5, 6, 7, 11, 25, 35, 36, and 37) and tribunals were granted authority to extend certain time limits at the sovereign's request (*see* Arts. 23 and 25); (4) in all provisions relating to administrative duties of a tribunal, references to the 'International Bureau' have been added where appropriate to reflect the structure of responsibilities within the PCA (*see* Arts. 4, 15, 25, 32, 33, 38, and 41); (5) all references to 'goods' or 'business days' have been omitted to reflect the exclusively public-law character of disputes arising under these Rules (*see* Arts. 2, 16, 26); (6) Art. 2 was modified to provide that notice shall be delivered through diplomatic channels, since states or the relevant agents may not have a 'residence' *per se*; and (7) in Art. 4 the term 'agent' was introduced instead of 'representative' in keeping with public law practice.

Article 8: Appointing authority and administration
As discussed,[35] Article 8 was expanded to clarify that an appointing authority operating pursuant to an agreement that incorporates these Rules is free to designate as arbitrators persons who are not members of the PCA. As noted, this is consistent with provisions of The Hague Conventions[36] and promotes flexibility by allowing appointing authorities to select the most highly qualified arbitrators in any dispute.

Article 13: Replacement of an arbitrator
The Rules have added a new paragraph to the UNCITRAL provisions on replacement of an arbitrator. Paragraph 3 provides that in the event that an arbitrator in a multi-member panel fails to participate in the arbitration, the remaining arbitrators may continue the arbitration if they deem it to be appropriate under all of the circumstances of the arbitration. This change reflects the emerging practice under the UNCITRAL Rules, and one which is generally favored by state parties.[37] The provision responds to the unusual circumstance in which an arbitrator seeks to resign solely in order to frustrate the proceedings. This modification clarifies practice under the UNCITRAL Rules, ensuring that a discontented arbitrator cannot delay proceedings indefinitely through such a tactic. Obviously, in most cases arbitrators have valid reasons for resigning from a tribunal or do so well before the tribunal has invested extensive resources in the arbitration or reached a conclusion on the proper disposition of the case. In those circumstances, the tribunal would accept the arbitrator's resignation and make arrangements for his replacement.

Article 15: General provisions
This Article has been clarified slightly to provide that requests for hearings will be entertained only at *appropriate stages* of the proceedings and only with respect to jurisdiction or the merits. These changes also reflect current practice under the UNCITRAL Rules, and are favored by state parties as a method of protecting against undue delay.

Article 16: Place of arbitration
Article 16 provides that, unless the parties agree otherwise, the location of the arbitration will be in The Hague. This provision was included in recognition of the physical location of the PCA and the practical realities of administrating a case outside of the Peace Palace. Unlike the UNCITRAL Rules, which leave site selection to the discretion of the parties in the first instance, the Optional Rules require that the International Bureau approve the choice of any location outside of The Hague based upon its evaluation of its ability to perform its functions in the chosen location. This

---

35. *See supra* note 27 and accompanying text.
36. *See supra* notes 19-20 and accompanying text.
37. *See* 5.1 *Preventing Delay and Disruption of Arbitration* ICCA Congress Series 242-67 (1991).

provision recognizes the limits on the International Bureau's ability to conduct cases outside of The Hague and is included for the benefit of parties considering making such a site selection.

Article 22: Further written submissions

The Expert Group amended this Article to grant parties the opportunity to express their views before a tribunal may require them to provide further written statements. This change was made to respect the dignity of sovereigns and was patterned after similar language in the Rules of the Court of the International Court of Justice.[38]

Article 24: Evidence and hearings

In deference to the sovereign character of parties to these disputes, the Expert Group changed the language of this Article to provide that a tribunal may 'call upon' (but not 'require') parties to produce materials relevant to the proceedings. The Expert Group did, however, add a provision that would allow a tribunal to take note of a party's refusal to comply with such an order as well as any reasons given for that refusal. This provision, which parallels Article 49 of the Statute of the International Court of Justice, permits the tribunal to draw adverse inferences about the failure to produce documents, and thus it protects parties from delay or frustration caused by the obstreperous behavior of adversaries who refuse to produce relevant materials for invalid reasons. As such, the modifications are favored in public international practice because they respect the integrity of the sovereign powers while at the same time deterring obstreperous conduct.

Article 26: Interim measures of protection

This Article was modified slightly to be consistent with a comparable provision of the Statute of the International Court of Justice (Article 41). The change eliminates certain references to 'goods' and other purely commercial matters which were deemed to be inappropriate in the context of state-to-state arbitration. In addition, the provision places limitations on a party's ability to invoke the tribunal's injunctive powers, by noting that such measures must be calculated to preserve the respective rights of either party. It also provides that the parties may agree not to permit the use of interim measures if they believe that this would frustrate their ability to resolve their dispute. The change is thus consistent with international practice.

Article 32: Form and effect of the award

The Expert Group deleted one portion of this Article as unnecessary in the context of public law disputes. That paragraph required a tribunal to file or register its award

---

38. Rules of the Court of the International Court of Justice, Art. 53.

as required by the law of the country in which it is issued. Because this provision would not apply to PCA awards, all references made to it throughout the document have been deleted.[39]

Article 33: Applicable law

The Expert Group concluded that because of the public law character of disputes being arbitrated under these Rules, it was appropriate to use the widely accepted standard of international law employed by the ICJ as the governing law in these disputes, unless of course, the parties agree to be governed by some different body of law. Absent an agreement by the parties to the contrary, Article 33 provides that the tribunal should apply the law as stated in Article 38 of the Statute of the International Court of Justice,[40] with one exception: it does not include the reservations of Article 59 of that Statute. The Expert Group declined to include that portion of Article 38 because of structural differences between the two institutions. The omitted portion provides that decisions of the ICJ have no binding force except between the parties and in respect of that particular case. This provision is important in the ICJ's case, because the ICJ is a continuing body that hears cases by other parties and new cases by past parties. By contrast, the tribunals created by the PCA are, by definition, *ad hoc*. These tribunals are temporary bodies, created to decide disputes with respect to one set of parties regarding one case. Once that tribunal has completed its work, it has no authority to bind any other parties or to take any other action. At that point, the tribunal is officially extinct. Thus, the Expert Group deemed it inappropriate to include a proviso that a tribunal's decisions have no collateral binding effect.

Articles 38-40: Costs

The Expert Group made two significant changes in the UNCITRAL provisions that define how costs will be assessed.[41] Under the UNCITRAL Rules, the costs of arbitration are borne by the unsuccessful party unless the tribunal determines to apportion them otherwise. This allocation of costs, however, is contrary to public law practice in general and may discourage claimants with a colorable argument from presenting their claims to the PCA. In addition, the Expert Group was concerned that

---

39. *See* corresponding changes in Art. 34, Para. 3, Art. 35 Para. 2, Art. 36, Para. 2, and Art. 37, Para. 3.
40. That Statute provides that the Court is to apply:
(a) international conventions, whether general or particular, establishing rules expressly recognised by the contesting states;
(b) international customs, as evidence of a general practice accepted as law;
(c) the general principles of law recognised by civilized nations;
(d) subject to the provisions of Article 59, judicial decisions and the teachings of the most highly qualified publicists of the various nations, as subsidiary means for the determination of rules of law.
41. Two less significant changes were made as well. In Art. 38, the Expert Group deleted a provision requiring an arbitral tribunal to fix its fees in accordance with Art. 39 and to state the fees of each arbitrator separately. The Experts noted that the first requirement was no longer applicable in light of modifications➜

in many state-to-state arbitrations, there may be some sensitivity about characterizing one of the parties as 'unsuccessful'. For these reasons, it revised Articles 38 and 40 to make them consistent with international public law practice which requires each party to bear its own costs.

Second, the Expert Group removed certain conditional language from UNCITRAL Rule 39 which did not apply in the context of the PCA Optional Rules. UNCITRAL Rule 39 provided that if an appointing authority had issued a schedule of fees pursuant to the rules of the institution that it represented the appointing authority should take that schedule into account to the extent that it deemed appropriate. The Expert Group expressed concern that such a practice would breed disparities in the fees assessed by PCA tribunals, since appointing authorities may be drawn from a variety of institutions with widely differing fee schedules. To the extent that appointing authorities were required to employ different fee schedules in PCA cases, this might result in similarly situated parties before the PCA paying different fees. To assure uniformity and predictability in the fees incurred by parties appearing before the PCA, the Group eliminated reliance upon outside fee schedules. Instead, Article 39 now provides that fees may be fixed in consultation with the Secretary-General of the PCA. The Secretary-General, it was noted, has an institutional interest in seeing that arbitral fees remain equitable in all PCA cases, to assure both parties and arbitrators that the tribunal's services have been properly valued.

Model arbitration clause. In addition to the UNCITRAL Rules, the experts modified the UNCITRAL Model Arbitration Clause to reflect practice before the PCA under these Rules. The Expert Group agreed that these model arbitration clauses would assist states parties who wished to avail themselves of the PCA's services.

The experts actually drafted two model clauses. The first model clause is directed towards parties who intend to submit future disputes arising from an agreement to arbitrate before the PCA.[42] The model clause states that the parties agree to submit to binding arbitration any dispute arising between them as to the interpretation, application, or performance of the relevant treaty or agreement. The Expert Group noted that there are several places in the Rules in which parties may choose among a variety of options, including the number of arbitrators, location of the arbitration and the languages to be used. The Expert Group thus approved a form of the model

---

made in Art. 39. The Experts also eliminated the requirement that arbitrators state their fees separately as an unnecessary precaution because the Secretary-General is available to consult on all fees and because the tribunal is bound by Art. 39 to set reasonable fees. Second, in Art. 39, the Experts modified the language of the UNCITRAL Rules slightly to clarify that disputes arising before the PCA need not concern claims for monetary compensation.

42. It is useful to note that in this Clause the Experts use the words 'treaty or other agreement' in place of the term 'contract'. This was done to confirm that these Rules apply in state-to-state disputes, and that the Rules may extend to 'less formal arrangements' between states - as contrasted with 'agreements' which are of course always treaties under the terms of the Vienna Convention on the Law of Treaties, Art. 1.

clause in which blanks were provided, allowing the parties to insert their choices.

The second clause assists parties, who are already disputants, and wish to enlist the PCA's services. It also directs the parties' attention to specific provisions of the Rules where they are called upon to express preferences for the language of the arbitration, the number of arbitrators, and the selection of an appointing authority. The Expert Group made clear in the introduction to the model clause that the parties are free to modify these model clauses as they see fit.

Multiparty treaties. Although the Rules are drafted in terms of disputes arising from traditional bilateral agreements, they provide that they may be adapted to resolve disputes arising from multilateral treaties as well. The only changes necessary for parties to such treaties seeking to take advantage of the PCA's rules are that the provisions for selecting arbitrators and allocating costs would need to be adapted to the particular circumstances of the agreement. The Optional Rules contain guidelines to assist the parties in drafting clauses for arbitration in multiple party disputes.

Other changes. Finally, other general changes in the UNCITRAL Rules were suggested, in addition to those ultimately adopted by the Expert Group. The Expert Group briefly considered these suggestions in relation to its central task of adapting the UNCITRAL Rules to the needs of the PCA. The Group agreed however that it should not act as a roving commission to 'improve' the UNCITRAL Rules generally, but rather should assure only that the Rules were modified as necessary to reflect the public international law character of disputes between states and the particular structure of the PCA, and to maximize party autonomy and flexibility. The Group noted that parties are free to modify the Rules if they are dissatisfied with any provision or wish to add further provisions. Accordingly, although other useful suggestions were discussed by the Expert Group, it ultimately confined itself to the changes described above as the ones necessary to accomplish the Group's general objectives.[43]

4.   CONCLUSION: THE PCA AND THE WORKING AND EXPERT GROUPS IN PERSPECTIVE

The ultimate task of the Working and Expert Groups was to formulate means by

---

43. *E.g.*, the Expert Group participants agreed in principle that the International Bureau should publish a schedule of fees and expenses to be charged in each case, but concluded that it was not necessary to determine the content of that schedule at this point. It was deemed that this was an administrative matter best left in the hands of the Secretary-General. The Expert Group also considered proposals that the UNCITRAL Rules be modified to permit revision or appeal of awards, and/or to require that challenges of arbitrators be submitted to outside authorities. Participants noted that these changes are relatively controversial, and thus promulgating them would deviate from its general policy of basing the PCA Rules on the UNCITRAL Arbitration Rules with only necessary modifications.

which the PCA could be restored to its proper place in world affairs and thereby to facilitate the peaceful resolution of disputes among international parties. As discussed above, the Working and Expert Groups' efforts have produced significant strides towards accomplishing this objective. In particular, the use of modernized Optional Rules will allow the PCA to fill a void in the current array of peaceful dispute resolution mechanisms, both by increasing the autonomy of parties and by serving the cause of peaceful dispute settlement to all who require it, including non-member and non-state parties.

The formulation of new rules to assist parties in arbitrating disputes before the PCA is an important step towards attaining these objectives, but it is only a step. In order for the PCA to re-establish itself in the international community, it will need to make other important structural changes and ultimately gain the confidence of parties who may appear before it. In particular, the following challenges still lie ahead: (1) the PCA, as an institution, will need to become more engaged in the work of the international community generally; (2) flexible aspects of The Hague Conventions will have to be utilized to enlarge the range of cases and subjects that the Court will entertain; and (3) the PCA will need to develop unique competencies within the field of arbitration to sustain it in the long-run.

4.1.   Prompt outreach

The most immediate task facing the PCA is to re-establish its presence within the arbitration community. The Secretary-General should, quite properly, be congratulated on his recent efforts to promote the work of the PCA by publishing the *New Directions* booklet as well as the recent brochure entitled "The Permanent Court of Arbitration: What It Is and What It Can Do", and by making numerous presentations, including one before the United Nations.[44] The Secretary-General must, of course, continue in his efforts, and emphasize the PCA's role as a facilitator that provides support and assistance to disputing parties.

Timing in this effort is critical. The PCA will need to capitalize immediately upon international attention if it wishes to maintain the interest of the international community long enough to accomplish its proposed changes. Public attention has been drawn to the PCA and other international law institutions by the confluence of the Secretary-General's initiatives, the United Nations' Declaration of the Decade of International Law, rapidly changing events in Eastern Europe, and the emergence of relatively new areas of international conflict, such as transboundary pollution and privatization of industry. Advances are being made on numerous fronts in international law, and, if the PCA is prepared to respond to those changes, it could serve a

---

44. *Annual Report, supra* note 2, at 9.

crucial role in anticipating areas of potential conflict and constructing services to address efficiently disputes in those areas. Thus, the Secretary-General should make every effort to place the PCA in the forefront of international arbitration while this window of opportunity is open.

Fortunately, the International Bureau need not wait until all proposed reforms are in place before it can effectively promote within the international community the PCA as a proper forum for arbitrating existing disputes. The PCA already has several attractive features to recommend it. Its assets include its universal character, its broad jurisdiction, its vast research facilities, the amenities of the Peace Palace, and the PCA's capacity to provide flexible rules of procedure to accommodate state claimants. Thus, even where the PCA's services parallel those of other arbitral institutions, the PCA system may offer unique benefits due to these considerable resources. Given its relatively small docket of cases, it can -at least in the short run- promise parties immediate processing of their cases. And, states parties choosing to take advantage of the optional rules of procedure will have the benefits of choosing their appointing authority and having their arbitrators drawn from throughout the world without restriction.

In raising the international community's awareness of the improvements in the PCA system, it will be important for the International Bureau to emphasize that -in taking steps to modernize and upgrade its performance- the PCA has not abandoned any existing obligations or compromised its ability to perform tasks in the present. The International Bureau has retained its useful role in providing facilities and services for *ad hoc* arbitrations under Article 47 of the 1907 Convention. Present efforts thus represent a broadening, rather than a shifting, of the PCA's contemporary role. Potential parties should be made aware that the new initiatives will close certain gaps in the PCA system to bring it closer to the original conception of The Hague Conventions. This system includes not only arbitration services under modernized rules, but also the provision of dispute resolution facilities and services for disputing parties, including good offices, commissions of inquiry, mediation and conciliation. Such a broad range of services is both necessary to and consistent with the PCA's original mandate of providing a central place for peaceful dispute resolution.

This message will ultimately only be as effective as its medium. In order to apprise the international community of both the PCA's present capacities and expanding resources, the International Bureau and other international figures concerned with the success of the PCA will need to aggressively disseminate materials that concisely explain the workings of the PCA, its rules, and the method by which parties can avail themselves of PCA services. Members of the Expert Group may, in particular, contribute in this effort by preparing materials for distribution within their own agencies and organizations regarding developments in the PCA.

4.2.   Flexible application of the Hague Conventions

The members of the Expert Group and the International Bureau need to continue their work to improve the functioning of the PCA by exploring ways to adapt the PCA to current trends under the flexible provisions of The Hague Conventions. At the Expert Group's suggestion, the International Bureau has already prepared revisions in the PCA's 1962 Rules designed for cases between a state and a non-state party. This will likely be a fruitful area for arbitration and one which a modernized PCA will be well-equipped to handle.

In addition, in recognition of the time lag that may exist between present efforts to update the Court's membership and the influx of cases by parties who wish to rely upon the Court (and not a 'special arbitration' panel), the PCA should follow the Expert Group's proposal to add 'Associate Members' to the PCA list. The use of Associate Members would increase the roster of learned people serving the Court itself without requiring any amendment of The Hague Conventions. In addition, it will further the PCA's goal of reaching out to the international community.

In proposing other changes, the Expert Group should remain cognizant that -in the interest of timing and efficiency- it is best to avoid changes that would require amending the 1907 Convention. Every effort must be made to effect changes quickly through authoritative interpretations of the provisions of the Conventions, and through actions within the competence of the Administrative Council and the International Bureau.[45]

The PCA will need to continue to draw upon creative resources such as the Expert Group in order to remain current with developments in international arbitration and to help it fashion innovative solutions to future problems.

4.3.   Unique competencies

In order to succeed in the long-term, the PCA must do more than merely duplicate the work of other international arbitral centers. The PCA needs to offer unique services to disputing parties, particularly in state/non-state cases, where there already exist numerous other regional centers equipped to handle such cases. The PCA can avoid direct competition in state/non-state cases by providing services that are both different in kind and in degree from those already provided by others. These may include developing special competence is emerging fields of international dispute such as the privatization of industry in the former socialist states, using the flexible procedures of The Hague Conventions to tailor arbitrations to the special needs of the parties, and attracting top-flight experts to serve as resources in streamlining the length and cost of arbitrations. The first step in this process will be to publish the new

---

45. *Anual Report, supra* note 2 Para. 24, at 17.

rules of procedure in state/non-state cases, which have recently been drafted by the International Bureau.

In the state-to-state context, the PCA will have to be sensitive to its relations with other public law institutions, and in particular with the International Court of Justice. Cooperation with the ICJ is critical to the PCA's success. The ICJ can lend its prestige and resources to the PCA, and -by respecting areas of specialization developed by the PCA- it can foster an efficient distribution of cases between the two institutions. In addition, because the PCA and the ICJ acting in chambers have equivalent competence to receive certain disputes, it is important for both institutions to recognize the ways in which they provide alternative means for resolving those disputes. There is a sound prospect for good relations between the ICJ and the PCA; the two institutions already have a long tradition of cooperation, including the role of the national groups of the PCA in nominating the members of the ICJ.

Finally, the PCA must move into current voids in international law quickly. First, the PCA should follow through on its present efforts to develop special competence in the field of international environmental law. This may include creating a database of arbitral materials and resources in that field, as well as maintaining a list of expert consultants to assist its tribunals. Second, it should move quickly to examine ways to attract countries that traditionally have not taken advantage of arbitration, such as developing nations, or nations in the process of adapting to Western arbitration systems, such as the countries of Eastern Europe. One obvious method of attracting such countries is to reduce the cost of arbitration. The PCA could take the lead in the international arbitral community generally by developing methods for reducing the expense of arbitration and for providing financial assistance to countries that are unable to afford arbitration.[46]

In all of these endeavors, the PCA must not lose sight of its goal: to offer parties a relatively easy and efficient method of resolving their problems, and thereby to discourage disputants from taking such matters into their own hands. The work necessary to accomplish this goal is daunting. But the experience of the Working and Expert Groups demonstrates that leaders in the field of arbitration believe it can be done; the PCA can serve a valuable role in the area of peaceful dispute resolution, by attracting cases for arbitration that are presently going unresolved and by increasing the level of satisfaction of parties with the process of arbitration. It is not clear that this is a 'new direction' for the PCA. Rather, it appears to be an original path, discovered anew. It is hoped that by traveling this direction, the PCA will again become a valuable asset in the universal goal of peaceful dispute settlement.

---

46. The International Bureau could begin this effort immediately by offering administrative assistance to developing countries in the early stages of forming agreements - such as printing, translating, and distributing treaties. This would reduce the cost of preparing arbitration agreements and, by ensuring that they are professionally prepared, greatly reduce the risk of expensive or time-consuming delays later in the application of those agreements.

STRUCTURE, PROCESS, OUTCOME: THOUGHTS ON THE 'ESSENCE' OF INTERNATIONAL ARBITRATION

M.C.W. Pinto[*]

1.   INTRODUCTION

The Hague Peace Conference of 1899 was attended by 27 states, the Conference of 1907 by 43, the overwhelming majority being from Europe and America. Among the participants were four from Asia: China, Japan, Persia and Siam. Their delegates, trained in the best European legal and diplomatic traditions, were assisted by European experts in explaining their positions on 'projects' (or drafts) of European or American origin.

No state from Africa attended either Hague Conference.

A third Hague Conference, which the Foreign Ministers of the Non-aligned countries propose should convene on the eve of the new millennium, and is likely to be attended by nearly 200 states, most of them from Asia and Africa. While the Conference may be expected to endorse many of the international dispute settlement concepts, structures and processes which five centuries of western economic dominance have considerably refined and propagated, it seems inevitable that the international instruments adopted by the conference will be significantly influenced by the positions taken by states from Asia and Africa, and so moved closer to the goal of universal acceptance. A Working Group of the Non-aligned countries' Coordinating Committee on the Peaceful Settlement of Disputes has undertaken the task of examining existing international instruments with a view precisely to drawing up a draft convention on the peaceful settlement of disputes that might, for the first time, become acceptable to all.

This paper invites reflection on one method of settling disputes, viz. international arbitration. It will suggest that the 'judicial' model of international arbitration, or the assimilation of arbitration to judicial settlement that evolved among the states which engaged in the process most frequently during the twentieth century, may not accord with the ancient character of the process, or arbitration as it is generally understood among states today; that the idea that arbitration in international law is not essentially different from judicial determination, may only prevail among those states; that certain essential features of arbitration continue to set it apart from judicial

---

[*] Attorney of Supreme Court of Sri Lanka; of the Inner Temple, Barrister-at-Law.

S. Muller and W. Mijs (eds.), The Flame Rekindled, 43–66.

determination of a dispute in international law; and that any future universal conference on dispute settlement ought to focus upon those features in an effort to clarify the nature and scope of arbitration as understood by states generally, and to develop it in ways that enhance its use and effectiveness.

2.   THE 'TRUE NATURE' OR 'ESSENCE' OF INTER-STATE ARBITRATION

A distinguished array of authors consider arbitration in international law virtually indistinguishable from judicial determination. Thus, Lauterpacht is critical of:

> [...] the tendency to provide for recourse to arbitral tribunals on the vague but persistent assumption that arbitral tribunals, although bound to apply law, need not somehow apply strict law; that their function lies midway between the application of law and adjudication *ex aequo et bono*; and that, therefore, the reference to these of disputes other than those concerning respective rights introduces the possibility of the law being changed in accordance with justice and political requirements.[1]

He argues that

> Even if arbitration within the state were wholly non-judicial this fact would be irrelevant for the determination of *the true nature of international arbitration*. For the function of arbitration is different in international and municipal law. In the latter it supplements -in a manner which is not essential to the life of the community- the rule of law by yet another legal institution; in international relations it lies at the very basis of the rule of law. Although voluntary in its origin, it fulfills the same function as normal judicial settlement within the state. [Emphasis added, *MP*][2]

Lauterpacht concludes that the judicial character of international arbitration is a matter of historical fact and of positive international law.[3]

What then *is* the 'true nature' of international arbitration, and is there a basis for the 'vague but persistent assumption' that arbitration tribunals, unlike courts, need not apply 'strict law'? The distinguishing characteristics of arbitration most frequently mentioned, are its 'voluntary' nature, and another, which derives from it, its 'flexibility'.

By 'voluntary nature' is meant the liberty of a state to decide whether or not to agree to submit a dispute to arbitration in order to settle it. This, in turn, implies that

---

1. H. Lauterpacht, The Function of Law in the International Community 379 (1933). *See also* J.H. Ralston, International Arbitration from Athens to Locarno 22 *et seq.* (1929) and the authorities cited in these works.
2. H. Lauterpacht, *supra* note 1 at 381, n. 2.
3. *id.*, at 381.

a state may choose whether or not another state is an acceptable party with which to engage in arbitration. Such a choice is often made by reference to whether or not there exists a bond of commonly held cultural values which would include legal traditions that are similar (or are recognized to be sound) and would be influenced by the existence of a common language or at least common language roots. This does not mean, of course, that the decision to arbitrate, or the choice of the other arbitrating party, would not be influenced to a greater or lesser extent by other factors, such as the relative bargaining power or the relative strength of a case.

The 'essence of arbitration' was a subject much discussed at the Hague Conference of 1907. Marschall von Bieberstein, for Germany, opposing 'obligatory arbitration' as being virtually a contradiction in terms because it would preclude the choice of contractants, had this to say:

> What constitutes the essence of arbitration? It is good understanding [...]. Now, all good understanding results from a disposition of the mind and of the soul. This is true both in private life and in international life. This disposition is inseparable from the personality and from the individuality of the contracting states, of their relations, of the community of sentiments, of interests and of traditions. [...] To exclude the choice of one's contractants [...] would mean the destruction of the ideal principle which forms the center of arbitration and which we must guard and care for [...].[4]

While the liberty to submit or not to submit disputes to arbitration, and the liberty to choose one's contractants might set arbitration apart from judicial proceedings in municipal law, or from some ideal of an international court with comprehensive compulsory jurisdiction, they would hardly be distinguishing characteristics when comparing it with current and former international courts, the jurisdiction of which is, and has been, based on consent. While declarations under provisions like those of Article 36(2) of the Statute of the International Court of Justice or Article 48 of the Hague Convention of 1907 might have the effect of limiting choice as to contractants to some degree, there is no obligation to make such declarations in the first place, so that use of the mechanism remains essentially 'optional'.

The element of 'flexibility', it is said, also sets arbitration apart from judicial proceedings. By flexibility is meant the adaptability of the institution to the exigencies of a particular situation or context, the nature of the dispute, or the needs or wishes of the parties. It is no more than a function of the 'voluntary' nature of arbitration, since after parties have taken the initial decision to resort to arbitration, 'flexibility' affords them a variety of auxiliary choices in the design of the actual arbitral mechanism, especially as to its *structure* and *process*. In this arbitration differs from court proceedings in both municipal and international law.

4. J.B. Scott, *The Proceedings of the Hague Peace Conferences,* trans. of the Official Texts, II The Conference of 1907, Meetings of the First Commission 49-50 (1921).

International and domestic courts are both organs established by the community, functioning according to rules and practices that admit of little variation by agreement between the parties. They are of a fixed composition, although the discretion conferred on the International Court of Justice to form a chamber for dealing with a particular case, and the element of party approval in its implementation, may have introduced an 'arbitral' attribute of flexibility.[5]

At the Hague Conference of 1907, 'justice' (a term used in place of 'court') was often contrasted with 'arbitration'. The following observations of Ruy Barbosa, delegate of Brazil, rejecting the proposal before the Conference to establish a system of 'obligatory arbitration' administered by a court of fixed composition, are illustrative:

> [...] justice and arbitration are both indispensable. Both have their legitimacy, their function, and their character. But in what way do they differ from each other? First of all, as to the source whence they come. Next, as to the social element that nurtures them. And lastly, as to the juridical form which they assume.
>
> The juridical form of justice is permanent and unalterable. It is the law that establishes it. With regard to arbitration, the juridical form is variable and casual. It is the agreement between the parties which decides that form. Justice emanates from sovereignty and imposes itself upon obedience. Its organs are created by power. The parties must submit to it. Arbitration, on the contrary, has its source in liberty. It is the work of a convention; it has no other authority except that admitted by the contractants, and its magistrates are those voluntarily chosen [...].[6]

The 'fixed' character of courts, excluding the parties' autonomy of choice as to judges, is emphasized in statements at the Conference by advocates of the establishment of a permanently constituted settlement mechanism different from the Permanent Court of Arbitration, and variously described in such terms as 'a really permanent tribunal', a 'veritable permanent court' (Marschall von Bieberstein) or, indeed, an 'International Court of Justice' (J.B. Scott, for the United States of America). It is implied in Scott's remark that the Permanent Court of Arbitration "[...] is not permanent because it is not composed of permanent judges [...] [and] [...] it is not a court because it is not composed of judges",[7] as well as in Asser's mildly macabre comment in the same vein, that "[i]nstead of a permanent court, the Convention of 1899 gave but the phantom of a court, an impalpable specter, or to be more precise yet, it gave us a recorder with a list".[8]

---

5. Statute of the International Court of Justice, Article 26, Para. 2.
6. *Supra* note 4, at 660.
7. *Supra* note 4, at 319.
8. *Supra* note 4, at 234.

3.   STRUCTURE

The aspect of flexibility to which most people frequently refer is the right of states to choose the person or persons who will carry out the arbitration of their dispute. Thus, the President of the Conference of 1907, Leon Bourgeois of France, drew attention to "[...] the right of choosing one's own judges, *a right which is of the very essence of arbitral justice*".[9] [Emphasis added, *MP*]

Mr. Beldiman (Roumania) spoke of the 'fundamental difference' between the International Prize Court, to have been established by Hague Convention No. XII of 1907, and what he called 'properly so-called *arbitral* justice' [original emphasis] in the following terms:

> The latter rests upon the free selection of judges by the states which decide to submit their controversy to arbitration; and it is precisely this freedom of sovereign states to constitute, by a common accord and for each case, the court to which they entrust the judgement of their dispute - it is this full freedom which is *the very essence of international arbitration*. On the other hand, the Prize Court will be an international tribunal organized in advance with judges irremovable for the duration of their appointment, and intended to act, in exceptional and well determined circumstances, upon the decisions of the national courts of each contracting state. [Original emphasis][10]

However, the 1907 Convention did take a cautious step in the direction of limiting the fullness of this freedom. By Article 45, disputing states are initially free to agree upon the number of members of a tribunal and their identity, with some emphasis on choice from among those inscribed on the 'general list' of the Permanent Court of Arbitration. Upon the failure to agree, the disputants are required to establish a five-member tribunal consisting of two members appointed by each (only one of whom may be a national of the appointing state or chosen from its PCA nominees) and an umpire chosen by a majority of the members so appointed. Where the latter cannot form a majority concerning choice of the umpire, that choice is to be made by a third state agreed between the disputants, or jointly by two such states each appointed by a disputant. Thus, while the element of choice of arbitrators is maintained, that choice might sometimes be exercised indirectly.

Neither the Convention of 1899, nor that of 1907, makes provision for a self-contained and self-executing procedure for the appointment of arbitrators in situations where one disputant failed to cooperate, or cooperate fully, in the exercise of its power of appointment. This lacuna, which made the arbitral process open to frustration was nevertheless deliberately left unfilled, testimony to the essential voluntary nature of the process, and equally, its vulnerability.

---

9. *Supra* note 4, at 2. In similar vein, Mr. Carlin (Switzerland) at 144-5; Mr. Brun (Denmark), at 147, and many others.
10. *Supra* note 4, at 14.

4.   PROCESS

The flexibility inherent in the *process* of arbitration is also considered to distinguish it from determination of a dispute by an international court. Thus, it might be said that states submitting to arbitration have, in principle, the liberty (1) to require that all stages of the proceedings remain private, and that the award should not be published; (2) to require that only a specified and defined aspect of the dispute be dealt with, precluding the tribunal, by their mere agreement, from taking cognizance of other aspects of the dispute that a court might have the authority, and perhaps the duty to examine; (3) to give directions to the tribunal as to the rules of law to be applied; and (4) to prescribe the general scope of the tribunal's procedural jurisdiction, concerning *e.g.* such matters as intervention in the proceedings by third parties, indication of provisional measures, and the rendering of an award on default of appearance, or other measure to be taken upon failure by a party to cooperate.

But to suggest that states have the right to set up a dispute settlement mechanism of their own with some or all of these features, is merely to affirm the liberty of states to contract, and not necessarily to demonstrate that, any settlement process they agree on is 'arbitration' because they decide to call it by that name. The latter term should continue to mean only that process, separate and distinct from judicial determination of a case, that is understood by the generality of states to have the attributes of arbitration properly so called.

As noted above, the Hague Conventions of 1899 and 1907, with the cumulative support of some 76 states parties, most widely accepted as the paradigm of inter-state arbitration, do make provision, on failure of disputants to cooperate, for a certain measure of automaticity directed toward constitution of the tribunal. However, they stop short of prescribing a system of appointment that would guarantee the constitution and functioning of the tribunal, in disregard of failure of a disputant to cooperate, and it was suggested that such an omission is unlikely to have been merely the result of an oversight. Situations such as that discussed by the International Court of Justice some 40 years later in the *Interpretation of Peace Treaties case with Bulgaria, Hungary and Romania (Second Phase)*[11] could hardly have been beyond contemplation by the distinguished delegates to the Hague Conferences, recalling as they must have done, the constitutional problems that had beset international arbitration since its very inception in the Jay Treaty.

11. Interpretation of Peace Treaties with Bulgaria, Hungary and Romania (Second Phase), 1950 I.C.J. Rep. 227, at 228-9. In its Advisory Opinion the Court held that where provisions on the constitution of a commission require that each party first appoint a member, and thereafter agree upon a third-country member, a power of appointment arising on default of agreement on the latter, conferred on the Secretary-General of the United Nations, could only be exercised after the party-appointed members were in place and had attempted to reach agreement. Failure by a party to appoint its 'national' member could thus, in the absence of express provision in the *compromis* governing the situation, halt constitution of the commission and frustrate the entire settlement process.

4.1. The role of law

Similarly, the Hague Conventions do not make a specific provision as to the nature of the law governing the dispute submitted to arbitration. That the Conventions contemplate the submission of 'questions of a legal nature' to arbitration is clear from Article 38 of the Convention of 1907 (Article 16 of the Convention of 1899). It is also provided that 'respect for law' is to be 'the basis' of the settlement arrived at, and that the members of the tribunal will act as 'judges' (Article 37 of the Convention of 1907; Article 15 of the Convention of 1899) in a process that could involve the taking of evidence, written pleadings and oral argument, followed by deliberation in private and a reasoned award that the parties will, by the fact of their recourse to the process, be presumed to have agreed to submit to in good faith. The Conventions do not, however, go so far, as do provisions on international courts (Article 38 in both the Statute of the Permanent Court of International Justice and the Statute of the International Court of Justice), as to prescribe the governing law, and in terms direct its application in deciding disputes before them.

The ordinary meaning and context of these provisions indicate a difference in the roles envisaged for law in describing respectively arbitration and judicial determination of a dispute. It was the function of the International Prize Court, co-eval with arbitration under the Convention of 1907, as it was later of the Permanent Court of International Justice (and at the present time, of the International Court of Justice) to decide disputes in accordance with and by the application of, law. It follows that decision of a dispute by reference to principles that are thought to fall outside strict law, e.g. *ex aequo et bono*, is only to be contemplated, as provided for in the Statutes of the two Courts, where the disputants have agreed to it. On the other hand, in arbitration under the Conventions of 1899 and 1907, differences are to be settled 'on the basis of respect for law', a phrase which, when given its ordinary meaning would seem to assign to 'law' a basic but by no means exclusive function, and to imply the admissibility of decisions *ex aequo et bono* unless the parties agree to exclude it.[12]

Of the different interpretations given to the phrase 'on the basis of respect for law', one authority observes:

> The Anglo-American jurists before the First World War who favoured the establishment of an international court were inclined to construe the words as 'in strict accordance with the law'. To them arbitration was merely the imperfect forerunner of a judicial body modelled on the lines of a municipal court. Yet, to many arbitrators in this early period, states' submission to arbitration provided an opportunity for reconciliation of national interests, and as the awards in the *Casablanca case* and the *North Atlantic Fisheries case* show, the arbitrators were prepared to waive a strict

---

12. Discussed in text *infra* 5.

application of the law in order to achieve an acceptable settlement. Today this difference of approach continues.[13]

International arbitration had been the forerunner of international courts. With the establishment of such a court in prospect, the distinct and separate nature of international arbitration was formally recognized. Thus, Article 12 of the Covenant of the League of Nations offered Members a choice of 'arbitration' or 'judicial settlement' as a means of resolving a 'dispute likely to lead to a rupture' in their relations. The following comment by Verzijl clearly implies the existence of a general conviction that the process of arbitration as understood in international law differed from that of judicial determination of a dispute, as well as the nature of that difference:

> When the idea of a real adjudication between states finally attained realization in 1920, the blue print for it was already prepared: the future Court should not perform a mediatory or conciliatory task, but it should be genuinely and in duty bound to administer existing law without regard to persons and without distorting the law from considerations of a political or expedient nature. In the Statute of the Court this principle was elaborated in an express enumeration of the rules and principles according to which justice be administered.[14]

4.2. Procedure

In keeping with the essentially voluntary nature of inter-state arbitration, the Hague Conventions contain only basic provisions on constitution of a tribunal (which, as has been noted, are open ended) and procedures for the conduct of the arbitration. The disputants are thus left to agree upon certain matters, however important. A checklist of such matters, to be agreed upon in the essential *compromis* to be concluded between the disputants, is offered by Article 52 of the Convention of 1907.

Thus, the Hague Conventions make no attempt to suggest to parties, much less require, that they adopt any particular mode of arbitration. Disputing states were left to elaborate upon the basic provisions of the Conventions - a process that presupposes the existence of a minimum of contact and cooperation between them or the existence of an intermediary - and to conclude the *compromis* that would regulate proceedings. While privacy of the process and equality of treatment of the parties are of the essence, the tribunal receives no directions as to the governing law or decisions *ex aequo et bono*, nor is it empowered to indicate provisional measures[15] or to issue

---

13. H. Fox, *Arbitration, in* International Disputes: the Legal Aspects, Report of a Study Group of the David Davies Memorial Institute of International Studies, at 102.

14. J.H.W. Verzijl, VIII International Law in Historical Perspective 106.

15. Of this power, conferred on the International Court of Justice by Article 41 of its Statute, Verzijl could write in 1976: "It is incontestable that the authors of the Statute have by this provision vested the court with a considerable power which surpasses by far the normal attributions of arbitrators"; *id.*, 150.

awards on default of appearance by a disputant. The Convention of 1899 even requires that the award bear the signature of every member of the tribunal, and would presumably be defective without it. No provision is made for dissenting opinions. The possibility of third party intervention is limited to cases of interpretation of multilateral conventions, and any power of the tribunal to revise an award must be agreed in the *compromis*.

By including only basic provisions on the structure of a tribunal and the arbitral process, the Hague Conventions sought to preserve the autonomy of the disputants, an aspect of the essential voluntary nature of international arbitration. In the decades that followed, states on either side of the Atlantic, which were in the vanguard of the development of the international arbitral process, impatient of the relatively imprecisely delineated and vulnerable nature of arbitration as outlined in the Hague Conventions, as well as the tendency of arbitrators to render decisions *ex aequo et bono* and 'waive strict application of the law', began to see these not as essential features of the arbitral process, inherent in it and derived from its voluntary character, but rather as anomalies in a settlement mechanism, in their view indistinguishable from the Permanent Court of International Justice (except in the matter of choice of judges), that should be remedied.

4.3. Toward 'judicial arbitration'

From this 'Atlantic' view of the nature of international arbitration two sets of initiatives developed: (1) to give the process the broadest possible application through a system of compulsory arbitration, or one that would require states to commit themselves in advance to arbitrate their disputes; (2) to develop comprehensive procedural rules that would turn the commitment to arbitrate into a self-sustaining and inexorable series of adversarial phases such as might follow the institution of proceedings before a court.

4.3.1. Compulsory arbitration

Already at the Hague Conference of 1907, a proposal for establishing a system described by some as 'compulsory arbitration' was rejected on grounds that it denied the essentially voluntary nature of arbitration, amounted to a contradiction in terms, and was, in any event, utopian. Discussion at the Conference foreshadowed controversies that were to persist throughout the half-century that followed. At issue were concessions to be made to the sensitivities of states through restoring a measure of autonomy within the 'obligatory' system by permitting them (a) to limit the undertaking to arbitrate to 'legal' disputes, and further, (b) to exclude from such commitment, disputes affecting 'honour', 'independence' or 'vital interests'.[16]

16. These exceptions generated extensive, but hardly conclusive, academic discussion. *See, e.g., id.,* 90 *et seq.*

The comments of Marschall von Bieberstein (Germany) on both issues have a timeless relevance:

> Arbitration is obligatory in matters of a *legal* order. What is the meaning of this word? It has been said that it may exclude 'political matters'. Now it is absolutely impossible, in a world treaty, to trace a line of demarcation between these two notions. A question may be legal in one country, and political in another one. There are even purely legal matters which become political at the time of a dispute. One of our most distinguished colleagues told us the other day, on another occasion, 'that politics is the realm of international law'. Do we desire to distinguish 'legal' questions from technical and economic questions? This would also be impossible. The result is that the word 'legal' states everything and states nothing, and in matters of interpretation the result is just the same. It has been asked: Who is to decide in case of some dispute, whether a question is or whether it is not legal? So far we have had no answer. Yet, this word 'legal' is the nail on which we have hung the whole system of obligatory arbitration along with the list and with the table. If this nail is not solidly fastened, everything hung on it will fall to the ground.
>
> As to the terms dealing with the exceptions, to wit: the honor, the independence and the vital interests, [...] I have shown that in a world treaty they are of no importance whatever. The evil, it is true, is palliated by the clause stating that each party will itself decide as to the exception which it has set forth. Then the other evil arises, because there is no longer any obligation. These two articles begin with the imperative words 'thou shalt' and end with the reassuring words 'if thou so desirest'. [...] here we have two articles not containing a single term which clearly defines the duties and the rights resulting therefrom, two articles which vacillate between the extreme poles of obligation and of privilege, and it is desired to recommend these dispositions to the world as 'the most efficacious means of settling international disputes'. For in these words arbitration has been defined in the Convention of 1899.[17]

Article 12 of the Covenant of the League of Nations offered Members a choice of submitting disputes to arbitration or to judicial settlement (in contemplation of the establishment of the Permanent Court of International Justice), or to enquiry by the League's Council, but deprived the provision of much of its authority through Article 13 which qualified the undertaking on submission to arbitration or judicial settlement so as to cover only disputes which Members 'recognize to be suitable' for such treatment. The inclusion of a paragraph listing disputes 'generally suitable for submission to arbitration or judicial settlement' (a list of what would be later characterised as 'legal disputes' in Article 36(2) of the Statute of the Permanent Court of International Justice) did little to strengthen the system. A Protocol of 1924 which would have created a residual settlement process, *inter alia*, giving the Council a role

17. *Supra* note 4, at 50.

in bringing reluctant disputants to accept arbitration or recourse to the Court and determining questions that threatened to frustrate the settlement effort, failed to gain sufficient support and was abandoned.

The idea of a comprehensive and compulsory dispute settlement system revived in the General Act for the Pacific Settlement of International Disputes of September 26, 1928 and was revised April 28, 1949. Under the General Act, 'disputes of every kind between two or more Parties' which are not settled through diplomacy are to be submitted to a residual procedure of conciliation. However, all 'legal disputes' (described simply as 'disputes with regard to which the parties are in conflict as to their respective rights' and by reference to article 36 of the Statute of the Court) are, by Article 17, to be submitted to the Permanent Court of International Justice (the International Court of Justice under the 1949 revision). The terms in which the General Act provides for recourse to arbitration may well reflect the dissatisfaction of those who favoured development of that process in the 'judicial' mode as being unable to convert the generality of states to that view: for whereas arbitration had hitherto been the method of choice for resolving 'legal' disputes, the General Act declares arbitration the process applicable to non-legal disputes, a term of similarly indeterminate scope.

Notwithstanding the Convention's directive that arbitration should henceforth be the means of settling non-legal disputes unresolved by conciliation, Article 28 requires the tribunal 'in regard to the substance of the dispute', to apply 'the rules [...] enumerated in Article 38 of the Statute of the [Court]', permitting decisions *ex aequo et bono* only if no such rule were applicable to the dispute; and provides constitutional and procedural safeguards against frustration of the process through failure of a party to cooperate, including reference to the President of the Court as appointing authority.

In the event, the General Act of 1928 was acceded to only by 35 states. Many accessions were subject to reservations provided for in respect of specified broad categories of disputes and some states excluded application of the arbitration provisions altogether. Revised in 1949 to adapt the system to the existence of the United Nations, it was ratified by only some 7 states, one state specifically excluding the application of the provisions on arbitration.

The European Convention on the Peaceful Settlement of Disputes of 1957 follows the General Act in requiring submission to the Court of 'international legal disputes', a category further elaborated in terms similar to Article 36(2) of the Statute of the International Court of Justice; submission of *all* disputes to conciliation; and submission of *non-legal* disputes unresolved through conciliation, to arbitration. While it provides constitutional and procedural safeguards against frustration of the process through failure of a party to cooperate, the Convention offers, as to the basis of the award, a flexibility reminiscent of the pristine character of arbitration, through residual application of the principle *ex aequo et bono* in Article 26:

> If nothing is laid down in the special agreement or no special agreement has been made, the tribunal shall decide *ex aequo et bono*, having regard to the general principles of international law, while respecting the contractual obligations and the final decisions of international tribunals which are binding on the parties.

It had been characteristic of the views of advocates of the evolution of international arbitration in the 'judicial' mode that to allow application of the principle *ex aequo et bono*, without qualifying or circumscribing it by reference to legal rules would confer too free a discretion on the arbitrator, a discretion that, as one authority observed "can easily be transformed into arbitrariness".[18] The residual application of the principle *ex aequo et bono*, wherein the Convention may have followed earlier bilateral Scandinavian and other European precedents, seems to stand at one end of the range of attitudes to arbitration, testimony to the 'good understanding' anticipated to prevail among like-minded and culturally similar parties. The European Convention, in force since 1958, has been ratified by 12 members of the Council of Europe, not including, however, France and the countries of the Eastern Mediterranean.

4.3.2. Comprehensive procedures

The efforts of the 'Atlantic' movement to cast international arbitration in the judicial mould were aimed not only at securing general commitment to recourse to arbitration, but also at developing comprehensive procedures similar to those of a court, designed to cure the process of its vulnerability to frustration through non-cooperation by a party. As was noted above, the results of those efforts are to be seen in a succession of instruments such as the abortive Protocol of 1924, and the General Acts of 1928/1949 all of which received only limited support. The International Law Commission's Model Rules on Arbitral Procedure completed in 1958, may represent the climax of those efforts, in particular, in the manner in which they provide meticulously against frustration of the process as the result of failure of a disputant to cooperate in it.

Thus, the Model Rules seek to assure conclusion of a comprehensive *compromis* and constitution of the tribunal as well as its continued effectiveness, and to regulate aspects of arbitral procedure. As to the basis for the tribunal's decision, the Rules specify 'the law to be applied' along the lines of Article 38 of the Statute of the International Court of Justice, conferring the power to decide *ex aequo et bono* only "if the agreement between the parties so provides [...]".

If the Model Rules are the highwatermark of legal scholarship in the field of inter-state arbitration, they also represent a point far removed from what the majority of states are willing to apply in settling their disputes. While in the UN General

---

18. A. Mérignac, *Traité theorique et pratique de l'arbitrage international* 290. Quoted *in* L.B. Sohn, *The Function of International Arbitration Today*, I Hague Recueil (1963), at 9, 42, in his discussion of the nature of decisions *ex aequo et bono*.

Assembly, one group of states which included the United States, the United Kingdom and some, but not all of the Western European states, were willing to adopt the Commission's recommendations, a very large number of representatives including those from the developing countries and the states of Eastern Europe, opposed them on the ground, *inter alia*, that they violated what in their opinion was a basic principle of arbitration, *viz.* retention of sufficient party autonomy. In the event, the Commission's work was, by Assembly resolution, merely brought to the attention of Governments for their consideration, use as appropriate, and for further comment that might facilitate review of the Rules in the future.[19] The Commission's Special Rapporteur himself summarized a wide spectrum of critical views as follows:

> The Commission's draft would distort traditional arbitration practice, making it into a quasi-compulsory jurisdictional procedure, instead of preserving its classical diploma-tic character, in which it admittedly produces a legally binding, but final, solution, while leaving Governments considerable freedom as regards the conduct and even the outcome of the procedure, both wholly dependent on the form of the *compromis*.[20]

States have thus far shunned the Model Rules, preferring to incorporate in their bilateral treaties a reference to the less comprehensive procedures of the Hague Conventions.

The 1982 UN Law of the Sea Convention's procedures for constituting an arbitral tribunal resemble those of the Hague Conventions for setting up the Permanent Court of Arbitration, in that appointment to the Tribunal is to be made from lists of nominees of each Member State maintained by the Secretary-General of the United Nations, and frustration of the process through non-cooperation by one of the parties is minimized through devices such as conferring a power of appointment on third parties. However, in provisions of rare stringency, the Convention states that 'the absence or abstention of less than half of the members shall not constitute a bar to the tribunal reaching a decision' (Annex VII, Article 8), and empowers the tribunal to make an award on default of appearance by one party (Annex VII, Article 9). The arbitration process prescribed by the Convention thus seems to go further than ever toward subjecting inter-state disputes to a compulsory judicial-type procedure further, in some respects, than even the procedure prescribed for the commercial arbitration of certain sea-bed disputes, to which the UNCITRAL Arbitration Rules apply (Annex III, Article 5, Para. 4).

The UN Convention on the Law of the Sea contains the only provisions on compulsory dispute settlement which, despite their comprehensiveness and stringency,

19. U.N. G.A. Res. 1262 (XIII).
20. 9 (II) Y.B.I.L.C., at 2 (1957).

have received general acceptance at a diplomatic conference which included representatives from countries with different legal, social and economic systems, as well as different levels of economic development. This may be a reflection of the limited nature of the subject-matter of the disputes to be submitted to the system; the flexibility of the system as a whole, which does not compel acceptance of any particular settlement mechanism; the fact that the rules of law to be applied had, to a considerable extent, been negotiated and agreed upon at the Conference on the Law of the Sea or were to be negotiated at such conferences in the future, and possibly the level of understanding and confidence that had evolved among the participants over some 10 years of association. It is unlikely that inclusion in the Convention's system of a tightly drawn arbitral mechanism indicates a trend toward extended acceptance of arbitration in its 'judicial' mode.

4.4.   'Flexibility' and the filling of gaps and loopholes

In contrast to the positions of states which conceive of arbitration in the judicial form, epitomised in the Model Rules of the International Law Commission, are those of states which view arbitration as a mechanism which, while it involves a final and binding judgement on the basis of respect for law, would allow substantial scope for party autonomy prior to the rendering of an award, and see in it a useful, if fragile process. For the latter, 'flexibility' of the process would imply that there could be an appeal to the autonomy of the will of the parties at all stages of the arbitration prior to the issuance of the award, leaving the process vulnerable to interruption, if, for example, circumstances, or a party's perception of them, should alter radically. As one authority has observed:

> [I]t is scarcely necessary to review the many stages at which a state may call a halt to an arbitration; a state's consent may be refused to the recognition of any dispute requiring submission to arbitration, to the signing of the *compromis* which defines the terms of reference and powers of the arbitrator, to the constitution of the tribunal either by failure to appoint its own national member or by failure to agree to the neutral members. Even when the arbitration tribunal has been properly constituted and has opened its proceedings a state may block progress by failure to appear, refusal to afford the tribunal the necessary information or facilities for investigation and, in the event of some change in the membership of the tribunal, refusal to appoint or agree to the appointment of a substitute. Consent, not only given at the beginning of the arbitration proceedings, but continued throughout the proceedings until the tribunal retires to make its award, is, therefore, an essential ingredient to the completion of any arbitration.[21]

Such a view was, and continues to be, widely held, and moreover causes its adherents

---

21. *See* H. Fox, *supra* note 13, at 101.

to lean away from filling gaps as the chief means of developing arbitration. Writing of the future of international arbitration in 1917 against the background of the Hague Conferences, Sir Thomas Barclay remarked the reluctance of even 'states of the first rank' to agree to enlargement of the scope of arbitration, observing:

> [W]e must not overlook the fact that there is something to be said in favour of providing a loophole by which either Contracting Party can escape in any particular emergency from its obligations. Treaties between nations, unfortunately, are not exactly in the same position as contracts between individuals. The best sanction they have is the sense of honour and justice of the Contracting Parties, and it may be argued that it will always be better to let a state escape from a Treaty through its own provisions than by violating them.[22]

The Netherlands Government, which had been host to the Conferences of 1899 and 1907, and whose dedication to the rule of law and concern for the development of arbitration could scarcely be questioned, expressed its misgivings as to the Commission's Model Rules in the following terms:

> A highly important characteristic difference between [arbitration and adjudication] is to be found in the greater prerogatives of the parties allowed for in arbitration, in regard to both the composition of the tribunal as well as the course of the procedure. From this special characteristic of arbitration follows the undesired consequence that it is rather easy for an unwilling party to find an excuse for shirking its engagements. For that very reason, the barring of this way out has been under study since the first Hague Conference, 1899. The draft convention of the International Law Commission has paid much attention to the same matter with a view to setting up some watertight rules rendering impossible any future attempt at evasion by a state which once accepted binding arbitration. However praiseworthy this ambition is, yet some doubt may arise whether in this way arbitration will not be divested of one of its specific characteristics and whether this may not entail the impossibility for arbitration to maintain itself beside international judicature. In other words: may not arbitration lose its attractiveness for the states?[23]

Another commentator, observing that the Commission's work had been principally shaped and directed by a perceived need to repair procedural defects, warns of the change in the essence of arbitration that could result:

---

22. T. Barclay, New Methods of Adjusting International Disputes and The Future 67 (1917), at 68.
23. 5 (II) Y.B.I.L.C. 235 (1953). Julius Stone expressed a similar opinion: "The features of arbitration law which offer so many avenues of escape and which serve in the Commission's eyes as excuses for 'shirking' international undertakings, may be the very features which attract states to enter into social undertakings". J. Stone, Legal Controls of International Conflicts 736 (1954).

> The Commission has sought to create a type of arbitration which it terms 'judicial arbitration', and which is proposed as a means for correcting these procedural defects [...]. The difficulty with the approach adopted by the Commission, however, is that, by including these proposals with a purported codification of the rules of international arbitral procedure in a single document [...] the effect [...] is, in essence, to *supplant* rather than to *supplement* the process of international arbitration in its existing stage of development [...]
>
> The process of international arbitration, in its present form, has grown up as one of a number of media for the pacific settlement of international disputes. It exists for that purpose and that purpose alone. It is not an end in itself *and its perfection should not be dictated by logic but rather by so fashioning it that it will retain its attractiveness to governments as a means for the solution of disputes.*[24] [Emphasis added, MP]

Finally, we may note in this connection the advice of Charles de Visscher, at the time Honorary President of the *Institut de Droit International*, and a former Judge of the International Court of Justice who, while praising the technical quality of the Commission's Model Rules, warned that the draft,

> [b]y endeavouring [...] to plug up all the openings and to foresee every loophole, in a word, to enclose arbitration within a rigid framework, runs the risk of hindering its development. As the Netherlands Government observed, perfectionist aspirations threaten to end up by 'petrifying' the evolution of arbitral practice.[25]

Any future study of international arbitration ought, it would seem, to focus not merely on the search for procedural perfection that, for various reasons, has characterised the efforts of a particular group of states, but first on reaching a consensus among the whole of the international community as to the essence of arbitration, and then on the complex task of finding ways of developing it without compromising its 'voluntary' character.

5.   OUTCOME

Similarity of outcomes as between international arbitration and judicial determination of a dispute is frequently described in formal terms. Both processes are based on the application of law to a dispute, calling for a reasoned conclusion ('award' or 'judgement'), and implying that that conclusion is final and binding on the parties. Thus, outcome is not an element generally discussed in distinguishing the two processes. While some studies suggest that such a distinction could be drawn in real

24. K.S. Carlston, *International Arbitration Procedure*, 19 The Arbitration Journal 84 (1957), at 85.
25. Charles de Visscher, *Reflections on the Present Prospects for International Adjudication*, 50 AJIL 469-470 (1956).

terms, there may be difficulties involved in demonstrating this, since both award and judgement emerge from deliberations that are private, and remain secret.

Early writings on arbitration are more candid. Already in the 17th century Grotius had quoted Aristotle as saying that:

> an equitable and moderate man will have recourse to arbitration rather than to strict law [...] because an arbitrator may consider the equity of the case, whereas a judge is bound by the letter of the law. Therefore arbitration was introduced to give equity its due weight.

"Equity", Grotius went on to explain, "includes everything, which it is more proper to do than to omit, even beyond what is required by the express rules of justice".[26] A modern authority renders Aristotle's words in English as follows:

> The equitable man [...] is not a stickler for his rights in a strict sense, but takes less than his share though he has the law on his side [...]. Equity bids us to be merciful to the weakness of human nature [...], not to consider [...] this or that detail so much as the whole story. It bids us [...] to settle by negotiation and not by force; to prefer arbitration to litigation - for an arbitrator goes by the equity of a case, a judge by the strict law, and arbitration was invented with the express purpose of securing full power for equity.[27]

We are told that the spirit of negotiation and compromise contributed in no small measure to the settlements achieved in arbitrations under the Jay Treaty and the Treaty of Ghent. The representative of the United States of America is quoted as saying of the award of the King of the Netherlands in the *North-eastern Boundary case* dealt with under the latter treaty:

> An umpire, be he a King or a farmer, rarely decides on strict principles of law: he has always a bias to try if possible to split the difference, and, with that bias, he is very apt to consider any previous proposal from either party as a concession that his title was defective, and as justifying a decision on his part that will not displease too much either party, instead of one founded on a strict investigation of title.[28]

As summarized by one commentator: "the arbitrator desires to settle the dispute and to satisfy the parties through a decision which will ensure peace. He decides the

---

26. H. Grotius, *De jure belli ac pacis*, Book III, Chapter XX.47, trans. by A.C. Campbell (1901) at 398, quoting Aristotle, Rhetoric I, 13.
27. J. Frank, Courts on Trial: Myth and Reality in American Justice 378-379 (paperback ed. 1973).
28. Gallatin, United States Minister to the Court of St. James, in a letter to Secretary of State Henry Clay, October 30, 1826, quoted *in* P.E. Corbett, Law in Diplomacy 146-147 (1959).

matter not according to law, but disposes of it *ex aequo et bono*".[29]

The transition from frank acknowledgement that arbitration is a mechanism that emphasizes *settlement* of a dispute through a decision which, although based on respect for law, 'will not displease too much either party', to the development of a concept of 'judicial' arbitration that emphasized the *application of law* to the dispute, that occurred among some 'Atlantic' states, was closely connected with their dedicated efforts to create a system of 'compulsory arbitration' as a step toward, the establishment of an international court on the domestic model. That transition is evident in an address by Secretary of State Elihu Root at the opening of the National Arbitration and Peace Congress in New York in 1907. Contrasting 'impartial judgement', such as is exercised by judicial officers everywhere, with 'an international arbitration [...] often regarded as an occasion for diplomatic adjustment', he calls for the establishment of a court of permanent judges, 'who will have no other occupation or interest but the exercise of the judicial faculty'.[30] On the latter view, an arbitral process which led to a settlement incorporating a 'diplomatic adjustment' could not be regarded as impartial and would not be in conformity with judicial standards and would be fundamentally flawed. It was a short step to saying that such a process should not be considered arbitration at all, and that only 'judicial' arbitration should be arbitration properly so called.

By the time Rapporteurs Borel and Politis presented their report to the *Institut de Droit International* in 1927, the 'Atlantic' concept of arbitration seems to have gained currency to the extent that they too, seem to imply that arbitration in the judicial mode is '*l'arbitrage proprement dit*'. The observations that follow show, however, that that view was far from generally accepted even within the essentially western schools of thought of the time:

> *Très souvent, les tribunaux d'arbitres ne s'attachent pas à l'application du droit comme tel; leurs sentences sont fondées, soit sur l'équité, soit sur des considérations pratiques conduisant les arbitres à la solution jugée la plus opportune. [...] Peu à peu, cependant, la notion de l'arbitrage, en tant qu'institution véritablement judiciaire, s'affermit [...]. Mais encore aujourd'hui le terme arbitrage conserve, dans les ouvrages de droit international et dans le langage officiel, un sens général, embrassant*

---

29. H. Wehberg, The Problem of an International Court of Justice 14 (1918), quoting Pohl. The Secretary-General of the Permanent Court of Arbitration, in a Note to Member States dated March 3, 1960, reproduced *in* 54 AJIL 933 (1960), urged that "in cases where parties agreed to settle their differences *ex aequo et bono*, the arbitral tribunal is definitely a more appropriate organism" than the International Court of Justice; and that "the decision *ex aequo et bono* can be of value in cases where the settlement of non-juridical differences is concerned". In doing so, the Secretary-General found support in the opinion of Charles de Visscher that "Settlement *ex aequo et bono* definitely fits the arbitral function better than the properly judicial one".
30. Quoted by J.B. Scott, *supra* note 4 at 317.

les cas où la solution, à strictement parler, présente plutôt le caractère d'une médiation obligatoire.[31]

Although the British Government joined the United States in supporting the proposal at the Conference of 1907 for the establishment of a permanent 'Court of Arbitral Justice' several distinguished publicists of the period from Britain did not share the view that arbitration would be tainted if it did not maintain a strictly judicial character or even that the concept 'arbitration' comprehended a range of settlement mechanisms, including one that was 'truly judicial'. On the contrary, their writings, based on a review of existing arbitral practice, imply that an outcome that had in it an element of compromise was actually characteristic of the international arbitral process.

Thus, Sir Thomas Barclay, having reviewed cases that had been the subject of arbitrations under the auspices of the Permanent Court of Arbitration reached the following conclusions:

> [...] the decisions have been based less on the idea that the mission of the arbitrators is to give their decision in strict accordance with law, than on that they must find a method of closing the matter with the minimum of ill-feeling on either side [...] in international cases, to steer between the arguments of Parties who regard their case with equal conviction of justice being on their side, is more strictly in conformity with the objects of arbitration than to give a strictly legal decision which, if a grievance resulted, would discourage recourse to this method of settling differences [...].
> The best, perhaps after all, that we can get from an International Court of Arbitration is not necessarily justice, but a settlement which closes the incident or grievance and permits of its being eliminated from both national and international preoccupations and becoming as soon as possible a thing in the past.[32]

Oppenheim, then Whewell Professor of International Law at Cambridge, himself confirms that

> [...] an arbitral tribunal is not a court in the real sense of the word, for its decisions are not necessarily based on rules of law, and it does not necessarily deal with legal matters. An arbiter, *unless the terms of reference otherwise provide* [emphasis added], decides *ex aequo et bono*, whilst a judge founds his decision on rules of law and is only applied to on legal issues [...]. The experience which we have so far had of arbitral tribunals shows that they make praiseworthy efforts to arrive at a finding which shall

---

31. E. Borel and N. Politis, *L'Extension de l'Arbitrage Obligatoire et la Competence Obligatoire de la Cour Permanente de Justice Internationale*, II Annuaire de l'Institut de Droit International 669 *et seq.* and 681 (1927)
32. T. Barclay, *supra* note 22, at 85, 86, 91.

as far as possible satisfy both parties, and that they have in view a compromise rather than a genuine declaration of law.[33]

Such statements suggest that, notwithstanding the efforts of some countries to create for international arbitration a 'judicial' model, emphasis on a 'settlement which closes the incident' and a decision characterized by compromise remained of the essence of the outcome anticipated from the arbitral process.[34] The statement by Oppenheim indicates how far the movement among the 'Atlantic' states toward a judicial model for arbitration had obscured in the process an essential element affecting its outcome: whereas an arbitrator was presumed to have the authority to decide *ex aequo et bono* unless the arbitrating parties agreed otherwise, the Commission's Model Rules, following other Atlantic models, sought to re-affirm the very opposite principle, *viz.* that the arbitrator may decide *ex aequo et bono* only if the parties expressly so agreed.

The views of the great majority of states from Asia and Africa on the matter remained unexpressed and, at least until after the Second World War, not even subjected by them to internal study directed at policy formulation. The fate of the Commission's draft when reviewed by the states represented at the General Assembly in 1958 (relatively few at the time, prior to the decolonizations of the 1960s) tells its own story.

6. PARTY AUTONOMY AND MODEL ARBITRATION RULES

The authority to decide whether or not to submit a dispute to international arbitration is an incident of party autonomy and, in the case of inter-state disputes, of state sovereignty. The 'voluntary' nature of arbitration, considered to be of its essence, enables disputing states to arrange a settlement process that will be 'arbitration' if the parameters of that process are present. They may similarly arrange for conciliation, or for the establishment of an *ad hoc* court. But if arbitration is chosen, each party has the right to expect that the process called by that name will be characterized by certain features of structure, process and outcome that are of the essence of arbitration.

Submission of a dispute to arbitration implies at least two sets of limits on the

---

33. L. Oppenheim, The Future of International Law 46-47 (1921).
34. The outcome of one of the most important of arbitrations has been similarly characterized. According to one author "[...] the jurisprudential value of the awards of the Iran-U.S. Claims Tribunal are open to doubt on the ground that they were based on an agreement settling a political dispute and that there was an effort made by the Tribunal to approach issues in a manner favouring compromise rather than provoking contention".
M. Sornarajah, The Pursuit of Nationalized Property 200 (1986). While the 'jurisprudential value' of the tribunal's awards has been otherwise widely acclaimed and requires no comment here, one may recall Garner's observation that "[...] the principal function of arbitration is to settle international differences and not to develop a body of international law". J.W. Garner, Recent Developments in International Law 524 (1922).

subsequent exercise of party autonomy: (1) the parameters or essential features of what is generally understood to be arbitration; and (2) the willingness of the other disputing party to agree on details of the organization of the settlement process. The 'autonomy' of a disputing party is therefore no more than the freedom to *negotiate agreement* on aspects of the process, not the freedom to introduce into it any element that serves its own interests or conforms to its special view of arbitration.

Between disputants of comparable economic strengths, with cultural affinities in matters such as legal tradition and language, bargaining strength may be expected to be balanced, and there would evolve from the negotiation the 'good understanding' that Marschall von Bieberstein thought should constitute the essence of arbitration. On the other hand, negotiation of an agreement to arbitrate as between disputants with widely disparate economic strengths and little cultural affinity may well result in an agreement reflecting the position of the stronger side as to the structure, and process of the settlement mechanism and foreshadow a similarly weighted outcome.[35] It is in the latter circumstance that the existence of model rules of arbitral procedure that are intended merely for the convenience of parties could, depending on their scope and content, fail to serve both disputants equally.

Although the application of a set of model rules might be agreed in advance by the disputants, subject to modification as to matters of detail, any such modification must likewise be the subject of agreement between them. However, adoption of model rules as the 'basis' for a negotiated agreement between them, will tend to have the effect that those rules *will apply unless both disputants agree to change them.* From the moment of the adoption of the rules as a basis, the playing field is no longer level and the implications of bargaining strength are enhanced. It is thus of the first importance that model arbitration rules offered by institutions concerned with settlement of inter-state disputes be drawn up after the views of all states of the community, as to their scope and content, have been taken into account. Rules which, in the view of the generality of states, would regulate matters that disputants should be left to agree upon uninfluenced by advance prescriptions, or that are not consistent with the general understanding of the 'essence' of arbitration, should be excluded. In this way, the effect of difference in the disputants' relative bargaining strengths - manifest to some degree in all aspects of international arbitration because of its contractual foundation and 'party autonomy'- would be minimized and moderated.

From the fate of the International Law Commission's Model Rules and others of similar scope, it would seem that, when such sets of rules exceed a certain degree of 'comprehensiveness' they risk being considered 'rigid', *i.e.* impairing party autonomy through offering prescriptions that may accord with the expectations of one side only, and may thus be shunned by some of the very states whose convenience they were

35. As to the theoretical basis for the view that a just outcome of an arbitration, interpreted as an outcome that is of mutual advantage to arbitrating parties, will reflect their relative bargaining strengths, *see* B. Barry, Theories of Justice 9 *et seq.* (1989).

intended to serve. Accordingly, when such model rules are discussed at some future conference, states may want to limit the scope of the rules to those basic provisions on structure, process and outcome that attract widespread and substantial support.[36] They may, however, want to attach to the rules, a separate list of matters as to which disputants are directed to negotiate agreement with a view to preserving the integrity of the process, developing in this way the technique followed in Article 52 of the Hague Convention of 1907. The latter might refer to various options for dealing with situations in which an arbitrating party or an arbitrator has failed to cooperate, and the role assigned to law in the settlement process. Alternative formulations may be included for the convenience of parties. Such a two-tiered approach would be more consistent with balanced treatment of the disputants than were the comprehensive texts inspired by the 'Atlantic' model, while being fully in accord with the 'voluntary' nature of arbitration, thought to be of its essence. The appeal of arbitration as a means for settling disputes between parties of disparate bargaining strengths would also be extended.

7.   DIRECTIONS FOR DEVELOPMENT

Recognition of the problems associated with the use of arbitration in its 'judicial' mode to resolve disputes between states inspired several proposals as to ways in which the arbitral process might be developed and applied. Several such proposals were reviewed by Professor Sohn, whose own proposals deserve, and have received careful attention. Having recalled the proposal of Lord David Davies (1934) for an arbitral tribunal deciding 'on the basis of equity and good conscience, political disputes, including those which have to do with the revision of treaties', a proposal for a Permanent Court of International Equity to decide non-legal disputes, prepared by Strupp (1937) and another group of proposals for mechanisms for inquiry and the rendering of advisory conclusions that would assist in resolving inter-state disputes through bringing about 'peaceful change' on the basis of consent (1937), Professor Sohn expresses his own preference for referring "non-legal disputes to an international arbitral tribunal empowered to decide *ex aequo et bono* either in all cases or, at least, in so far as there is no rule of international law applicable to the particular dispute".[37]

In implementing the proposal, he would not rely upon cumbersome machinery requiring that a special tribunal to be selected in each case, but would prefer the establishment of a permanent arbitral tribunal, perhaps called the 'Court of Arbitral

36. As Charles de Visscher observed, "It is better to recognize [the reality that political tensions make states reluctant to submit disputes to arbitration] clearly than to wander afield in the search for procedural reforms which remedy nothing". *See supra* note 25, at 474. *See also* the conclusions of one of the few Asian scholars to address the subject: "The road to progress lies not in framing rigid rules of procedure to make arbitration effective, but in creating conditions which may prove congenial for resolving disputes". M.A. Chaudhri (ed.), The Prospects of International Arbitration 19 (1966).
37. L.B. Sohn, *supra* note 18, at 98.

Justice', on which states would be invited to confer jurisdiction in non-legal disputes. The Tribunal would also be given an advisory competence, under which the Security Council and the General Assembly of the United Nations might have recourse regarding the merits of important disputes.

Professor Sohn emphasizes the importance of the personal attributes of the members:

> To a large extent the prestige and influence of the tribunal would depend on its composition [...] the tribunal should be composed of elder statesmen having a worldwide reputation and of other persons well-known for their ability, integrity and impartiality.[38]

As to its working,

> The proposed tribunal could investigate carefully all the relevant facts and prepare a decision or an advisory opinion which would try to balance the interests of both sides. In a case in which one side would have to make a greater sacrifice than the other, the tribunal might arrange for a reasonable compensation or for some other benefit, either temporary or permanent, which would make it easier for that side to accept the award or opinion.
> The proposed solution might also require some other states not directly involved in the dispute to take certain action in the interest of peace which would make the suggested settlement more acceptable to the parties.[39]

While the 1957 European Convention referred to above, and proposals like those of Professor Sohn may well indicate directions in which inter-state arbitration should evolve if it is to increase its appeal to governments and enhance the prospect of acceptability to states generally, it might be useful if, as a preliminary step, the arbitral process could be subjected to careful analytical study, perhaps in connection with preparatory work for the third Hague Peace Conference contemplated for 1999. Such a study, which might, for example, take place under the aegis of the United Nations, the Non-aligned countries' Coordinating Committee on the Peaceful Settlement of Disputes, the Asian-African Legal Consultative Committee, or the Permanent Court of Arbitration, should be the work not only of legal experts, but also of experts in such fields as political science, international relations, the sociology of law, language and conflict resolution, as well as legal anthropology.[40] The study could focus on relevant aspects of the relationship between the parties to a dispute, with a view to arriving at a commonly held perception of the essentials of the arbitral process. This, in turn, could lead to a better appreciation of the expectations of the parties as to what could be achieved through arbitration, and lay the foundation for a genuine consensus as to the implications of a state's agreement to submit to the process. The objective of

38. *Id.*, at 99.
39. *Id.*, at 100.
40. Study of the role of arbitrator would be of central importance in a study of arbitration as an institution.

→

the study would be to reconcile views on these subjects as an essential pre-requisite to formulating rules which all states might be invited to accept. Those rules would not, then, be based necessarily on a concept of international arbitration held by any particular state or group of states, but upon a common perception of the arbitral process derived from scientific inquiry to which the relevant disciplines, including, in particular, the legal, will have contributed.[41]

A proposal for such a study to be carried out on an inter-disciplinary basis, may well be met with scepticism, if not indifference, by international lawyers, and possibly dismissed as a 'soft' approach to problems that call for legally oriented solutions characterised as 'realistic' and 'practical'. On the other hand, it is difficult to avoid the conclusion that the latter type of 'solution' has not enjoyed conspicuous success world-wide through encouraging states to settle their disputes through arbitration. Today, in many important fields of endeavour, there is a preference for taking initiatives on the basis of the best available scientific evidence and advice. The attempt to develop an acceptable mechanism for settling disputes among states preventing friction and promoting harmony among them, should surely not be accorded less thoughtful treatment. We should pay heed to the warning of Ruy Barbosa, eloquent delegate of Brazil to the Conference of 1907: "Progress there will ever be in arbitration. We must ever develop it. But to develop it more and more, we must not change its nature".[42]

Simon Roberts concludes a discussion of dispute settlement in a range of societies with this description of differences between the roles of 'arbitrator' and 'adjudicator' which appears equally applicable in the international sphere: "Because the arbitrator depends for his authority to make a decision upon the disputants' agreement that he should do so, he must be sensitive towards their opinions as to what an acceptable decision might be; otherwise the chances of his decision being complied with, and of his being approached to deal with subsequent quarrels, will be small. Such considerations are not present in the case of the adjudicator who hears and decides a dispute by virtue of his office in the community. Not only is he entitled to hear the dispute but he is also likely to have force at his disposal to ensure compliance with his decision if the parties do not like it. Only in the much longer term can unpopular decisions affect his legitimacy"; S. Roberts, Order and Dispute: An Introduction to Legal Anthropology 78 (1979). For a criticism of the 'anthropological approach', *see* J. Frank, *supra* note 27.

41. Not only should the study cover aspects of the structures, processes and outcomes associated with international arbitration, such as those discussed or referred to above, but it might also usefully address the cultural dimensions of a state's approach to international arbitration as part of the effort to arrive at a common perception of the nature of the arbitral process. It cannot be denied that arbitration, as a process established and intended to function in accordance with the agreement of disputing parties, and distinct from determination of a dispute by a court as the organ established by the community, has existed in some form in all cultures. It seems likely therefore that attitudes to international arbitration in different countries would be influenced by a culturally distinct view of the essence of arbitration. Such views ought to be heard and taken into account before a common understanding is reached regarding the implications of recourse to 'arbitration'. However, some scholars have tended to discount the relevance of culture to the development of international law in general; *see* W. Friedmann, The Changing Structure of International Law 313-314 (1964), and dispute settlement in particular; *see* R.P. Anand, International Courts and Contemporary Conflicts 315 (1974).

42. *See supra* note 4, at 662.

SOME REFLECTIONS ON THE NATURE OF ARBITRATION

Howard M. Holtzmann*

The Secretary-General of the United Nations, Dr. Boutros Boutros-Ghali, in his perceptive Introduction to this second *Special Issue* of the *Leiden Journal of International Law* notes that the occasion of this publication provides an opportunity for "reflections on international dispute settlement". I respond to this opportunity by offering ten personal reflections based on experiences gained from participating for some years in the arbitral process as a lawyer, as a co-draftsman of a number of arbitration rules and laws, and, for the last decade, as an arbitrator on an international tribunal.

I.

When reflecting on the nature of arbitration between states, the first question that comes to mind is "compared to what?" That train of thought invariably leads to comparing arbitration with adjudication by an international court, a comparison that has been the subject of extensive analysis in the literature from Aristotle to contemporary commentators.[1] In such analyses an initial question that is often explored is whether arbitration between states is a judicial process designed to reach a decision based on the application of legal principles, or whether it is an extension of a diplomatic process aimed at finding a middle ground that, it is hoped, will be perceived as fair and acceptable to the parties.[2] To this long-debated question, I have

---

* Judge, Iran-United States Claims Tribunal. The author was a member of the United States delegation to UNCITRAL when it adopted the UNCITRAL Arbitration Rules, and was a member of the Working Group, the Expert Group and the Drafting Committee that considered the PCA Optional Rules discussed herein. The views expressed herein are his own, and do not necessarily reflect those of the United States or the PCA. The author is grateful to Charles R. Eskridge, III, for his assistance in preparing this article.
1. All who consider this subject must be indebted to M.C.W. Pinto for his remarkable survey of the comparative conceptual bases and the historical development of international arbitration in *The Prospects for International Arbitration of Inter-State Disputes, in* A.H.A. Soons (ed.), International Arbitration: Past and Prospects 63-99 (1989) [hereinafter *Pinto*]. These views are further developed *in* Pinto, *Structure; Process and Outcome: Thoughts on the 'Essence' of International Arbitration*, LJIL *Special Issue* (1993) 43.
2. *See, e.g., id.,* 64-65, 71.

S. Muller and W. Mijs (eds.), The Flame Rekindled, 67–79.

two observations and one more fundamental comment. First, 'diplomatic' and 'judicial' approaches often lead to similar results, for decisions based on application of legal principles may result, by application of those principles, in parties receiving less than total victory or complete defeat. Second, compromised decisions are not always advantageous, because reasoned arbitral awards shown to be grounded on legal principles can (even if disappointing) often be more easily accepted, intellectually or politically, than decisions that cannot be seen to have objective motivation. Third -and most importantly- the question of the nature of arbitration need not be debated at all, for arbitration is whatever the parties mutually agree that it should be. If parties want their disputes to be decided in accordance with established procedures and by application of defined legal principles they are free to say so, or, alternatively, they are equally free to agree upon other procedures and guidelines for decision.

This leads to the observation that the essence of the nature of arbitration can be summed up in two words: *party autonomy*. Arbitration differs from judicial process in the extent of the freedom of the parties mutually to agree on (i) the persons who will decide the dispute, or at least the method for choosing those persons, (ii) the procedure to be followed in the case, and (iii) the principles, legal or otherwise, that are to govern the decision. Given the primacy of party autonomy in the arbitral process, the reflections that follow will often revert to that freedom.

II.

In order to provide convenient bases for comparing adjudication by an international court with determination by an arbitral tribunal, I will refer, on the one hand, to the Statute[3] and Rules of Court[4] of the International Court of Justice ('the ICJ Statute' and 'the ICJ Rules of Court', respectively), which are the paradigm for judicial resolution of disputes between states, and, on the other hand, to the new Permanent Court of Arbitration Optional Rules for Arbitrating Disputes Between Two States adopted October 20, 1992 ('the PCA Rules'), which are the most recent rules for arbitration of state-to-state disputes.[5]

Because the PCA Rules are referred to as a principal basis of comparison in these reflections, it may be useful briefly to review the process of consultation and consensus by which they were drafted. That process creates confidence in the professional quality of the PCA Rules and gives promise of their acceptability to states in all social and legal systems, as well as in all stages of economic development.

3. Statute of the International Court of Justice, signed at San Francisco on June 26, 1945.
4. Rules of Court, adopted on April 14, 1978.
5. The PCA Rules include 'Guidelines' to assist states in adapting them for use in resolving disputes that involve more than two parties.

The project to develop the new PCA Rules had a strong pragmatic motive: states were not using the old rules, which had been written almost a century earlier in the 1899 Hague Convention for the Pacific Settlement of International Disputes, and which had been amended only once when certain changes were made by the 1907 Hague Convention bearing the same name.[6] While the longevity of the Permanent Court of Arbitration made it appear permanent,[7] it had not for decades administered any arbitrations under the procedural rules laid down in the 1899 or 1907 Conventions. Faced with this circumstance, the energetic PCA Secretary-General, P.J.H. Jonkman, set about seeking the reasons for the disuse and embarked on a search for solutions.

It soon became apparent that the problem lay in the antiquated procedures, not in the viability or acceptability of the PCA as an institution.[8] Indeed, the PCA had rarely, if ever, been busier. It was heavily engaged in providing important administrative and supporting services to several international arbitral tribunals, and, in a growing number of disputes, it was performing its responsibilities under the UNCITRAL Rules to designate an appointing authority in cases in which the parties were unable to agree upon the arbitrators and had not designated an appointing authority to do so.

6. Convention for the Pacific Settlement of International Disputes, concluded at The Hague on July 29, 1899 [hereinafter *the 1899 Convention*]; Convention for the Pacific Settlement of International Disputes, concluded at The Hague on October 18, 1907 [hereinafter *the 1907 Convention*].

7. John Scott Brown had quipped 70 years earlier that the PCA "is not permanent because it is not composed of permanent judges [...] [and] is not a court, because it is not composed of judges". *See* Pinto, *supra* note 1, at 73 n. 18, quoting J. Scott (ed.), 2 The Proceedings of The Hague Peace Conference: Conference of 1907, at 319.

8. A brief explanation concerning the use of the term 'Permanent Court of Arbitration' and its abbreviation, PCA, may be helpful. Strictly speaking, they refer to the body consisting of approximately 300 persons, four selected by each state that is a party to the 1899 or 1907 Convention. 1899 Convention, Arts. 20, 23; 1907 Convention, Arts. 41, 44. Pursuant to those Conventions, an 'International Bureau' serves as the secretariat of the Permanent Court of Arbitration. 1899 Convention, Art. 22; 1907 Convention, Art. 43. The Secretary-General heads the International Bureau. The "direction and control of the International Bureau" is entrusted to the Administrative Council "composed of Diplomatic Representatives of the Contracting Powers accredited to The Hague and of The Netherland [*sic*] Minister of Foreign Affairs, who will act as President". 1899 Convention, Art. 28; 1907 Convention, Art. 49. Notwithstanding that the Permanent Court of Arbitration technically consists solely of its members, in common usage, 'Permanent Court of Arbitration' and PCA are widely used to refer also to the entire system established by the 1899 and 1907 Conventions, particularly the International Bureau, the Secretary-General and the Administrative Council. Actions by the International Bureau, the Secretary-General or the Administrative Council are commonly referred to as acts of the PCA. Thus, for example, the arbitration rules discussed herein are entitled the 'Permanent Court of Arbitration Optional Rules for Arbitrating Disputes Between Two States', although they were drafted by the International Bureau under the direction of the Secretary-General and approved by the Administrative Council, without having been submitted to or approved by the members of the Permanent Court of Arbitration. That action was in accordance with the power of the Administrative Council to adopt regulations. 1899 Convention, Art. 28; 1907 Convention, Art. 49.

It also had increasing activity in appointing arbitrators or designating appointing authorities under other rules.[9]

In these circumstances, the Secretary-General in May 1991 convened a Working Group to consider steps for improving the functioning of the Permanent Court of Arbitration. The activities of the Working Group and of the Expert Group and Drafting Committee that were convened to implement the Working Group's conclusions are described in detail in Jeffrey Bleich's cogent contribution to this *Special Issue*[10] and need not be repeated here. Suffice it for the purpose of these reflections to note that the Working Group and the Expert Group included 26 persons from 22 countries, working under the constructive chairmanship of Judge Manfred Lachs of the International Court of Justice. These individuals represented a broad spectrum of legal systems -civil law, common law and Islamic law- and came from a wide range of geographic regions and social and economic systems. Several brought practical experience as legal advisers to foreign ministries; seven served on the International Court of Justice; one had long experience as a judge of the Court of Justice of the European Community; and at least six were currently involved in state-to-state arbitration proceedings. In addition, the Secretary-General sought the views of other prominent individuals in the field of international law.[11]

In a 'Background Paper' circulated to the Working Group in advance of its meeting, the Secretary-General raised the provocative question of whether the PCA system is a "venerable anachronism or neglected asset".[12] The widely diversified group that he had assembled had no difficulty in agreeing that the PCA system was both 'venerable' and an 'asset', but that its procedures had become an 'anachronism'. To remove the anachronisms that characterized it and to overcome the neglect from which it suffered, they recommended that the PCA system should be modernized by adopting new optional rules of procedure, and that these should be modeled on the UNCITRAL Arbitration Rules with such changes as were needed to

9. *See, e.g.*, the Secretary-General's description of the PCA staff and facilities and his account of its current activities in *Extract of the 90th Annual Report of the Administrative Council of the Permanent Court of Arbitration - 1990, reprinted in* International Bureau of the Permanent Court of Arbitration, The Permanent Court of Arbitration - New Directions 60-63 (1992) [hereinafter *New Directions*]. The activities reported for that year included providing continuing support services to the Iran-United States Claims Tribunal, and also to the arbitral tribunal dealing with the arbitration between the United States and the United Kingdom concerning Heathrow Airport User Charges, and to an arbitral tribunal dealing with a case before the International Centre for Settlement of Investment Disputes involving the Arab Republic of Egypt; entering into a Memorandum of Agreement with the Multilateral Investment Guarantee Agency (MIGA) providing, *inter alia*, for administration of arbitrations and acting as appointing authority under MIGA's rules; and acting in connection with appointing arbitrators in a number of international cases.
10. J. Bleich, *A New Direction for the PCA: The Work of the Expert Group*, LJIL *Special Issue* (1993), 17.
11. A list of the members of the Working Group appears *id.*, at 19 n. 4, and a list of members of the Expert Group and the other persons with whom the Secretary-General consulted is found in *id.*, at 30 n. 28.
12. P.J.H. Jonkman, *Background Paper, reprinted in New Directions, supra* note 9, at 19.

reflect the public international law character of disputes between states, and diplomatic practice appropriate to such disputes [...] [and to] indicate the role of the Secretary-General and the International Bureau of the [PCA].[13]

The choice of the UNCITRAL Arbitration Rules as a model was logical and, in my view, fortunate. The PCA was already familiar with the UNCITRAL Arbitration Rules as a result of its experience in designating appointing authorities under those Rules,[14] and because of the administrative support that it had been giving in arbitral proceedings that use them.[15] Moreover, the General Assembly of the United Nations had indicated that the UNCITRAL Arbitration Rules had been "prepared after extensive consultation" and were "acceptable in countries with different legal, social and economic systems".[16]

The breadth of the acceptance of the new PCA Rules is further demonstrated by the fact that they were adopted by consensus of the PCA Administrative Council after a draft text had been circulated for comment to the 75 states that were then parties to the 1899 or the 1907 Conventions, a group that is widely representative of the international community.[17] A number of these states submitted written comments, many of which were reflected in modifications made by the Secretary-General after consultation with an informal Drafting Committee that he formed to assist him.

While one can be optimistic that the extensive process of consultation that produced broadly-based approval of the new PCA Rules will result in their wide use by states, it bears emphasis that the PCA Rules -consistent with party autonomy- are '*Optional* Rules', and it remains to be seen how many states will opt to utilize them. Nevertheless, the provenance and pedigree of the PCA Rules makes them a suitable model of modern rules for the purpose of comparing arbitration with court proceedings.

III.

The adoption by the PCA of the UNCITRAL Arbitration Rules as the basis for its new procedures for arbitration of disputes between states is a milestone in the steady decline of the old perception that there are fundamental differences between the procedural aspects of international public law arbitration and international commercial arbitration. The Introduction to the PCA Rules emphasizes this development:

---

13. PCA Rules, Introduction.
14. UNCITRAL Rules, Art. 6.
15. *E.g.*, Iran-U.S. Claims Tribunal.
16. U.N. G.A. Res. 31/98, adopted on December 15, 1976 (Arbitration Rules of the United Nations Commission on International Trade Law); *see also* U.N. GAOR, Thirty-first Session, Supplement No. 17 (A/31/17), Chapt. V, Sect. C.
17. A list of states parties, as of August 1991, appears in *New Directions, supra* note 9, at 43-44.

> Experience in arbitration since 1981 suggests that the UNCITRAL Arbitration Rules
> provide fair and effective procedures for peaceful resolution of disputes between states
> concerning the interpretation, application and performance of treaties and other
> agreements, although they were originally designed for commercial arbitration.

The usefulness of similar arbitral procedures for disputes between states and those
involving private parties is underlined by no less an authority than Professor Pieter
Sanders.[18] In his contribution to this *Special Issue*, Professor Sanders suggests that
the PCA adopt rules for arbitration between states and non-state parties that are also
based on the UNCITRAL Arbitration Rules. Albert Jan van den Berg has recently
made a similar suggestion.[19] If that recommendation is followed, as I hope it will be,
the PCA will have similar procedures for all types of disputes.

One benefit of the convergence of public and private arbitral procedures is that
practitioners in each of these areas are now able to draw on each other's experiences.
There are, for example, thousands of international commercial arbitrations each year,
administered by dozens of arbitral centers under a wide variety of rules. Much study
by practitioners and scholars is being directed to methods and techniques for making
the conduct of those cases quicker, more efficient and less costly. Those concerned
with improving the process of arbitration between states should not ignore the lessons
to be learned from developments in international commercial arbitration.

Similarly, it may be noted in passing that experience in conciliation of commercial
disputes under procedures such as the UNCITRAL Consolidation Rules may well
provide valuable guidelines for resolution of disputes between states.

IV.

When comparing arbitration with adjudication by an international court, using the
ICJ Statute and the PCA Rules as examples, it may be useful to begin by emphasizing
similarities rather than differences. One such similarity is that neither the ICJ Statute
nor an arbitral tribunal under the PCA Rules has compulsory jurisdiction; both have
only such jurisdiction as may have been conferred by states parties. Thus, jurisdiction
may be conferred on the ICJ for defined existing disputes, for future disputes
generally, or for particular types of disputes, such as those arising out of the
interpretation or performance of a specified treaty.[20] Similarly, the PCA Rules
provide that they apply only where the states parties have agreed that the dispute shall

---

18. Sanders, *Private Parties and the Permanent Court of Arbitration*, LJIL *Special Issue* (1993), 91.
19. A.J. van den Berg, *The Permanent Court of Arbitration at the Peace Palace, The Hague - A New Role
for International Commercial Arbitration?*, *in* M. Sumampouw *et al.* (eds.), Law and Reality: Essays on
National and International Procedural Law 22 (1992).
20. ICJ Statute, Art. 36.

be referred to arbitration under those Rules.[21] As under the ICJ Statute, the PCA Rules are intended to apply where parties agree to submit an existing dispute to arbitration, or where they agree in a treaty or other agreement to arbitrate any future disputes arising thereunder.[22]

Thus, insofar as competence to resolve a dispute, both the ICJ Statute and the PCA Rules are similarly dependent on the will of the parties.

V.

Another similar aspect of the ICJ Statute and the PCA Rules is that both prevent a party that has agreed to jurisdiction of the tribunal from frustrating the proceeding by refusing to participate. Thus, the ICJ Statute provides that if a party does not appear or fails to defend its case, "the other party may call upon the Court to decide in favour of its claim", although the Court must, before doing so, satisfy itself that it has jurisdiction and that the "claim is well founded in fact and law".[23] Likewise, the PCA Rules prevent a party from frustrating the proceeding or preventing an award by refusing to participate. To overcome obstructive tactics by a party, the PCA Rules provide three safeguards: (i) if a party fails to respond without showing sufficient cause, "the arbitral tribunal shall order that the proceedings continue";[24] (ii) if a party fails to appear at a hearing "without showing sufficient cause for such failure, the arbitral tribunal may proceed with the arbitration";[25] and (iii) if a party fails to make timely production of evidence without showing sufficient cause, "the arbitral tribunal may make the award on the evidence before it".[26]

Both the ICJ Statute and the PCA Rules also include provisions to prevent a party-appointed judge or arbitrator from frustrating the process by refusing to participate in hearings or deliberation. While the ICJ Statute provides that if the Court does not include on the Bench a judge of the nationality of a party, that party may choose an *ad hoc* judge,[27] the ICJ Rules of Court state that *ad hoc* judges "shall not be taken into account for the calculation of the quorum",[28] thereby preventing a party-appointed judge from blocking a decision by his or her absence. To this same end, the PCA Rules expressly state:

21. PCA Rules, Art. 1, Para. 1.
22. Annexed to the PCA Rules is a model clause that states may insert in a treaty or other agreement to provide for arbitration of all future disputes that may arise thereunder, and another model clause for use in submitting an existing dispute to arbitration.
23. ICJ Statute, Art. 53.
24. PCA Rules, Art. 28, Para. 1.
25. PCA Rules, Art. 28, Para. 2.
26. PCA Rules, Art. 28, Para. 3.
27. ICJ Statute, Art. 31, Para. 3.
28. ICJ Rules of Court, Art. 20, Para. 3. Moreover, the ICJ Statute provides that "[a]ll questions shall be decided by a majority of judges *present*". Art. 55, Para. 1 [emphasis added, *HH*].

> If an arbitrator on a three- or five-person tribunal fails to participate in the arbitration, the other arbitrators shall, unless the parties agree otherwise, have the power in their sole discretion to continue the arbitration and to make any decision, ruling or award, notwithstanding the failure of one arbitrator to participate. In [making this determination] the other arbitrators shall take into account the stage of the arbitration, the reason, if any, expressed by the arbitrator for such nonparticipation, and such other matters as they consider appropriate in the circumstances of the case.[29]

This provision makes explicit the power of arbitral tribunals to prevent frustration of their proceedings by a party-appointed arbitrator. This power is well-recognized under international law and has been held to be implicit under the UNCITRAL Arbitration Rules.[30] This power to prevent disruption of orderly arbitration proceedings flows from the requirement of good faith inherent in the international obligations of states, as well as the application of the principle of *pacta sunt servanda* to agreements to arbitrate.

Thus it can be seen that the ICJ Statute and Rules of Court and the PCA Rules are both concerned with preserving the integrity of their respective proceedings. The PCA Rules are, in this respect, less stringent because they give discretion to the other arbitrators to decide whether or not to continue the proceedings and to render an award in the absence of one arbitrator, whereas the ICJ Statute contemplates continuation of the proceedings, and rendition of a judgment will occur by virtue of operation of the ICJ Statute. Moreover, under the PCA Rules, states parties have the general power to agree to modify the Rules,[31] which is further underscored by the specific provision in the above-quoted Article that it shall apply "unless the parties agree otherwise".[32] Thus here, as elsewhere, the over-riding principle of party autonomy governs the arbitral procedure.

While it has been suggested that some states may prefer rules that permit them to

---

29. PCA Rules, Art. 13, Para. 3.
30. *See, e.g.*, S.M. Schwebel, International Arbitration: Three Salient Problems 296 (1987): ("the weight of international authority, to which the International Court of Justice has given its support, clearly favours the authority of an international arbitral tribunal from which an arbitrator has withdrawn to proceed and to render a valid award"); *Reports* of S.M. Schwebel and K.-H. Böckstiegel *in* A.J. van den Berg (ed.), Proceedings of the Xth International Arbitration Congress, Stockholm 1990, at 242 *et seq. See also* H.M. Holtzmann, *How to Prevent Delay and Disruption of Arbitration: Lessons of the 1990 ICCA Stockholm Congress, id.*, at 26-29, and sources cited therein. The United Nations Law of the Sea Convention also includes provisions to prevent frustration of arbitration. As cited and commented upon in Pinto, *supra* note 1, at 81-82, the Law of the Sea Convention states that "'[t]he absence or abstention of less than half the members [of the arbitral tribunal] shall not constitute a bar to the tribunal reaching a decision', (Annex VII, Art. 8) and empowers the tribunal to make an award on default of appearance by one party (Annex VII, Art. 9)".
31. PCA Rules, Art. 1, Para. 1.
32. PCA Rules, Art. 3, Para. 3.

block the arbitration at any stage, I find it hard to imagine a state in good faith agreeing to arbitrate and nevertheless insisting on reserving the right to walk away from that agreement whenever it perceives that it has a weak case or some other reason arises. And I find it equally hard to visualize a state being willing to accept a regime in which a good faith agreement to arbitrate can be so easily frustrated by the other side. I note in passing that, if either party were free to frustrate the proceeding, the economic burden of litigation cost would fall harder on the poorer state if, after it had already expended money on the preparation and presentation of its case, the other side were free to scuttle the process.

VI.

The provisions in the ICJ Statute and the PCA Rules relating to the law to be applied may appear, at first glance, similar, yet they are fundamentally different in significant respects. Article 38, Paragraph 1, of the ICJ Statute provides that the Court's "function is to decide in accordance with international law" and then sets forth the sources of international law that it shall apply. In contrast, Article 33 of the PCA Rules enshrines party autonomy by providing that the arbitral tribunal "shall apply the law chosen by the parties" and only "in the absence of an agreement [...] shall decide such disputes in accordance with international law".[33]

On the other hand, the power to decide *ex aequo et bono*, and the role of equity, are the same under the ICJ Statute and the PCA Rules. Thus, the ICJ Statute specifically states that the provision on governing law in the first paragraph of Article 38 "shall not prejudice the power of the Court to decide a case *ex aequo et bono*, if the parties agree thereto".[34] Indeed, this is one of the few instances of party autonomy in the entire ICJ regime. The PCA Rules include the identical wording concerning the power of an arbitral tribunal to decide *ex aequo et bono*.[35] In this connection, as Professor Brownlie has pointed out, "[t]his power of decision *ex aequo et bono* involves elements of compromise and conciliation",[36] in contrast to equity which refers to "considerations of fairness, reasonableness, and policy often necessary for the sensible application of more settled rules of law".[37] As Judge Hudson observed in his concurring opinion in *Diversion of Water from the River Meuse*, principles of

---

33. Art. 33 of the PCA Rules does, however, describe the sources of international law in exactly the same words as Art. 38, Para. 1, of the ICJ Statute.
34. ICJ Statute, Art. 38, Para. 2.
35. PCA Rules, Art. 33, Para. 2.
36. I. Brownlie, Principles of Public International Law 27, 4th ed. (1990).
37. *Id.*, at 26. While Brownlie points out some contexts in which *ex aequo et bono* and equity are considered synonymous, I share his view that this is not true with respect to Article 38 of the ICJ Statute. It follows that the same interpretation applies to the PCA Rules which, as noted, are identical to the ICJ Statute in this respect.

equity "have long been considered part of international law".[38] Equity is thus an element of international law, regardless of whether that law is applied by a court or an arbitral tribunal.[39]

I mention this last point because of the well-known view of Aristotle, quoted by Grotius, that "an arbitrator may consider the equity of the case, whereas a judge is bound by the letter of the law".[40] While that ancient view has been repeated by some later commentators, I agree with Professor Brownlie that equity has now been received into international law. Accordingly, an arbitral tribunal applying international law may apply equity in the same way as an international court.

VII.

The most fundamental difference between court adjudication and arbitral procedure relates to the establishment of the tribunal that will decide the dispute. Courts, of course, are established by the community in advance; thus, the judges of the ICJ are chosen by an elaborate system of nomination and election by both the General Assembly and the Security Council of the United Nations.[41] Even the ICJ provision described above that permits each party to designate an *ad hoc* judge in certain circumstances does not empower the parties to choose the majority that will decide the dispute.

By contrast, when parties agree to arbitration, they opt for a system in which they are free to agree upon the persons to whom they grant the power of decision. Effective arbitration rules, such as the PCA Rules, include safeguard mechanisms ensuring that if the parties are unable to exercise their autonomy by reaching agreement on the arbitrators, they have the freedom to choose the procedure by which an independent individual or institution will make that choice. Thus, for example, the PCA Rules establish a failsafe procedure to be used if a party fails to exercise its right to name one arbitrator, or if the parties fail to agree on choice of the remaining member or members of the arbitral tribunal. Under that mechanism the arbitrators necessary to constitute the tribunal will be designated by an appointing authority whom they have chosen, or, if they have not named an appointing authority or if the chosen authority

---

38. 1937 P.C.I.J. Rep., Judgment of June 28, Series A/B, No. 70, at 4. *See also* Dissent of Howard M. Holtzmann to the Tribunal's Decision Refusing to Accept as Filed Three Claims Received by the Registrar on January 20, 1982, *reprinted in* 1 Iran-U.S. CTR 129, at 130: "It is well established that international tribunals are not bound to make strict, literal interpretations when to do so is inherently unfair".
39. Judge Lachs' article in this Special Issue provides scholarly analysis and extensive citation in support of this position. *See* M. Lachs, *Equity in Arbitration and in Judicial Settlement of Disputes, LJIL Special Issue* (1993), 125.
40. Pinto, *supra* note 1, at 65, *quoting* H. Grotius, De Jure Belli ac Pacis, BkIII, Cap. XX.47, C. Dunne trans. (1901).
41. *See* ICJ Statute, Arts. 3-12.

fails to act, the Secretary-General of the PCA will designate an appointing authority.[42] Moreover, the parties are free to agree upon any particular qualifications that one or more arbitrators must possess, a power that is particularly useful if the states involved wish a certain type of dispute to be decided by individuals with specialized knowledge of the subject matter of the case. In this respect, the PCA Rules include total flexibility for the parties to search the world for the most qualified arbitrators, without any limitation that the persons chosen shall have been included on any list established in advance by states or others. Thus, in a major departure from the typical procedure under the 1899 and 1907 Conventions, the PCA Rules state that "[i]n appointing arbitrators [under the PCA Rules], the parties and the appointing authority are free to designate persons who are not members of the Permanent Court of Arbitration at The Hague".[43]

VIII.

Another basic difference between court adjudication and arbitration is the power of states parties in arbitration to choose, or design, the procedures to govern all aspects of the proceeding. This autonomy may be exercised in several different ways. First the parties are free to adopt established rules such as the PCA Rules; second, they may write their own rules; or third, they may leave establishment of the procedures to the discretion of the arbitral tribunal. Even when parties agree on established rules, which is by far the easiest route, they typically retain the power to vary those rules. Thus, for example, the PCA Rules, as noted above, not only include a general power for the parties to agree to modify the rules,[44] but a party may waive any provision or requirement of the PCA Rules by proceeding with the arbitration without promptly stating its objection to such non-compliance.[45] Moreover, in order to underscore the power of the parties over the procedures, the PCA Rules, like many other rules, in certain provisions often include phrases such as "unless the parties otherwise agree"[46] or "if the parties have not previously agreed"[47] - although those phrases can be considered surplusage in view of the general power of modification which the PCA Rules provide.

---

42. PCA Rules, Arts. 6-7.
43. PCA Rules, Art. 8, Para. 3.
44. PCA Rules, Art. 1, Para. 1.
45. PCA Rules, Art. 30.
46. *See, e.g.*, PCA Rules, Art. 13, Para. 3 (power of arbitral tribunal to proceed in absence of one arbitrator); Art. 16, Para. 1 (place of arbitration); Art. 25, Para. 4 (hearings to be *in camera*); Art. 26, Para. 1 (interim measures of protection); Art. 32, Para. 3 (request that award state reasons).
47. *See, e.g.*, PCA Rules, Art. 5 (number of arbitrators); Art. 6, Para. 3 (use of list procedure by appointing authority); Art. 17, Para. 1 (language of proceedings); Art. 25, Para. 3 (arrangements for translation and transcripts); Art. 33, Para. 1 (applicable law).

By contrast, court procedures are typically established in mandatory terms that cannot be varied by agreement of the parties. For example, the word "shall" recurs throughout the ICJ Statute and Rules of Court, without any possibility for the parties to agree to modify or waive those procedural requirements. The ICJ Rules of Court do, however, include a provision that the parties "may jointly propose particular modifications or additions to" most of the Rules, and the Court "may" adopt the proposals if it "considers them appropriate in the circumstances of the case".[48] This is but a small window of flexibility because it relates only to the Rules of Court, not to the ICJ Statute, and even in that limited sphere parties can only jointly 'propose', with the ultimate authority remaining firmly in the hands of the Court itself. Both the ICJ Statute and the Rules of Court provide that the Court will "ascertain the views of the parties" before making certain procedural determinations,[49] but that is an expression of the right of parties to be heard, not a grant of autonomy to them.

IX.

Shakespeare observed long ago that "comparisons are odorous".[50] I hope, however, that the comparisons between court and arbitral proceedings noted in these reflections will escape that condemnation, for comparison is an inescapable part of the process of choosing between available alternatives.

The comparisons made in these reflections do not in themselves point to either alternative as being superior. Is it better, for example, to have a court chosen by a painstaking international process in which all member states of the United Nations participate, or to permit states flexibility to choose who will decide their disputes, or to agree upon procedures for such choice? Is it more efficient to have a court already established, even if parties must take their place in the queue of the court's docket, or for states to have to expend the not-inconsiderable time and effort needed to establish an *ad hoc* arbitral tribunal? Is it preferable in a particular dispute, or class of disputes, to have a bench consisting of generalists "who possess the qualifications required in their respective countries for appointment to the highest judicial offices, or jurisconsults of recognized competence in international law",[51] or to have a tribunal that includes specialists in the subject matter of the dispute before it? Is it more convenient for parties to have the relative certainty provided by mandatory procedures, or to have the flexibility to mold procedures to the circumstances of

---

48. ICJ Rules of Court, Art. 101.
49. *See, e.g.*, ICJ Statute, Art. 39, Para. 1 (agreement as to language of the proceedings); Art. 52 (consent to receive evidence presented out of time); ICJ Rules of Court, Art. 31 (questions of procedure generally); Art. 46, Para. 1 (number and order of pleadings); Art. 51, Para. 1 (agreement as to language of the proceedings); Art. 56, Para. 2 (production of documents submitted after close of written proceedings).
50. W. Shakespeare, *Much Ado About Nothing*, Act III, Scene V.
51. These are the qualifications for ICJ Judges established in Art. 2 of the ICJ Statute.

particular cases?

There is no pre-ordained answer to any of these questions that is applicable to every dispute. Like a tapestry, the fabric of international law is enriched by the availability of varied colors and textures.

X.

One final reflection: the availability of effective modern arbitration as an alternative to court adjudication provides for the ultimate expression of party autonomy - the freedom for states to agree on which procedure they mutually prefer in particular circumstances.

THE INTERNATIONAL COURT AS CONSTITUTIONAL COURT AND THE BLURRING OF THE ARBITRAL / JUDICIAL PROCESSES

EDWARD MCWHINNEY*

1.   THE ATROPHY OF THE PERMANENT COURT OF ARBITRATION

The institutionalization of international conflict-resolution on a third-party basis, with the creation of a Permanent Court of Arbitration, was one of the high hopes of the political leaders at the First Hague Peace Conference in 1899. In the early phase, from creation of the Court in 1902 until the outbreak of World War I in 1914, 17 cases were initiated before the Court. There was a quite understandable gap, through the War years, until 1921; and then, in the decade until 1931, 7 further cases were brought before the Court. This was followed by another awkward *hiatus* as to cases throughout the 1930s, apparently because of the renewed international tensions in Europe that culminated in World War II. There were no cases before the Court during the War years, the seat of the Court being under belligerent occupation for most of that time. The fact remains, however, that since World War II and, indeed, since 1931, there have been only *two* cases (both minor ones) brought before the Court, (or *three*, if we accept the Court Registry's retroactive classification, in its 1990 Annual Report, of the continuing Iran-US Claims Tribunal, which had begun its work in 1981, as one of its own cases).[1]

Scientific-legal explanations for the remarkable decline in the work load of the Permanent Court of Arbitration, after its manifestly fruitful early phase until 1914, include obvious *macro*-international law causes. Among these is the abandonment of the dry light of legal reason and of recourse to third-party-based disputes-settlement, in favour of direct action, in periods of international tension such as the between-the-two-World-Wars era. This would be a more convincing explanation were it not for the fact that that other, parallel international tribunal in The Hague, the old Permanent Court of International Justice, newly established after World War I, experienced its

---

* Queen's Counsel; Barrister-at-Law; Barrister and Solicitor; Professor of International Law, Simon Fraser University, Vancouver: *Membre de l'Institut de Droit International; Membre-Associé de l'Académie Internationale de Droit Comparé.*
1. The preceding statistics are detailed in the Permanent Court of Arbitration's own yearbook: Cour Permanente d'Arbitrage, 90ème Rapport Annuel 42-49 (1990).

S. Muller and W. Mijs (eds.), The Flame Rekindled, 81–89.
© 1994 *Leiden Journal of International Law. Printed in the Netherlands.*

most successful and productive years, in terms of actual number of cases, during that same time period. A lot of the attraction, and certainly the uniqueness, of the Permanent Court of Arbitration was certainly lost to the new, judicial tribunal, particularly since the judges of the latter tribunal were also constitutionally legitimated by the fact of direct election by the main, legislative organs of the League of Nations which functioned for these purposes as electoral college. For 'like-minded states' (the Allied and Associated Powers who had been the victors in World War I and who dominated the League of Nations), the Permanent Court of International Justice proved to be an attractive new forum for regulation of their differences which usually went to lesser, subsidiary issues and never touched vital interests. For disputes that really did involve vital interests -particularly those between the victor states and the defeated states from World War I, turning on the justice and equity of the imposed peace-settlement under the Treaty of Versailles and related treaties- third-party settlement, whether judicial or arbitral, was never a realistic mode of changing international law and was hardly resorted to, except for the one, 'what-might-have-been', judicial testing before the permanent Court of International Justice in *Customs Régime between Germany and Austria*, in 1931.[2]

2.   PERSONAL REFLECTIONS AS A SOMETIME MEMBER OF THE PERMANENT COURT OF ARBITRATION

The author served as a member of the Permanent Court of Arbitration, and member of the Canadian National Group within the Court, from 1985 to 1991.[3] The Canadian National Group has had its own special ground rules, which have derived, in part, from the bi-lingual (French and English), and federal, character of the country. Thus the four members at any time of the National Group will always include at least one francophone from Québec; they will be drawn, as far as possible, from the different geographical regions of the country; they will fall into the four main professional-legal categories - the Foreign Ministry Legal Division, the federal judiciary, the practising Bar, and the academic-scientific legal community; and, finally, there will be respect for the new constitutional principle of 'gender equality' by now including at least one woman. Two other ground rules in which the Canadian National Group departs sharply from the well-evidenced practice of other National Groups: the members will serve for only the one, non-renewable term of six years; and they will

2. Customs Régime between Germany and Austria, 1931 P.C.I.J. Rep., Ser. A/B, No. 41, at 42.
3. For more detailed analysis of the Canadian National Group's practice, *see* Lee and McWhinney, *The 1987 Elections to the International Court of Justice*, 25 Can. Y.B.I.L. 379 (1987); McWhinney and April, *The 1990 Triennial Elections to the International Court of Justice and the 1989 Casual Election*, 28 Can. Y.B.I.L. 403 (1990).

not personally be eligible, during their term, for consideration or selection for nomination, themselves, as national candidates for election to the International Court of Justice. The latter ground rule was dictated by the desire to avoid seeming conflict of interest in those rare situations -at only forty year intervals, as it has turned out-when there should be a question of a possible Canadian candidacy for election to the Court. The ground rule as to service for only the one, non-renewable term of six years, seems to stem from a 'share-the-wealth' philosophy to filling of what are discretionary Government appointments; but it is harder to justify such a ground rule pragmatically insofar as it means that there is very little continuing wisdom and experience within the National Group as to the political gamesmanship in successfully sponsoring and electing candidates to the International Court of Justice, or even of bargaining and horse-trading with other countries in return for support of those other countries' own candidates for election.

This is the cold political reality of the International Court's judicial selection processes. During the author's own tenure as a member of the Canadian National Group, we took very seriously our collective responsibilities in vetting possible Canadian candidates for the International Court and also, (and much more often), assessing and ranking foreign National Groups' nominees who were seeking Canadian co-nominations and endorsements. During the author's own six-year term on the Canadian National Group, we were seised of two of the regular, triennial elections to the International Court; and we proceded to co-nominate, for each of those triennial elections, four foreign nationals already designated by their own National Groups. We were guided in our choices by considerations of a 'regional' character designed to ensure, variously, legal-systemic, linguistic, geographical, and political-ideological balance within the International Court; and seven of our eight co-nominations were successful in the subsequent Court elections. Where candidates who came from 'new', Third World countries were relatively unknown, we read their scientific-legal publications, in their original languages if need be. I would have to say that our approach worked very well in the case of foreign candidates, and less well perhaps in the case of Canadian candidates. The consultation (enjoined by Article 6 of the Statute of the International Court of Justice) with the "highest Court of Justice, [...] legal faculties and schools of law, and [...] national academies and national sections of international academies devoted to the study of law", proved, in my own personal experience, intellectually unproductive, insofar as those outside bodies, when they did choose to offer advice, almost never produced reasoned recommendations derived from empirically-based study of the various candidates' scientific writings or equivalent professional achievement. In the case of foreign candidates, the designated outside bodies seemed not to have enough knowledge and background in international law in general and too little ability to canvass scientific-legal writings in languages other than English (and perhaps French), to be persuasive or helpful. My conclusion, after the experience of my own term on the Canadian National Group, is that the function of nominating candidates for the elections to the International Court, as provided in Article 4 of the Court Statute, would better be entrusted to the Legal Division of the national Foreign Ministries, where the political factors in Court elections today could then be canvassed openly and without equivocation. It is, in the end, a high political choice that is involved, in which the, by now, historically-sanctioned claims of particular 'regional' blocs (legal-systemic, linguistic, geographical, and political-ideological) are usually dominant, particularly since candidates, for the most part, have scientific-legal or professional-legal claims. Only in contests *within* the one 'region' will considerations of the intellectual pre-eminence of individual candidates be likely to be controlling. The screening and nomination of candidates for election to the International Court has, in any case, nothing much to do with arbitration as international legal process, or with the special competence of the Permanent Court of Arbitration and its panels (lists) of potential arbitrators. It should be stripped away, as a decorative survival from another, earlier, 'Eurocentrist' era in the historical evolution of international law when the conflict of vital interests in litigation was not so apparent and when, in consequence, elections to the International Court were not so fiercely politically contested as today.

It should be added that, in addition to the two regular, triennial elections to the International Court for which the Canadian National Group was seised during my own tenure, we also passed on the electon, in 1989, to fill the casual vacancy created by the death of Judge Nagendra Singh (India). Canada, which was then an elected member of the Security Council, co-nominated a candidate from Sri Lanka, as did four other members of the Security Council. It is known that, in the period between close of nominations and the actual balloting in the Security Council and General Assembly, there was intensive diplomatic activity in behalf of the Indian candidate. Such diplomatic lobbying reflected a fairly general custom or convention, from past Court elections, that casual vacancies should be filled by election of someone of the same nationality as the previous incumbent. In the event, the Indian candidate, Judge Pathak, was elected, with the Sri Lankan candidate trailing far behind and receiving only two votes in the Security Council. It is clear that three states that voted in the Security Council chose to ignore the decision of their respective National Groups to co-nominate the Sri Lankan candidate, for those states voted otherwise in the recorded actual balloting.[4] Would it not be sensible, then, to concede to the national Foreign Ministries plenary powers as to the nomination of judges, in addition to the casting of votes in the actual balloting?

4. *See*, in this regard, McWhinney and April, *supra* note 3 at 403-5.

3.   **BLURRING OF THE ERSTWHILE DISTINCTION BETWEEN
      ARBITRATION AND ADJUDICATION**

I do not think any intellectually persuasive distinction can be made, today, between
arbitration and adjudication, viewed as processes of third-party decision-making.
Comparison might be made between the *jurisprudence* of the Permanent Court of
Arbitration (when it was still active), and that of the old Permanent Court of
International Justice, over the same time period up to World War II; but that would
simply highlight the fact that the old PCIJ was essentially a legalistic tribunal,
dominated by classical, 'black-letter-law' theories of legal interpretation and of the
judicial process generally. Since the Court revolution of *Namibia*, in 1971[5] against
the *South West Africa*,[6] ultra-positivist, single-vote-majority decision of 1966, the
'new' judicial majority within the new International Court of Justice has essayed
more consciously activist, policy-making conceptions of the judical role. When
positivism is rejected in favour of more dynamic, instrumental approaches to the
progressive development of international law, the test of wise policy becomes a
process of balancing competing societal interests, in which considerations of the
common good, and of equity in its original form unfettered by the dead weight of past
historical precedent, will prevail over strict and literal interpretation and the canons
of (logical) construction.[7]

Sometimes a tribunal will itself become confused by the signals and as to the exact
process in which it is engaged: in *Beagle Channel*,[8] a panel of five arbitrators,
composed, however, entirely of World Court judges, chose to apply the old, *South
West Africa*, 1966-type, positivistic approach and it rendered the parties justice in the
old, strict, 'logical' sense, overlooking the fact that the parties had come seeking
equity and not merely a mechanical re-statement of the pre-existing positive law,
whatever that might be. The arbitral role, at least in theory, connotes active
participation by the members of a tribunal in changing and re-writing old law deemed
no longer to be consonant with contemporary societal needs. To miss that essential
truth is to compound or exacerbate an existing problem, rather than to resolve it.

Sometimes, again, state parties, making use of a reform of Court procedures
intended, originally, to facilitate recourse to the Court's jurisdiction and to accelerate
its decision-making, may turn it in unexpected directions and also cross the line
between arbitration and adjudication in *a priori*, institutional terms. Thus, the

5. Legal Consequences for States of the Continued Presence of South Africa in Namibia (South West
Africa), notwithstanding Security Council Resolution 276 (1970), 1971 I.C.J. Rep. 16.
6. South West Africa, Second Phase, Judgment, 1966 I.C.J. Rep. 6.
7. Developed more fully, *in* E. McWhinney, Judicial Settlement of International Disputes: Jurisdiction,
Justiciability and Judicial law-making on the Contemporary International Court 16 *et seq.* (1991).
8. Beagle Channel Arbitration (Argentina *v.* Chile), Arbitration Award, (April 18, 1977), 17 I.L.M. 634
(1978).

institution of a Special Chamber within the International Court of Justice, long dormant and unused, was activated during the revived Cold War climate of the early 1980s, by the United States Administration's publicly expressed (and, in empirical terms, quite unfounded) mistrust of the International Court of Justice whose fifteen-judge *plenum* the United States stigmatised as being dominated by members from the Soviet Union and Eastern Europe (in bald, numerical terms, two judges out of fifteen).[9] In professing, nevertheless, its attachment to the principle of third-party, judicial settlement of international disputes, the United States Administration invoked the institution of the Special Chamber as its own favoured judicial arena, and as an alternative to the *plenum* or full Court. In the first instance of actual user of a Special Chamber, in *Gulf of Maine*,[10] for purposes of litigation between the United States and Canada, the two parties successfully insisted -in despite the letter of the Court Statute and Court Rules, and the clear legislative intent therein expressed- on being able not merely to direct the Court as to the *number* of judges to constitute the Special Chamber (as it happened, five judges), but on being able to impose on the Court the two parties' own particular agreed choices of the individual judges. The *plenum* of the Court's ruling in *Gulf of Maine*, acquiescing in the parties' dictate of the choice of the judges, does not appear as persuasive, legally, as the judicial Declaration and the individual Dissenting Opinions accompanying it.[11] The Court majority, in acquiescing so readily to the parties' dictate as to choice of judges, was undoubtedly influenced by the serious dearth of Court business at the opening of the 1980s, - one of the still-continuing political consequences of the ultra-positivist, single-vote-majority decision in *South West Africa, Second Phase*, in 1966. That particular condition of absence of Court case-load no longer exists today; and some of the unanticipated consequences of rendering, through a highly selective five-member panel, judgments that purportedly are binding on the fifteen-member full Court, are already apparent. The five-member panel for *Gulf of Maine*, a 'new' Law-of-the-Sea case *par excellence*, conspicuously omitted, through the two parties' dictate on choice of judges, those two members of the Court most highly qualified in law-of-the-sea matters, Judge Nagendra Singh and Judge Oda.[12] It may not be surprising that a later Opinion, filed by Judge Oda in a later law-of-the-sea case with which the full Court was seised, reads like a retroactive, authoritative judicial dissent to the Special Chamber ruling in *Gulf of Maine*;[13] or that, in a more recent Special

9. McWhinney, Judicial Settlement of International Disputes 58-9, 62-72 (1991).
10. Delimitation of the Maritime Boundary in the Gulf of Maine Area, (Canada *v.* U.S.A.), Constitution of Chamber, Order of January 20, 1982, 1982 I.C.J. Rep. 3; Judgment 1984 I.C.J. Rep. 246.
11. 1982 I.C.J. Rep. 3; *id.*, 10 (Oda J., Declaration); *id.*, 12 (Morozov J., Dissenting Opinion); *id.*, 13 (El-Khani J., Dissenting Opinion).
12. McWhinney, Judicial Settlement of International Disputes 79-80 (1991).
13. Continental Shelf (Libyan Arab Jamahiriya *v.* Malta), 1985 I.C.J. Rep. 13, 165-9 (Oda J., Dissenting Opinion).

Chamber decision also involving the law-of-the-sea, Judge Oda dissents, at length, to a key part of the holding rendered by the other four panel members (who included two *ad hoc* judges).[14] What does that do to the claimed authority of Special Chamber rulings?[15] Special Chambers within the International Court, -if the full Court's 1982 ruling, sanctioning a right of the parties to choose the judges to make up the panel, be maintained- take on one of the main elements that, classically, distinguished arbitral from judicial tribunals, namely the complete freedom of choice by the parties to agree between themselves on the composition of the arbitral tribunal. With a judicial tribunal, by comparison, the parties have no choice but to be bound by the existing composition and membership of the court, once they have submitted to the Court's jurisdiction. The parties cannot, and should not, be permitted to pick and choose as to the judges sitting on a Court. The obvious imperfections in the Court's analysis in its 1982 judgment in *Gulf of Maine* on this point; plus the ending of the Cold War (the original political *raison d'être* for the US Administration's deliberate by-passing of the full Court in favour of Special Chambers and the US insistence on choosing the judges for such Chambers); plus, finally, the unexpected extreme delays attending an institution (Special Chambers), that was supposed to accelerate and simplify the administration of international justice, have all combined, by the end of the decade of the 1980s and the beginning of the 1990s, to suggest that the Special Chambers, in their practical application, have been a reform *manqué* which may not persist - at least in its present form and regulation.

4.   IS THERE STILL A ROLE FOR INTERNATIONAL ARBITRATION TODAY?

Accepting the increasing blurring of the distinction, *qua* process, between international arbitration and international adjudication as the International Court moves, more and more, into judicial policy-making as distinct from the old, positivistic, strict-and-literal interpretation conception of its proper function, does something remain for the Permanent Court of Arbitration to do? The Arbitration Court needs, as we have said, to slough off the extraneous, but overly preemptive function of acting as a collection of national Foreign Ministry screening committees for purposes of appraising and recommending candidates for ultimate election to the International Court. Why not, as we have already said, leave all that to the national Foreign Ministries themselves, with the extra freedom that that will then give to confine the national lists for the Permanent Court of Arbitration, henceforward, to jurisconsults of recognised inter-

14. Land, Island and Maritime Frontier Dispute (El Salvador *v.* Honduras: Nicaragua Intervening), 1992 I.C.J. Rep., (Oda J., Dissenting Opinion).
15. S. Rosenne, *Equity, in* Bloed & van Dijk (eds.), Forty Years International Court of Justice 88 (1988); E. McWhinney, Judicial Settlement of International Disputes 80 (1991).

national distinction? The International Court's progress towards judicial policy-making has not, however, been attained in one single great leap forward, but rather on a step-by-step, trial-and-error, testing basis, with the occasional retreat into judicial self-restraint when a particular advance may seem too politically charged for the moment and worthy of extra time and reflection before being attempted.

This is reflected in the recent rulings in *Aerial Incident at Lockerbie*,[16] where the International Court was asked to pass on the constitutional competences of a coordinate United Nations organ, the Security Council, in a situation where it might be argued that the Security Council had itself acted in a 'judicial' capacity in issuing decisions with purportedly normative-legal consequences. It had already been established, in the court's *jurisprudence* evolving from the 1970s onwards, that there is no classical, constitutional separation-of-powers within the United Nations organisation, and therefore no necessary constitutional bar to the Court's being seised with a particular issue at the same time as its coordinate institutions, the Security Council and the General Assembly.[17] The limitations, if any, in the exercise of the Court's own international legal problem-solving competences would be found in considerations of constitutional comity, and of institutional cooperation and mutual support and deference and respect for special competence, on the part of Court, Security Council, and General Assembly equally.

Aerial Incident at Lockerbie, however, went significantly beyond these classical separation-of-powers arguments where no direct conflict or competition was in fact involved between the different UN organs; for it put the Court in the position, -if it were to grant the applicant state's request for what amounted to an injunctive form of relief against the respondent United Kingdom and United States- of directly challenging the Security Council. The Court, if it had taken that step, would very clearly have crossed the constitutional Rubicon and established itself, *de facto*, as a special constitutional Court -continental European, post-World War II- style, with the legal competence to exercise judicial review and constitutional control over the acts of the coordinate United Nations institutions, the Security Council and General Assembly, so as to ensure their conformity to the United Nations Charter. As one reads the official Opinion of Court and the supporting Special Opinions in *Aerial Incident at Lockerbie*, that was simply one constitutional bridge too far at this particular political moment in time, without any prior intellectual-legal canvassing

---

16. Questions of Interpretation and Application of the 1971 Montreal Convention arising from the Aerial Incident at Lockerbie (Libyan Arab Jamahiriya *v.* United Kingdom), Provisional Measures, Order of April 14, 1992, 1992 I.C.J. Rep. 3; *id.*, (Libya *v.* U.S.A.), 1992 I.C.J. Rep. 114.

17. *See,* especially, Judge Lachs' comment: "There is an old Roman law principle that if you resort to one method you cannot resort to other methods. Well, we have abandoned this -I was very active in abandoning it- and if there is a dispute, now you have to seek all methods, perhaps simultaneously, in order to solve it". Cited *in* Sturgess and Chubb, Judging the World 463 (1988). *See also* E. McWhinney, Judicial Settlement of International Disputes 142-147 (1991).

or preparation. With the dramatic changes to the Security Council and the General Assembly, since the ending of the Cold War and the disappearance of the old Soviet-Western equilibrium of forces or political balance-of-power on which United Nations decisions had been predicated for more than forty years, the issue of alternative, possibly Court-based, constitutional checks-and-balances to the powers of the two legislative organs of the United Nations can hardly be avoided in the future. The excellent individual judicial Opinions, both concurring and dissenting,[18] filed in *Aerial Incident at Lockerbie*, suggest that the judges are fully aware that the Court is entering on a new and testing phase, as constitutional Court, in the post-Cold War era.[19] It is to take on much of the intellectual-legal flexibility, and the conscious resort to the skills of pragmatism, and the invocation of equity in its original, creative sense before it had degenerated into a closed system of precedents, that were thought to inhere in arbitral tribunals, in the era when judicial tribunals (including the International Court itself) were deemed to be limited to strict-and-literal, 'logical' interpretation and the mechanical application of black-letter-law from past precedents. An International Court that is fully legitimated in its new, policy-making role by the fact of direct election of its judges by the Security Council and the General Assembly, and that is now perceived and recognised as fully representative in political-ideological, legal-systemic, linguistic and cultural, and geographical terms, enjoys a mandate for the progressive development of international law in charter terms that could hardly be approached by an arbitration tribunal whose members, by definition, are selected, *ad hoc*, for the particular case by the particular parties to that case.

---

18. 1992 I.C.J. Rep. 3, at 17 (Oda J., Declaration); 20 (Ni J., Declaration); 24 (Evensen, Tarassov, Guillaume and Aguilar Mawdsley, JJ., Joint Declaration); 26 (Lachs J., Separate Opinion); 28 (Shahabuddeen J., Separate Opinion); 33 (Bedjaoui J., Dissenting Opinion); 50 (Weeramantry J., Dissenting Opinion); 72 (Ranjeva J., Dissenting Opinion); 78 (Ajibola J., Dissenting Opinion); 94 (El Kosheri J. *ad hoc*, Dissenting Opinion).
19. *See* the prophetic analysis advanced by Wilhelm Wengler, in 1991, as to the case for judicial review of the Security Council when it acts in a judicial or quasi-judicial capacity in making determinations under Chapter VII of the Charter. Wengler, *International Law and the Concept of a New World Order, in* McWhinney, Zaslove, Wolf (eds.), Federalism-in-the-Making: Contemporary Canadian and German Constitutionalism, National and Trans-national (1992).

PRIVATE PARTIES AND THE PERMANENT COURT OF ARBITRATION

PROF. PIETER SANDERS*

1. INTRODUCTION

As early as 1952 I launched the idea of enhancing the use of the PCA by making its arbitration facilities accessible for arbitration between states and private parties.[1] A few years later I was requested by the Secretary-General, at that time, Prof. François, to draw up draft arbitration rules for this purpose. These rules, as elaborated by the International Bureau of the PCA, became the 1962 Rules of Arbitration and Conciliation for Settlement of International Disputes between Two Parties of Which Only One is a State, hereafter referred to as the 1962 Rules.[2]

At the time I wrote my article about the "Future of the PCA" (1952), the PCA could more or less be regarded as a sleeping beauty in the Peace Palace. The machinery offered by the Hague Conventions of 1899 and 1907 was seldom used.[3] Even the existence of the PCA was largely unknown. I became aware of this when, as consultant of UNCITRAL for its Arbitration Rules, I suggested calling upon the Secretary-General of the PCA to designate the Appointing Authority (AA), if no AA had been agreed upon by the parties. It needed quite some explanation about the PCA before the Secretary-General was inserted as designating authority in the final version of the 1976 UNCITRAL Arbitration Rules.

The successful UNCITRAL Arbitration Rules have certainly contributed to making the PCA better known in the private international arbitration world. In international arbitrations under the Arbitration Rules of UNCITRAL the Secretary-General of the PCA is regularly called upon to designate an Appointing Authority.

---

* Emeritus Professor, Erasmus University, Rotterdam, The Netherlands.

---

1. *De toekomst van het Permanente Hof van Arbitrage (The future of the PCA)*, 384 Arbitrale Rechtspraak 353-359 (1952).
2. These Rules are reproduced in the 1991 publication of PCA's International Bureau, The Permanent Court of Arbitration - New Directions, as Annex 3, at 45-54.
3. For the period 1902 until World War II, 23 arbitration cases appear on the list published as Annex 3 to the PCA's Annual Report 1991. For the period following World War II until the present-time, four more cases are reported.
In addition the Annual Report 1991 refers to four International Commissions of Inquiry (Annex 4) and three International Conciliation Commissions (Annex 5).

S. Muller and W. Mijs (eds.), The Flame Rekindled, 91–97.
© 1994 *Leiden Journal of International Law. Printed in the Netherlands.*

The Secretary-General currently also receives requests to make the premises and the staff of the PCA available for arbitrations in The Hague which are not governed by the Rules of the PCA. The international arbitration world seems to have found its way to the Peace Palace. The PCA has become less somnolent than before.

This also appears from references to the PCA or its Secretary-General made in international instruments. A very recent example of this may be found in the Agreement between the Russian Federation and the USA on Investment Incentives, Washington, April 3, 1992.[4] Article 5 of this Agreement indicates the Secretary-General as Appointing Authority: either Government may request him to make the appointment of an arbitrator under the circumstances as stated in this article. Here, the Secretary-General does not function as a designating authority, like under the UNCITRAL Arbitration Rules, but as the authority who makes the appointment. Nevertheless, in spite of all activities I mentioned and the growing awareness of the PCA's existence, its arbitration-machinery provided by the 1907 Convention is hardly used.

This situation may change. On initiative of the present Secretary-General a program has been elaborated to make its existence better known and to improve its machinery.[5] A Working Group has elaborated new Rules for Arbitration between States.[6] These Rules, based on the UNCITRAL Arbitration Rules as adapted for arbitration between states, have already been authorised for distribution by the Administrative Council of the PCA.

As a further part of the program for activating the PCA new Rules for Arbitration between a state and private parties may be elaborated. This forms the subject of my contribution.

2.   ARBITRATION BETWEEN STATES AND PRIVATE PARTIES

Since World War II, the use of international commercial arbitration has increased considerably. In many of these arbitrations a state or state controlled enterprise is involved.[7] As far as arbitration under the Rules of the International Chamber of Commerce (ICC) is concerned, the available estimates regarding their frequency vary from one sixth of all arbitrations registered in one year to one third.[8] Not only the ICC, but also the London Court of International Arbitration (LCIA) and the American Arbitration Association (AAA) and other general arbitration institutes

---

4. 4 I.L.M. XXVI 780 (July 1992).
5. *See* the publication mentioned in note 2.
6. On the work of the Expert Group, *see also* Bleich's contribution in this *Special Issue,* 17.
7. For types of disputes dealt with in these arbitrations *see* the arbitral awards published regularly in the 18 volumes of ICCA's Yearbook Commercial Arbitration 1976-1993.
8. Craig, Park and Paulsson *in* ICC Arbitration (2nd ed. 1990), at 8.

administer arbitrations between states and private parties. State arbitration is certainly not exceptional.

For a special category of disputes, investment disputes, the Washington Convention of 1965 on the Settlement of Investment Disputes between States and Nationals of Other States created the International Centre for Settlement of Investment Disputes (ICSID). In the context of arbitration between a state and private parties, the ICSID should be mentioned. However, for the problems encountered in state arbitration, arbitrations held under the auspices of the above-mentioned institutes and *ad hoc* arbitration, for example concerning oil-concessions, should in particular be considered.

One of the issues that may be raised in state arbitration is whether the state has the capacity to enter into an arbitration agreement. This capacity depends on its national law. As a rule national laws do not prohibit states from concluding an arbitration agreement. There are, however, exceptions. In *France*, for example, the state and public entities *(établissements publics)* may not enter into an arbitration agreement. However, the Supreme Court limited this prohibition to domestic cases.[9] In *Belgium*, Article 1676(2) of the CCP prohibits legal persons of public law from concluding an arbitration agreement. Exception is made for the state "when a Treaty authorises it to have recourse to arbitration".

The conclusion of an arbitration agreement is generally regarded as a waiver by the state of its immunity from jurisdiction. However, whether this also involves a waiver of immunity from execution is still debated although it may seem logical to reason that once a state has validly entered into an arbitration agreement, the state should also be bound by the outcome of the arbitration proceedings. An award, rendered against a state should be enforceable against property of the state unless this is earmarked for public services.

However, this reasoning is not generally recognised. The Washington Convention, for example, clearly distinguishes between immunity from jurisdiction and immunity from execution. For the latter reference is made to the law in force in the contracting state (Article 55). This distinction is also found in the Vienna Convention on Diplomatic Relations of April 18, 1961. Article 32(2) of the Convention states that a waiver of immunity from jurisdiction "shall not be held to imply waiver of immunity in respect of the execution of the judgment for which a separate waiver shall be necessary".

The plea of sovereign immunity and in particular immunity from execution has given rise to many court decisions. Special legislation, like the Foreign Sovereign Immunities Act of the USA and the State Immunity Act of the United Kingdom, has been enacted to regulate this issue. An abundance of literature exists on the subject. Harmonisation attempts have also been made, the most recent of which can be found

---

9. Cour de Cassation, May 2, 1966 in the Galakis case, 533 RCDIP (1967), with note by Goldman.

in the Draft Articles submitted by the International Law Commission in 1991 to the General Assembly of the UN with the recommendation to convene an international conference. This Draft, dealing with sovereign immunity in general, contains some provisions dealing with state immunity in arbitration. Article 18 of the Draft states that, in case the state enters into an arbitration agreement, this agreement may contain an express waiver of immunity from execution and may well be taken into account when drafting Special Rules of the PCA for arbitration between a state and private parties.

3.   SPECIAL RULES OF THE PCA FOR ARBITRATION BETWEEN A STATE AND PRIVATE PARTIES

Apart from the 1962 Rules of the PCA there are so far no special rules for this type or arbitration. Special Rules of the PCA would therefore be quite distinct from the general arbitration rules of the arbitral institutes (ICC, LCIA, AAA) referred to above.

The provision of a special set of arbitration rules for arbitration between a state and private parties would clearly distinguish the PCA Rules from the Rules of these institutes. They would also distinct from these other Rules as they would not originate from the international business community. Having been approved by the Administrative Council of the PCA, they may be more readily accepted by states. In addition, the insertion in these Rules of an express waiver of immunity from execution will demonstrate this special character and eliminate a difficulty which otherwise might be encountered.

Following the UNCITRAL Arbitration Rules, with some additions and modifications in view of state arbitration, will also distinguish the PCA-Rules from the above-mentioned Rules of the arbitral institutes. Two sets of Rules will then be offered by the PCA for optional use, one for arbitration between states (already distributed) and one for arbitration between a state and a non-state party, both based on the UNCITRAL Arbitration Rules. Following the UNCITRAL Arbitration Rules is particularly important in respect of developing countries who participated in the drafting of these Rules. This may make these countries more inclined to accept arbitration. Special Rules of the PCA based on the UNCITRAL Arbitration Rules may therefore offer a welcome addition to the already existing arbitration facilities.

4.   ADAPTATION OF THE UNCITRAL ARBITRATION RULES

Apart from the insertion of an express waiver of immunity from execution, only one subject will be mentioned here in respect of the adaptation of the UNCITRAL Arbitration Rules which will have to take place in case Special Rules are drafted as suggested above.

An advantage, if parties agree to arbitration instead of resorting to court proceedings, is the freedom of the parties to choose as arbitrators persons who are particularly qualified to decide their disputes. An arbitral tribunal is composed *ad hoc*, taking into account the character of the dispute.

The UNCITRAL Arbitration Rules recognise this freedom. The choice of a sole arbitrator is first of all left to the parties and, in case of a tribunal of three, each party appoints one arbitrator and the two arbitrators thus appointed choose the third (presiding) arbitrator. Only in case the parties cannot agree on the sole arbitrator or, in case of a panel of three, one of the parties does not appoint 'his' arbitrator or the two arbitrators cannot agree on the choice of the third (presiding) arbitrator, the Rules provide for the intervention of an Appointing Authority (AA). In that case the AA applies the list-procedure, proposing several names for each appointment. The parties thus regain influence on the choice, as they can express their preference by striking names from the list and numbering the remaining ones in the order of their preference. This procedure can be followed in the PCA Rules. It is in particular in respect of the designation of the AA that an adaptation is required.

UNCITRAL had to provide for the designation of an AA in case parties had not agreed on the AA. The Special Rules could avoid this intermezzo by stating that the Secretary-General of the PCA will act as AA unless the parties agree on another AA. The AA -as a rule the Secretary-General- will then follow the list-procedure as provided for in the UNCITRAL Rules (Article 6(3) for the sole arbitrator and in case of a tribunal of three, Article 7(2) for the second and Article 7(3) for the third arbitrator). In applying the list-procedure the Secretary-General should be free in proposing names and not be limited in his proposals to the names on an existing list of arbitrators of the PCA.

As to the number of arbitrators, the UNCITRAL Rules (one or three) could be followed. In international commercial arbitration a tribunal of five arbitrators is virtually unknown. The possibility, provided for in the PCA Rules for arbitration between states, to have five arbitrators should therefore not be kept in the Special Rules for arbitration in which private parties are involved.

It is not the place nor the time to deal here in detail with the adaptation of the UNCITRAL Arbitration Rules in order to make the Special Rules suitable for arbitration between a state and private parties. Apart from the appointment procedure an adaptation or addition may also be required on other points. I confine myself to the appointment procedure, essential for any arbitration.

5.   IMPLEMENTATION

Extension of the activities of the PCA by providing the possibility to arbitrate under newly established Special Rules based on the generally accepted UNCITRAL Arbitration Rules, will in my opinion be welcomed by both the states and the non-state parties. These Rules can be based on Article 47 of the 1907 Convention (Article 26 of the 1899 Convention) as the 1962 Rules were.

The Administrative Council may be prepared to authorise the issuance of such Rules. The Rules would fill a gap. On the other hand, the potental field of application is increasing as new types of disputes, for example regarding transborder pollution, may call as well for arbitration. The need for well drafted Special Rules therefore can, in my opinion, hardly be doubted.

6. WHAT ABOUT THE 1962 RULES OF THE PCA?

Should the 1962 Rules be withdrawn when the new set of Rules is launched? The 1962 Rules contain next to Arbitration Rules in Section I, Conciliation Rules in Section II and regulate, in Article 1 of Section III, the relationship between arbitration and conciliation: parties may agree to submit the dispute firstly to conciliation and, where the Conciliation Commission has found that the parties cannot be reconciled, then to the arbitration procedure.

In case the possibility of agreeing to conciliation, preceding arbitration, should be maintained, Section II of the 1962 Rules may also be reviewed and adapted to the UNCITRAL Conciliation Rules of 1980. In addition, the submission clause has to take into account the possibility of conciliation. Parties may then have a choice between (a) arbitration, (b) conciliation or (c) conciliation followed, in case of non-conciliation, by arbitration.[10]

It may be doubted whether these complications, in case conciliation would be maintained, are worth while. Contrary to arbitration, conciliation is seldom resorted to.[11] A choice will thus have to be made between on the one hand a completely new set of Arbitration Rules together with a new set of Conciliation Rules plus the optional clauses just mentioned or to withdraw the 1962 Rules and to limit the new set of Rules to arbitration only. In any case it cannot be avoided to deal with the question what will be the fate of conciliation as provided for in the 1962 Rules.

7. CONCLUSION

My contribution only deals with part of the initiative taken by the Secretary-General to reanimate the PCA. In this context a new set of Arbitration Rules, replacing the 1962 Arbitration Rules for Disputes between a State and Private Parties is recommended. These Rules should be based on the UNCITRAL Arbitration Rules

---

10. *See* the publication mentioned in note 2, at 55 under Submission Clause.
11. ICC Bulletin June 1991 reported that, while it received per year over 300 arbitration requests, requests for conciliation under its Rules amount to no more than 5-10 per year.

but then adapted, as the IRAN-US Claims Tribunal did when drafting the rules which govern these arbitrations.[12] Insertion in these Rules of a waiver by the state of immunity from execution is recommended. The new Rules will in any case replace the 1962 Rules as far as arbitration is concerned. The fate of conciliation, provided for in Section II and Section III of the 1962 Rules has to be considered.

It is expected that Special Rules of the PCA for arbitration between a state and non-state parties will be welcomed by the international community and will contribute to the increase in the activities of the PCA.

---

12. For the manner in which the UNCITRAL Arbitration Rules have been adapted by the IRAN-US Claims Tribunal and have been applied by the Tribunal, *see* Van Hof, Commentary on the UNCITRAL Arbitration Rules - Their Application by the Iran-US Claims Tribunal, published by Kluwer in cooperation with the T.M.C. Asser Institute, 1991, XIV, 369 pp.

THE INTERNATIONAL COURT OF JUSTICE AND INTERNATIONAL ARBITRATION

SHABTAI ROSENNE*

1. INTRODUCTION

The purpose of this article is to examine the attitude of the International Court of Justice toward questions concerning different aspects of the international arbitration process. This relates in particular to disputes over the obligation to submit an alleged dispute to arbitration, disputes over the validity or nullity of an award rendered in an international arbitration process, and appeals to the International Court from other bodies with a power of dispositive decision. These questions have arisen in many different circumstances. The matter is also important having regard to the presence of compromissory clauses in international treaties conferring jurisdiction on the International Court itself, but only after it is clear that a process of arbitration, as the preferred method of dispute settlement, is not going to be successful in the concrete case.[1]

It is first necessary to clarify what is meant by 'an award rendered in an international arbitration process'.

There are several forms for an international arbitration process. Taking the recent classification of Coussirat-Coustère and Eisemann, 'classic arbitration' refers to cases, usually between states, decided by an *ad hoc* body. Since the end of the Second World War arbitral awards and arbitration procedures exist for the settlement of disputes between (a) international intergovernmental organizations and between such organizations and states, a form of dispute settlement which is to some extent institutionalized in international treaties; (b) awards rendered by an international tribunal to decide a number of distinct claims, usually by an individual against a

---

* Member of the Permanent Court of Arbitration. Member of the Institute of International Law; honorary member of the American Society of International Law. Counsel for the Government of Israel in the arbitrations concerning *German Secular Property in Israel* (1962) and *Taba* (1988). This article was written during the winter of 1992.

1. *See, e.g.,* Article 14 of the Convention for the Suppression of Unlawful Acts against the Safety of Civil Aviation, Montreal 1971, 974 U.N.T.S. 177. This article will not consider specifically the problem of where the jurisdiction of the Court arises only after attempts to settle the dispute by negotiation or by arbitration (or by both) have not been successful. The Court seems to have regarded as a question of fact the issue whether negotiations to settle a current dispute, including negotiations to organize an arbitration procedure, have been exhausted or not.

S. Muller and W. Mijs (eds.), The Flame Rekindled, 99–124.
© 1994 *Leiden Journal of International Law. Printed in the Netherlands.*

foreign state; and (c) what are termed 'transnational arbitrations', that is arbitrations involving at least one party which is not a state or an international intergovernmental organization.[2] The kind of international tribunal formed to deal with a number of distinct claims against a foreign country includes the Mixed Arbitral Tribunals established by the Peace Treaties after the First World War,[3] the Conciliation Commissions established under the Peace Treaties of 1947 with Italy[4] and of 1951 with Japan[5] and the Iran-United States Claims Tribunal currently sitting at The Hague.[6] The 'transnational arbitration' is another kind of arbitration which has come to the fore since the end of the Second World War, although earlier examples can be found. This is an *ad hoc* arbitration between an individual (usually a corporation) and a foreign state or an international intergovernmental organization, the arbitrator or the third arbitrator (umpire), often being appointed by the President of the International Court of Justice in exercise of the so-called extra-judicial function.[7]

The expression 'international tribunal' indicates that the tribunal has an international character, usually in the form of a neutral president, and applies 'international law', either in the general sense set out in Article 38, Paragraph 1, of the Statute of the International Court of Justice, or in a particular sense specified in the agreement establishing the *ad hoc* tribunal. On the other hand, for the purposes of this article the term does not extend to a tribunal which is a judicial organ of an international organization of integration such as the Court of Justice of the European Communities (the Luxembourg Court). The term 'arbitration' is also not used here in any defined technical sense. Diplomacy frequently requires the use of other terms such as mediation or conciliation, perhaps technically not formally binding in the sense that an arbitral award is usually regarded as being final and without appeal, following Article 81 of the First Hague Convention of 1907.[8] I do not propose to be over-fastidious in the choice of illustrations.

2. *See* V. Coussirat-Coustère and P.M. Eisemann, III Repertory of International Arbitral Jurisprudence xxv (1991).
3. *See* Recueil des Decisions des Tribunaux Arbitraux Mixtes, 10 volumes, 1922-1930.
4. *See* XIII, XIV and XVI U.N.R.I.A.A., *passim.*
5. XIV U.N.R.I.A.A. 449.
6. *See* Iran-United States Claims Tribunal Reports, 27 volumes to date.
7. For an instance of this in the Permanent Court, *see* the Société Commerciale de Belgique case, 1939 P.C.I.J. Rep. (Ser. A/B, No. 78), at 50. On the basis of the title of jurisdiction the Court found that since the arbitral awards were final and without appeal, and since the Court had no mandate from the parties with regard to them, "it can neither confirm nor annul them either in whole or in part" (at 179). It did, however, find that the awards were "definitive and obligatory" (at 179). This gave rise to the Socobel *v.* The Greek State case in the Belgian Courts (1951), 18 I.L.R. 3. On this type of arbitration, *see* further, in particular, S.M. Schwebel, International Arbitration: Three Salient Problems (1987); S.J. Toope, Mixed International Arbitration (1990). On the extra-judicial function, *see* Sh. Rosenne, The Law and Practice of the International Court 633 (1965, 1985).
8. 205 Consolidated Treaty Series 233.

Of these three major types of arbitration, questions relating to inter-state arbitrations and of the obligation to submit an alleged dispute to arbitration -both an alleged dispute between states and an alleged dispute between a state and an international intergovernmental organization- have come before the International Court. Cases relating to the Mixed Arbitral Tribunals came before the Permanent Court of International Justice, by way of appeal.[9] Interesting attempts have been made to secure compliance with a judgment of the International Court itself as well as of awards of the Iran-US Claims Tribunal through domestic courts. It is convenient to treat the first type of arbitration dispute separately from the appeals cases before attempting to draw conclusions of more general application.

2. THE OBLIGATION TO SUBMIT A DISPUTE TO ARBITRATION

The principal cases in the International Court relating to aspects of 'classic arbitration' are the following: the *Interpretation of Peace Treaties between Bulgaria, Hungary and Romania Advisory Opinion*,[10] the *Ambatielos case*,[11] the *Case Concerning the Arbitral Award made by the King of Spain on December 23, 1906*,[12] the *Applicability of the Obligation to Arbitrate under Section 21 of the United Nations Headquarters Agreement of June 26, 1947, Advisory Opinion*,[13] and the *Arbitral Award of July 31, 1989 case*.[14] Both the contentious and the advisory jurisdiction of the Court have been invoked, an illustration of how diplomatic necessities are continually reaching into new methods of dispute settlement through the judicial or quasi-judicial process.

The cases which have been mentioned cover a wide range of fundamental aspects of international arbitration. They fall into two broad classes. The *Peace Treaties Advisory Opinion*, for instance, was the first to examine the relation of an alleged dispute to a compromissory clause, the obligation to submit that dispute to a properly constituted organ, and the constitution of that organ in accordance with the compromissory clause. The case has had a major influence on the development of the law for preventing the frustration of arbitration agreements. The *Ambatielos case* and the *Headquarters Agreement Advisory Opinion* also concerned the question whether

---

9. These include the Appeals from Certain Judgments of the Hungaro-Czechoslovak Mixed Arbitral Tribunal case, 1933 P.C.I.J. Rep. (Ser. A/B No. 56); Appeal from a Judgment of the Hungaro-Czechoslovak Mixed Arbitral Tribunal, The Peter Pázmány University case, 1933 P.C.I.J. Rep. (Ser. A/B, No. 61); Pajzs, Csáky, Esterházy case, 1936 P.C.I.J. Rep. (Ser. A/B, Nos. 66, 68) (appeal from a judgment of the Hungaro-Yugoslav Mixed Arbitral Tribunal).
10. 1950 I.C.J. Rep. 65, 221 (second phase).
11. 1952 I.C.J. Rep. 28 (Preliminary Objections), 1953 I.C.J. Rep. 10 (merits). For the final arbitral award, *see* XII U.N.R.I.A.A. 91.
12. 1960 I.C.J. Rep. 192. For the award of 1906, *see* XI U.N.R.I.A.A. 111.
13. 1988 I.C.J. Rep. 12.
14. 1991 I.C.J. Rep. 53. For the Award of July 31, 1989, *see* 94 RGDIP 204 (1990); English translation in 83 I.L.R. 1.

an alleged dispute (if such existed) came within the scope of the arbitral *compromis*. In each instance the question was answered in the affirmative, but only in the first did the arbitration actually take place.

On the other hand, the two Arbitral Award cases each concerned the validity, nullity or existence of the impugned award. These were not 'appeals' since each of the awards was final and without appeal, and the Court had no jurisdiction to determine the case on appeal.

Both categories of cases in the International Court are important for the distinction which they draw between recourse relating to the obligation to proceed to arbitration in given circumstances, the question of the validity of a final and binding arbitral award which has been rendered, and an appeal as such when the arbitral *compromis* makes provision for an appeal to the International Court. That aspect has arisen in the *Appeal relating to the Jurisdiction of the ICAO Council case.*[15]

The compromissory clause at issue in the *Peace Treaties case* reads:

> 1. Except where another procedure is specifically provided in any article of the present Treaty, any dispute concerning the interpretation or execution of the Treaty, which is not settled by direct diplomatic negotiations, shall be referred to the Three Heads of Mission acting under Article 35, except that in this case the Heads of Mission shall not be restricted by the time-limit provided in that article. Any such dispute not resolved by them within a period of two months shall, unless the parties to the dispute mutually agree upon another means of settlement, be referred at the request of either party to the dispute to a Commission composed of one representative of each party and a third member selected by mutual agreement of the two parties from nationals of a third country. Should the two parties fail to agree within a period of one month upon the appointment of the third member, the Secretary-General of the United Nations may be requested by either party to make the appointment.
> 2. The decision of the majority of the members of the Commission shall be the decision of the Commission, and shall be accepted by the parties as definitive and binding.[16]

The relevant facts can be summarized. In April 1949 the question of the observance of the human rights clauses in those treaties by the three states concerned had been referred by the Western Powers to the General Assembly of the United Nations. The General Assembly adopted a resolution expressing its grave concern at those accusations and recalled the obligations undertaken in the compromissory clauses of the Peace Treaties. Those three countries denied the charges and refused to appoint

---

15. 1972 I.C.J. Rep. 46.
16. Article 36 of the Treaty of Peace with Bulgaria; Article 40 of the Treaty with Hungary; Article 38 of the Treaty with Romania. On the nature of these clauses, *see* G.G. Fitzmaurice, *The Juridical Clauses of the Peace Treaties*, Academy of International Law, 73 Recueil des Cours, at 259, 362 (1947). The author explained that the articles of the treaties providing for the supervision of their execution and the settlement of disputes "may present a good many difficulties or ambiguities of legal interpretation".

representatives to the Commissions. At this, the General Assembly decided to request advisory opinions on two related sets of questions. The first set enquired first whether the diplomatic exchanges between the states concerned "disclose disputes subject to the provisions for the settlement of disputes contained in the Treaties"; and second, in the event of an affirmative reply, whether the three states were "obligated to carry out the provisions of the Articles in the Peace Treaties for the settlement of disputes, including the provisions for the appointment of their representatives to the Commissions".

The second set of questions, in the event of an affirmative reply to the second question above within thirty days of the delivery of the first advisory opinion and the designation had not been made, asked whether the Secretary-General was "authorized to appoint the third Member of the Commissions". In the event of an affirmative reply to that question, the fourth question enquired whether a Commission so composed would be "competent to make a definitive and binding decision in settlement of the dispute".

The first advisory opinion is complicated because the three states (and others) raised a series of objections to the giving of the advisory opinion. Some of those objections related to the advisory competence itself and are not relevant here. Others, however, related to the compromissory clauses, including one to the effect that the advisory procedure would take the place of the procedure envisaged in the Treaties. On these the Court made the following statement of principle:

> The Court is not called upon to deal with the charges [...] since the Questions [...] relate neither to the alleged violations of the provisions of the Treaties [...] nor to the interpretation of the articles relating to these matters. The object of the Request is more limited. It is directed solely to obtaining from the Court certain clarifications of a legal nature regarding the applicability of the procedure for the settlement of disputes by the Commissions [...]. The interpretation of the terms of a treaty for this purpose [...] is a question of international law which, by its very nature, lies within the competence of the Court.
>
> [...]
>
> [T]he object of this Request is to facilitate [the procedure instituted by the Peace Treaties for the settlement of disputes] by seeking information for the General Assembly as to its applicability in the circumstances of the present case.
>
> [...]
>
> [T]he present Request [...] is solely concerned with the applicability to certain disputes of the procedure for settlement instituted by the Peace Treaties, and it is justifiable to conclude that it in no way touches the merits of those disputes. Furthermore, the settlement of those disputes is entrusted solely to the Commissions [...]. Consequently,

> it is for these Commissions to decide upon any objections which may be raised to their jurisdiction in respect of any of these disputes, and the present Opinion in no way prejudges the decisions that may be taken on those objections. It follows that the legal position of the parties to those disputes cannot be in any way compromised by the answers that the Court may give to the Questions put to it.

The Court then turned to Question I. The Court had little difficulty in deciding that disputes existed and that those disputes

> must be considered to fall within those provisions [for the settlement of disputes] if they relate to the interpretation or execution of the Treaties, and if no other procedure of settlement is specifically provided elsewhere in the Treaties. Inasmuch as the disputes related to the question of the performance or non-performance of certain obligations provided in the Treaties, they are clearly "disputes concerning the interpretation or execution of the Peace Treaties".

Since no other procedure was specifically provided in the Peace Treaties, "the disputes must be subject to the methods of settlement contained in the articles providing for the settlement of disputes". This led to an affirmative answer to Question I.

The Court interpreted Question II as meaning that, in view of the disputes which had arisen and which had so far not been settled, were the three countries "obligated to carry out, respectively, the provisions of" the relevant settlement articles of the Treaties. The Court summarized those provisions and examined the diplomatic documents presented to it. It found that "all the conditions for the commencement of the stage of the settlement of disputes by the Commissions have been fulfilled".

> In view of the fact that the Treaties provide that any dispute shall be referred to a Commission "at the request of either party", it follows that either party is obligated, at the request of the other party, to cooperate in constituting the Commission, in particular by appointing its representative. Otherwise the method of settlement by Commissions provided for in the Treaties would completely fail in its purpose.[17]

It is notable that the Court made no reference to any precedents of the Permanent Court. This stands in sharp contrast to some of the pleadings and the separate and dissenting opinions, which relied strongly on the *Eastern Carelia case*.[18]

The three states took no action after the Court's first advisory opinion, and in due course it became necessary for the Court to give its answer to question III. Referring in particular to the second part of Paragraph 1 of the compromissory clause and to

17. 1950 I.C.J. Rep. 65.
18. 1923 P.C.I.J. Rep. (Ser. B, No. 5).

Paragraph 2, the Court analyzed the relevant part of Paragraph 1. It defined the point at issue as being whether the provision empowering the Secretary-General to appoint the third member of the Commission applied in the present case where "one of the parties refuses to appoint its own representative to the Commission". The Court declined to interpret the expression 'third member' as being the neutral member as distinguished from the two commissioners appointed by the parties. The implication was that the failure of the parties within the stipulated period to select the third member by mutual agreement would not satisfy the condition required for the appointment of the third member by the Secretary-General. The Court said:

> The Secretary-General's power to appoint a third member is derived solely from the agreement of the parties as expressed in the disputes clause of the Treaties; by its very nature such a clause must be strictly construed and can be applied only in the case expressly provided for therein. The case envisaged in the Treaties is exclusively that of the failure of the parties to agree upon the selection of a third member and by no means the much more serious case of a complete refusal of cooperation by one of them. The power conferred upon the Secretary-General to help the parties out of the difficulty of agreeing upon a third member cannot be extended to the situation which now exists.

The Court pointed out that were the Secretary-General to appoint the third member in these circumstances, the result would be the constitution of a two-member Commission. "A Commission consisting of two members is not the kind of commission for which the Treaties have provided". The Court also explained that such a commission could only decide by unanimity, contrary to the provision for a majority decision in Paragraph 2.

In reaching this decision, the Court rejected contentions based on the maxim *ut res magis valeat quam pereat*. It distinguished the present case from the situation that arises when an arbitration commission may make a valid decision although the original number of its members as fixed in the arbitration agreement is later reduced by such circumstances as the withdrawal of one of the commissioners. It also rejected arguments based on the view that a negative answer to question III would seriously jeopardize the future of the large number of arbitration clauses drafted on the same pattern as that which appears in the Peace Treaties.

Having answered question III in the negative, it became unnecessary for the Court to deal with question IV.[19]

Although this case was at the time subject to considerable criticism, there can be little doubt of its wisdom: in the context of the 'Cold War' as it was then taking shape, it is certain that a positive answer to question III, whatever the answer to question IV,

19. 1950 I.C.J. Rep. 221.

would have become a source of great embarrassment to the Secretary-General of the day, Mr Trygve Lie, who had already encountered difficulties in his relations with one of the permanent members of the Security Council. It is likely to have severely damaged the standing of the Court.

The next in this series of cases was the *Ambatielos: Obligation to Arbitrate case*, brought by Greece against the United Kingdom. Greece asked the Court to declare that a certain claim should be submitted to arbitration under arbitration treaties in force between the two countries. The case was complicated by a preliminary objection raised by the United Kingdom to the effect that the Court lacked jurisdiction to decide that question.

In the course of dealing with the preliminary objections, the Court was faced with a contention that if it accepted jurisdiction, there might be a conflict between a decision of the Court finding that there was an obligation to submit the difference to a Commission of Arbitration and an eventual decision by that Commission. The Court dismissed such an idea, saying:

> The Court would decide whether there is a difference between the Parties [...]. Should the Court find that there is such a difference, the Commission of Arbitration would decide on the merits of the difference.[20]

In the second phase, subtitled *Merits: Obligation to Arbitrate*, that paragraph constituted the point of departure. The Court continued by saying:

> The Court must refrain from pronouncing final judgment upon any question of fact or law falling within the "merits of the difference" or the "validity of the claim". If the Court were to undertake to decide such questions, it would encroach upon the jurisdiction of the Commission of Arbitration. The task of the Court will have been completed when it has decided whether the difference between Greece and the United Kingdom with regard to the validity of the Ambatielos claim is or is not a difference as to the validity of a claim on behalf of a private person based on the provisions of the Treaty of 1886 and whether, in consequence, there is an obligation binding the United Kingdom to accept arbitration.

One of the contentions of the United Kingdom was that the claim was not a claim the substantive foundation of which lay in the 1886 Treaty, and that, before the Court could decide upon arbitration, it would have to determine whether the claim was actually or genuinely based on the 1886 Treaty. Rejecting this argument, the Court said:

> The Court cannot accept this contention. It would necessarily lead to passing on a point

20. 1952 I.C.J. Rep. 28, at 44.

which constitutes one of the principal elements of the Ambatielos claim and consequently to the substitution of the Court for the Commission of Arbitration. The Court cannot substitute itself for the Commission of Arbitration. The question of violation or non-violation of the Treaty of 1886 goes to the very roots of the Ambatielos claim. To decide whether the facts alleged by the Hellenic Government, if true, would constitute an actual violation of the Treaty of 1886 would be to pass upon "the validity of the claim" and "the merits of the difference", which are reserved exclusively for the Commission of Arbitration, and concerning which this Court, according to its own earlier Judgment, is without jurisdiction. It cannot be assumed that the Declaration of 1926 [regarding outstanding claims when a new Treaty was negotiated] contemplates that the verification of the allegations of fact of the Hellenic Government should be the duty of the Commission of Arbitration, while the determination of the question whether the facts alleged constitute a violation of the Treaty of 1866 should form the task of another tribunal. Such a division of functions would imply a division of the merits of the claim, which is authorized neither by the Declaration [of 1926] nor by the previous Judgment of this Court.

[...]

In the absence of any manifestation of a common intention of the Parties to the contrary, the Commission of Arbitration cannot be deprived of a part of its competence and no other body can be invested with the authority to determine definitively the validity of the treaty basis of the Ambatielos claim.

[...]

The fact that a claim purporting to be based on the Treaty may be eventually found by the Commission of Arbitration to be unsupportable under the Treaty, does not of itself remove the claim from the category of claims which, for the purpose of arbitration, should be regarded as falling within the terms of the Declaration of 1926.

The Court pointed out that in order for it to decide that the Greek Government's claim was based on the 1886 Treaty within the meaning of the Declaration of 1926, it was not necessary for the Court to find that the Government's interpretation of the Treaty was the correct one: indeed the Court was without jurisdiction to do this. It was enough to find that those arguments were of a sufficiently plausible character.

The validity of the arguments presented by the Hellenic Government, as well as those presented by the United Kingdom Government, would be determined by the Commission of Arbitration in passing upon the merits of the difference. If the interpretation given by the Hellenic Government to any of the provisions relied upon appears to be one of the possible interpretations that may be placed upon it, though not necessarily the correct one, then the Ambatielos claim must be considered, for present proceedings, to be a claim based on the Treaty of 1886.

The Court would use its power of appreciation to resolve the legal problem presented by the parties, but it could not "carry its power of appreciation to the extent of deciding the merits of the difference".[21]

The last case in this series is the advisory opinion entitled *Applicability of the Obligation to Arbitrate under Section 21 of the United Nations Headquarters Agreement of June 26, 1947*. The situation here was unusual. Legislation of the United States of America was interpreted by the United States authorities as requiring them to initiate action to close the offices of the Palestine Liberation Organization (PLO) in the United States, including the offices of its Permanent Observer Mission to the United Nations in New York. In the course of correspondence with the United States over this, the Secretary-General had determined that a dispute had come into existence concerning the interpretation of the Headquarters Agreement. The compromissory clause of that Agreement was in the usual terms: any dispute concerning the interpretation or application of the Agreement not otherwise settled should be referred for final decision to a tribunal of three arbitrators, one to be named by the Secretary-General, one by the Secretary of State, and the third to be chosen by the two, or if they should fail to agree upon a third, by the President of the International Court of Justice. The Secretary-General called on the United States to cooperate in the organization of the arbitration and appointed a former President of the Court as his arbitrator. In later resolutions, including the resolution requesting the advisory opinion, the General Assembly had affirmed the position of the Secretary-General that a dispute existed with the United States. The Court was asked whether, in the light of the facts as reflected in various reports of the Secretary-General, the United States was "under an obligation to enter into arbitration in accordance with section 21 of the [Headquarters] Agreement".

Although it is arguable that the determination by the Secretary-General and by the General Assembly that a dispute existed may have limited the Court's freedom of action in that respect, the advisory opinion follows its predecessors in the methodology of its reasoning. The Court pointed out that it was not called upon to decide whether the measures adopted by the United States in regard to the Observer Mission of the PLO to the United Nations did or did not run counter to the Headquarters Agreement. The question put to the Court was not about either the alleged violations of the provisions of that Agreement or the interpretation of those provisions. The question was directed solely to the determination whether under the Agreement the United Nations was entitled to call for arbitration and the United States was obliged to enter into that procedure. "Hence the request for an opinion concerns solely the applicability to the alleged dispute of the arbitration procedure provided for by the Headquarters Agreement".

The Court then explained what it would have to do in order to answer that

21. 1953 I.C.J. Rep. at 17-19.

question. "[T]he Court has to determine whether there exists a dispute between the United Nations and the United States, and if so whether or not that dispute is one concerning the interpretation or application of the Headquarters Agreement within the meaning of "the compromissory clause". If it finds that there is such a dispute it must also, pursuant to that section, satisfy itself that it is one not settled by negotiation or other agreed mode of settlement".

On the question of whether a dispute existed, the Court had little difficulty -and perhaps little choice- in giving an affirmative answer. Unlike what had occurred in the *Peace Treaties Advisory Opinion*, however, it relied heavily on precedents, including the *Mavrommatis Palestine Concessions case*,[22] the *Peace Treaties case*, the *South West Africa cases*[23] and the *Case Concerning Northern Cameroons*,[24] to establish that the opposing attitudes of the parties clearly established the existence of a dispute.

In the course of the negotiations the United States had taken the position that as it had not yet concluded that a dispute existed, the matter being pending in the United States courts, it did not believe that arbitration "would be appropriate or timely". The Court rejected this argument, explaining that it could not allow considerations as to what might be "appropriate" to prevail over the obligations that derived from the compromissory clause. On the other hand, the Court did not think that there was any need to determine the date at which the dispute came into existence, once it had reached the conclusion that there was such a dispute at the date on which the opinion was given. In this way it avoided the issue of the "timeliness" of the approach to the Court by the General Assembly.

The Court next turned to the question whether the dispute was one which concerned the interpretation or application of the Headquarters Agreement. Repeating what it had done in previous cases, the Court said:

> It is not [...] the task of the Court to say whether the enactment, or the enforcement, of the [impugned United States enactment] would or would not constitute a breach of the provisions of the Headquarters Agreement; that question is reserved for the arbitral tribunal [...].

After a discussion of that aspect the Court turned to the issue of whether the dispute was one "not settled by negotiation or other agreed mode of settlement". Examining the correspondence with the United States, the Court agreed that in the circumstances the Secretary-General had exhausted such possibilities of negotiation as were open to him, and that there was no other agreed method of settlement contemplated by the

22. 1924 P.C.I.J. Rep. (Ser. A, No. 2), at 11.
23. 1962 I.C.J. Rep. 319, at 328.
24. 1963 I.C.J. Rep. 15, at 27.

parties. The Court could not regard the proceedings in the domestic courts of the United States as an "agreed mode of settlement" within the meaning of the compromissory clause, notwithstanding that the United Nations wished to be admitted "only" as *amicus curiae* before the *District Court for the Southern District of New York*.[25]

Given the political background of this case, the outcome is no cause for surprise, and given the political environment, the jurisprudential value of the case as a precedent in other political circumstances is circumscribed. What is interesting is to see how once again the Court was meticulous in maintaining a sharp distinction between what its powers and competences were in the case, and those of the arbitration tribunal should it be established. In this respect the Court did not break new ground. However, its reaffirmation of established patterns of proceeding is a useful reinforcement of its general approach to maintaining the integrity of the international arbitration system when that is what the compromissory clause requires.

3.   THE VALIDITY OR NULLITY OF AN AWARD

The first of the cases concerning the validity or nullity of an arbitral award was the *Arbitral Award made by the King of Spain on December 23, 1906 case*.[26] The following statement of principle is relevant to the issues discussed here:

> [T]he Court will observe that the Award is not subject to appeal and that the Court cannot approach the consideration of the objections [...] to the validity of the Award as a Court of Appeal. The Court is not called upon to pronounce on whether the arbitrator's decision was right or wrong. These and cognate questions have no relevance to the function that the Court is called upon to discharge in these proceedings, which is to decide whether the Award is proved to be a nullity having no effect.[27]

One of the questions which the Court had to decide was whether the award was sufficiently reasoned. On this point too the Court made an important statement of principle. The Court said that an examination of the impugned award showed that it "deals in logical order and in some detail with all relevant considerations" and that it "contains ample reasoning and explanations in support of the conclusions arrived at by the arbitrators".

25. 1988 I.C.J. Rep. 12. This notwithstanding, the United States Court had the last word in settling this dispute. *See* United States *v.* The Palestine Liberation Organization and Others, 695 Fed. Supp. 1456 (Southern District New York, 1988). The Court declined to follow the advisory opinion and held that it should decide the question solely by reference to United States law. It went on to hold that the United States legislation did not require the closing of the office of the Permanent Observer Mission in New York. In that way the matter was finally settled.
26. 1960 I.C.J. Rep. 192, at 214.
27. *Id.*, 216.

The issue next arose in the *Arbitral Award of July 31, 1989 case* brought by Guinea-Bissau against Senegal concerning the existence and the validity of the arbitral award rendered between the same parties on July 31, 1989, on the basis of an arbitration agreement of March 12, 1985. By that agreement, the arbitration Tribunal was requested to answer two questions: the first related to the legal force of a pre-decolonization agreement of 1960 between the former colonial powers regarding maritime delimitation; and the second, to be answered "[i]n the event of a negative answer to the first question", concerned the delimitation between the two countries. The arbitration agreement also required the Tribunal to annex a map to its award. In its award, the Tribunal concluded that the 1960 agreement was valid and could be opposed to both parties; that it had to be interpreted in light of the law in force in 1960; and accordingly that it did not apply to delimit those maritime spaces which did not exist then, notably the exclusive economic zone, fishery zone or whatever. Accordingly the Tribunal did not find it necessary to answer the second question, or to append a map to its award. The operative clause was adopted by two votes to one, but the President, who had voted with the majority, appended a declaration which was partially affirmative and partially negative.

Guinea-Bissau challenged the validity and the very existence of this award in its application instituting the proceedings in the *Arbitral Award of July 31, 1989 case*. The challenge was based on a number of grounds including that one of the arbitrators was absent when the award was read, that in fact the award was not supported by the majority of the Tribunal, that the Tribunal had committed an *excès de pouvoir* through inadequate reasoning and by not including a map in the award - all grounds touching fundamentals of international arbitration procedure. In its judgment the Court appears to have gone as far as it could in rejecting all these contentions to uphold the validity of the award, and in so doing also to lay the basis for the final settlement of the dispute through negotiations or through further proceedings in the Court itself.

The jurisdiction of the Court was said to be based on the two declarations accepting the jurisdiction under Article 36, Paragraph 2, of the Statute. The declaration of Guinea-Bissau was unconditional: that of Senegal included reservations which could have influenced the Court's jurisdiction. However, during the proceedings the parties agreed that there was a distinction between the substantive dispute relating to maritime delimitation, and the dispute relating to the arbitral award, and that only the latter dispute was before the Court and came within the jurisdiction. On this aspect the Court said (Para. 25):

> the Court would emphasize that, as the Parties were both agreed, these proceedings allege the inexistence and the nullity of the Award [...] and are not by way of appeal from it or application for revision of it.

Here the Court cited from its judgment in the *Arbitral Award Made by the King of Spain case*. The effect of this holding came out later in the judgment.

At a session of the Tribunal in which the award was pronounced, one of the arbitrators was absent. Guinea-Bissau alleged that the absence of that arbitrator "lessened the Tribunal's authority". On this the Court said (Para. 29) that it was not disputed that this arbitrator had been present when the award was adopted, and that the absence of the arbitrator "could not affect the validity of the Award which had already been adopted".[28]

The first contention regarding the inexistence of the award was that because of its President's declaration the award was not "supported by a real majority". The Court explained its understanding of the President's declaration (Paras. 31, 32), and continued:

> 33. Furthermore, even if there had been any contradiction [...] between the view expressed by President Barberis and that stated in the Award, such contradiction could not prevail over the position which President Barberis had taken when voting for the Award. In agreeing to the Award, he definitively agreed to the decisions, which it incorporated, as to the extent of the maritime areas covered by the 1960 Agreement, and as to the Tribunal not being required to answer the second question in view of its answer to the first. As the practice of international tribunals shows, it sometimes happens that a member of a tribunal votes in favour of a decision of the tribunal even though he might individually have been inclined to prefer another solution. The validity of his vote remains unaffected by the expression of such differences in a declaration or separate opinion of the member concerned, which are therefore without consequence for the decision of the tribunal.

Three factors were adduced in support of the contentions that the award was a nullity: insufficiency of reasoning; the absence of a reply to the second question; and the absence of a map in the award. The Court proceeded to analyze the main elements of the award (Para. 68), after which it turned to the arguments of Guinea-Bissau contesting the existence and validity of the award.

Dealing with the argument based on the absence of an answer to the second question, the Court said:

> 41. The Court recognizes that the structure of the Award is, in that respect, open to criticism. Article 2 of the Arbitration Agreement put two questions to the Tribunal [...]. Consequently, it would have been normal to include in the operative part of the Award

28. This corresponds to the Court's own practice. Article 9 of the Resolution concerning the Internal Judicial Practice of the Court of April 12, 1976 and Articles 94 and 107 of the Rules of Court distinguish between the adoption of a judgment or advisory opinion, and its being read in open Court. For that resolution, *see* Sh. Rosenne, *Documents on the International Court of Justice* 441 (1st bilingual ed., 1991). The judgments of the European Court of Human Rights as a matter of course indicate when the judgment was adopted and when it was read in open Court or otherwise published.

[...] both the answer given to the first question and the decision not to answer the second. It is to be regretted that this course was not followed. However, when the Tribunal adopted the Award by two votes to one, it was not only approving the content of Paragraph 88 [the operative part], but was also doing so for the reasons already stated in the Award and, in particular, in Paragraph 87. It is clear from that paragraph, taken in its context, and also from the declaration of President Barberis, that the Tribunal decided by two votes to one that, as it had given an affirmative answer to the first question, it did not have to answer the second. By so doing, the Tribunal did take a decision: namely, not to answer the second question put to it. The Award is not flawed by any failure to decide.

On the question of adequacy of reasons, the Court said:

This reasoning is brief, and could doubtless have been developed further. But the references in Paragraph 87 to the Tribunal's conclusions and to the wording of Article 2 of the Arbitration Agreement make it possible to determine, without difficulty, the reasons why the Tribunal decided not to answer the second question. [...] That statement of reasoning, while succinct, is clear and precise (Para. 43).

Although critical of the structure of the award, this passage does not depart from the essentials stated by the Court earlier in the *King of Spain case*.

Guinea-Bissau had challenged the validity of the reasoning of the Tribunal to the effect that it was not required to answer the second question. On this, the Court first recalled (Para. 46) the consistently held rule that in the absence of agreement to the contrary, an international tribunal has the right to decide as to its own jurisdiction and for this purpose has the power to interpret the instruments which govern its jurisdiction. Pointing out that Guinea-Bissau was in fact criticizing the interpretation of the Arbitration Agreement by the Tribunal and proposing another interpretation, the Court said (Para. 47):

the Court does not have to enquire whether or not the Arbitration Agreement could, with regard to the Tribunal's competence, be interpreted in a number of ways, and if so to consider which would have been preferable. By proceeding in that way the Court would be treating the request as an appeal and not as a *recours en nullité*. The Court could not act in that way in the present case. It has simply to ascertain whether by rendering the disputed Award the Tribunal acted in manifest breach of the competence conferred on it by the Arbitration Agreement, either by deciding in excess of, or by failing to exercise, its jurisdiction.

The Court then proceeded to examine that aspect and rejected the contentions of Guinea-Bissau. Accordingly the Court rejected (Para. 60) contentions that the award was inexistent and absolutely null and void, and on a counter-submission by Senegal found that the Arbitral Award "is valid and binding" for both parties, "which have the obligation to apply it".

A notable feature of this judgment is its measured criticism of the arbitration agreement itself, which was inadequate to settle the dispute between the two countries (Paras. 44-65). It is rare for the International Court to do this.

Taken as a whole, this judgment is an important instance of judicial control being exercised over the details of an arbitration procedure, including the drafting of the *compromis* and the formation and promulgation of the award. The categoric operative part of this judgment also has the effect of bringing the application of the award within the framework of Article 94 of the Charter, and in imposing on both parties the obligation to comply with it.

4.   APPEALS TO THE ICJ

The Permanent Court had three instances of appeal from decisions of a Mixed Arbitral Tribunal, one of which was discontinued.[29] These are not on all fours with appeals in international litigation between states, as the parties in the cases in the Mixed Arbitral Tribunals were not identical with the states parties in the proceedings in the Permanent Court. This notwithstanding, for present purposes it seems that the principles applied by the Permanent Court in the two relevant judgments are applicable in cases between states.

In the *Peter Pázmány University case*, the relevant treaties provided for an appeal from the Hungaro-Czechoslovak Mixed Arbitral Tribunal "from all judgments on questions of jurisdiction or merits". On this the Court said:

> There can be no doubt that this Article confers jurisdiction upon the Court.
>
> [...]
>
> Having thus established that it has jurisdiction in the present case, the Court must observe that this jurisdiction does not extend to certain objections which have been made by the Czechoslovak Government in the present proceedings before the Court and which, according to that Government, relate to the proceedings before the Mixed Arbitral Tribunal.
>
> According to the terms of Article X of the Paris Agreement No. II, the Parties agree to submit to the Court "questions of jurisdiction or merits". In view of the fact that its jurisdiction is limited by the clear terms of this provision, the Court has no power to control the way in which the Mixed Arbitral Tribunal has exercised its functions as regards procedure.

29. Appeals from Certain Judgments of the Hungaro-Czechoslovak Mixed Arbitral Tribunal case, *supra* note 9.

The jurisdiction of the Tribunal was based on various provisions of the Treaty of Trianon, and in particular on Article 250. The Court did not feel called upon to deal separately with the question of the Tribunal's jurisdiction and of the merits, and examined whether the conditions required by Article 250 were fulfilled in this case before drawing the necessary inferences for the decision.[30]

The consequence of this was that the Permanent Court in effect examined *de novo* the various contentions advanced in its proceedings before reaching the conclusion that the judgment of the Mixed Arbitral Tribunal had been "rightly decided".

In the *Pajzs, Csáky, Esterházy case* the Hungaro/Yugoslav Mixed Arbitral Tribunal had declared that certain applications could not be entertained by it for reasons connected with its interpretation of the same Article 250 of the Treaty of Trianon. The Permanent Court therefore first considered whether under the various relevant treaties it could entertain the appeal, a question answered in the affirmative. The Court then turned to the merits, and found that the judgments under appeal were not delivered in proceedings before the Mixed Arbitral Tribunal for which the Permanent Court had an appellate jurisdiction. It therefore decided that the appeals could not be entertained, in that way in effect upholding the decision of the Mixed Arbitral Tribunal.[31]

The only instance of an appeal from a decision of an international organ competent to determine differences between States was the *Appeal Relating to the Jurisdiction of the ICAO Council case* between India and Pakistan.[32] This was an appeal by India from a decision of the Council of the International Civil Aviation Organization (ICAO) on the basis of article 84 of the Convention on International Civil Aviation of 1944 (The 'Chicago Convention').[33] That provision of the constituent instrument of ICAO empowers the Council to decide "any disagreement between two or more of the contracting parties relating to the interpretation or application" of this Convention which could not be settled by negotiation.

> Any such contracting State may [...] appeal from the decision of the Council to an *ad hoc* arbitral tribunal agreed upon with the other parties to the dispute or to the Permanent Court of International Justice [...].[34]

---

30. 1933 P.C.I.J. Rep. (Ser. A/B, No. 61), at 221.
31. *Supra* note 9.
32. 1972 I.C.J. Rep. 46.
33. 15 U.N.T.S. 295. For the current version containing all the amendments, *see* ICAO Doc. 7300/6 (1980).
34. By virtue of Article 37 of the Statute of the International Court of Justice, that Court now replaces the Permanent Court of International Justice in this provision. For the Rules of the ICAO Council for the Settlement of Differences, *see* ICAO Doc. 7782/2 (1975). Reproduced *in* K. Oellers-Frahm and N. Wühler, Dispute Settlement in Public International Law: Texts and Materials 489 (1984).

The Council had been seized of a dispute between India and Pakistan on the basis of that provision. In the course of those proceedings, the Council was faced with objections by Pakistan to its jurisdiction and it decided in favour of assuming jurisdiction. India appealed from that decision to the Court.

From the start the Court emphasized:

> 11. It must [...] be stated at the outset that with these various matters [concerning the substance of the dispute submitted to the ICAO Council] and with the dispute as placed before the Council, and the facts and contentions of the Parties relative to it, the Court has nothing whatever to do in the present proceedings, except in so far as these elements may relate to the purely jurisdictional issue which alone has been referred to it, namely the competence of the Council to hear and determine the case submitted by Pakistan [*i.e.*, to the Council]. Subject to this necessary exception, the Court must avoid not only any expression of opinion on these matters of substance, but any pronouncements which might prejudge, or appear to prejudge, the eventual decision, whatever it might be, of the Council on the ultimate merits of the case, if the Council is held to be competent to entertain these - *see also* the *case of Interpretation of Article 3, Paragraph 2, of the Treaty of Lausanne*, Advisory Opinion, 1925, PCIJ, Ser. B, No. 12, at 18.

Before coming to the question of the Council's jurisdiction, the Court had to deal with some objections by Pakistan to its own jurisdiction to entertain the appeal. The chief of these was that Article 84 only allowed an appeal to the Court from a decision of the Council on the merits of the dispute referred to the Council, and not from a decision concerning the Council's jurisdiction to entertain the reference, whether such jurisdiction was affirmed or rejected by the Council. In the course of this, Pakistan contended that because of the principle of the *compétence de la compétence*, the Council's jurisdiction decisions are conclusive and unappealable. The Court dismissed this shortly, pointing out that it prejudged the question. "[I]f on other grounds it appears that these decisions must be held appealable, this principle could not be permitted to prevail without defeating a priori all possibility of appeal" (Para. 15).

Another contention was that Article 84, on its correct interpretation, only provides for an appeal to the Court against a final decision of the Council on the merits of any dispute submitted to it, and not against decisions of an interim or preliminary character. Dismissing this, the Court said:

> 18. This view would certainly have to be regarded as correct in respect of any procedural or otherwise genuinely interlocutory decisions of the Council, such as a decision about the manner in which a case was to be presented to it; as to the time-limits within which the written pleadings were to be deposited; or as to the production or admissibility of documents or other evidence, etc. The Court however thinks that a

decision of the Council relative to its jurisdiction to entertain a dispute does not come within the same category as the matters just mentioned, even though, like them, it necessarily has a preliminary character; - for although, in the purely temporal sense, a preliminary question is involved, that question is, in its essence, a substantial question crucially affecting the position of the parties relative to the case, notwithstanding that it does not decide the ultimate merits.

Accordingly the Court considered that for the purpose of the jurisdictional clause, final decisions of the Council as to its competence should not be distinguished from final decisions on the merits.

The Court noted some further points in support of that view.

Although a jurisdictional decision does not determine the ultimate merits, it is a decision of a substantive character inasmuch as it may decide the whole affair by bringing it to an end. A decision which can have that effect "is scarcely of less importance" than a decision on the merits, which it either rules out entirely or permits by endorsing the existence of the jurisdictional basis "which must form the indispensable foundation of any decision on the merits. A jurisdictional question is therefore unquestionably a constituent part of the case, being regarded as being on a par with decisions on the merits as regards any right of appeal".

For the party raising a jurisdictional objection, its significance lies in the possibility which it may offer of avoiding not only a decision, but even a hearing, on the merits. Here an essential point of legal principle is involved, namely that a party should not have to give an account of itself on issues of merits before a tribunal which lacks jurisdiction in the matter or whose jurisdiction has not yet been established.

Many cases before the Court itself had shown that although a decision on jurisdiction can never directly decide any question of merits, the issues involved are by no means divorced from the merits. A jurisdictional issue may often have to touch upon the latter, or at least involve some consideration of them. That illustrated the importance of the jurisdictional stage of a case and the influence it may have on the eventual decision on the merits, "a factor well known to parties in litigation".

Not only do issues of jurisdiction involve questions of law, but those questions may be as important and complicated as any that arise on the merits:

> They may, in the context of an entity such as ICAO, create precedents affecting the position and interests of a large number of states, in a way which no ordinary procedural, interlocutory or other preliminary issue could do. It would indeed be hard to accept the view that even the most routine decisions of the Council on points of interpretation or application of the Treaties [invoked in the Council proceedings] should be automatically appealable, while decisions on jurisdiction, which must *ex hypothesi* involve important general considerations of principle, should not, despite the drastic effect which [...] they are capable of having.

The final consideration was that supposing an appeal were made from the final decision of the Council on the merits, it would hardly be possible for the Court either to affirm or reject that decision if it found that the Council had all along lacked jurisdiction to go into the case.

In addition to the difference submitted to the Council under Article 84 of the Chicago Convention, Pakistan had also submitted a 'complaint' under the jurisdictional clause of the related Air Services Transit Agreement of 1944.[35] That jurisdictional clause did not directly contain a provision for appeal to the Court from the decision of the Council. In the Court Pakistan had contended that accordingly the Court could not deal with the Council's decision on this complaint in these appeal proceedings. In principle the Court did not deny this contention. It pointed out that the findings and recommendations of the Council on complaints "would not be about legal rights or obligations: they would turn on considerations of equity and expediency such as would not constitute suitable material for appeal to a court of law" (Para. 20).

However, the Court was not prepared to say that a complaint could never deal with matters that would primarily form the subject of an application, or allege illegalities as having caused the injustice or hardship complained of. To that extent the complaint would necessarily assume the character of an application. It would be a paradox if a complaint were non-appealable unlike an application even though the issues involved were almost identical. In the present case the application and the complaint made exactly the same charges of breach in almost identical language; and made the same request except that the application also asked for damages. Accordingly this particular complaint alleged injustice and hardship resulting from action said to be illegal and in those circumstances the Council's decision assuming jurisdiction in respect of Pakistan's complaint was also appealable "in so far as it covers the same ground as the 'Application'" (Paras. 23-24).

In consequence the Court rejected Pakistan's objections on the question of the competence of the Court and found that it had jurisdiction to entertain India's appeal.

Turning to the appeal itself, the Court made the following statement of principle:

> 27. The Court now turns to the substantive issue of the correctness of the decisions of the Council [...]. The question is whether the Council is competent to go into and give a final decision on the merits of the dispute in respect of which, at the instance of Pakistan, and subject to the present appeal, it has assumed jurisdiction. The answer to this question clearly depends on whether Pakistan's case, considered in the light of India's objections, discloses the existence of a dispute of such a character as to amount to a "disagreement [...] relating to the interpretation or application" of the Chicago Convention or of the related Transit Agreement [...]. If so, then *prima facie* the Council

---

35. 84 U.N.T.S. 389. The Council's Rules for the Settlement of Disputes contained a section dealing with these complaints, *see* previous note.

is competent. [...] The fact that a defence on the merits is cast in a particular form cannot affect the competence of the tribunal or other organ concerned - otherwise parties would be in a position themselves to control that competence, which would be inadmissible. As has already been seen in the case of the competence of the Court, so with that of the Council, its competence must depend on the character of the dispute submitted to it and on the issues thus raised - not on those defences on the merits or other considerations, which would become relevant only after the jurisdictional issues had been settled. It is desirable to stress these points because of the way, perfectly legitimate though it was, in which the Appeal has been presented to the Court.

On the merits of the appeal, the Court proceeded to examine *de novo* the arguments of the parties, to reach the conclusion that the Council was competent to entertain the application and complaint of Pakistan. In consequence, the Court rejected India's appeal against the Council's decision assuming jurisdiction in those respects.

The Court concluded its reasoning with an important statement regarding the relationship between the appeal and alleged procedural irregularities in the Council proceedings:

> 45. The Court [...] does not deem it necessary or even appropriate to go into this matter, particularly as the alleged irregularities do not prejudice in any fundamental way the requirements of a just procedure. The Court's task in the present proceedings is to give a ruling as to whether the Council has jurisdiction in the case. This is an objective question of law, the answer to which cannot depend on what occurred before the Council. Since the Court holds that the Council did and does have jurisdiction, then, if there were in fact procedural irregularities, the position would be that the Council would have reached the right conclusion in the wrong way. Nevertheless, it would have reached the right conclusion. If, on the other hand, the Court had held that there was and is no jurisdiction, then, even in the absence of any irregularities, the Council's decision to assume it would have stood reversed.

In the Rules of the Permanent Court of International Justice and in the initial Rules of the International Court of Justice, a provision had been included regarding appeals to the Court.[36] In the current Rules of 1978 this was changed, and Article 87 is now entitled 'Special Reference to the Court'. It provides in general terms that when in accordance with a treaty or convention in force a contentious case is brought before the Court "concerning a matter which has been the subject of proceedings before some other international body", the provisions of the Statute and of the Rules governing contentious cases shall apply. It will be noted that this seemingly circuitous provision only applies to contentious cases although there is nothing to

---

36. This was introduced in the Rules of Court of 1936 as Article 67; repeated in the Rules of 1946, Article 67; Rules of 1972, Article 72.

prevent such cases coming before the Court for an advisory opinion.[37] This provision incorporates the judicial practice of the *ICAO Council Appeal case* which was treated in all respects as any other contentious case. The previous Rules had their origin in the provisions for appeal from the decisions of the Mixed Arbitral Tribunals established by the Peace Treaties of 1919. In substance Article 87 of the current Rules may not differ much from its predecessors, except that specific references to 'appeal' have been dropped, giving the Rule a somewhat broader conceptual framework. This may open new perspectives for the contentious jurisdiction of the Court.

5.   COMPLIANCE WITH ARBITRAL AWARDS AND THEIR ENFORCEMENT

The sensitivity displayed by the Court and the caution with which it has approached questions relating to arbitral procedure and arbitral awards stand in contrast to the difference between Article 13 of the Covenant of the League of Nations and Article 94 of the Charter of the United Nations in the matter of compliance with arbitral awards and their enforcement. Under Article 13 of the Covenant, the Members of the League of Nations agreed that they would carry out in full good faith any award that may be rendered [sc. by the Permanent Court or by an arbitral tribunal] and that they would not resort to war against a Member of the League which was complying with such an award.[38] In the Charter, all reference to arbitration has been dropped from Article 94 which reads:

> 1. Each Member of the United Nations undertakes to comply with the decision of the International Court of Justice in any case to which it is a party.
> 2. If any party to a case fails to perform the obligations incumbent upon it under a judgment rendered by the Court, the other party may have recourse to the Security Council which may, if it deems necessary, make recommendations or decide upon measures to be taken to give effect to the judgment.

This is all the more surprising considering the express mention of arbitration in Article 33 of the Charter on the means to be employed for the peaceful settlement of disputes.

---

37. In this connection it may be noted that by Article 102, Paragraph 2, of the Rules regarding advisory proceedings, the Court "shall also be guided by the provisions of the Statute and of these Rules which apply in contentious cases to the extent to which it recognizes them to be applicable".
38. This provision was invoked once, in connection with the non-compliance by Bulgaria with the arbitral award in the Central Rhodopia Forests case. For that award, *see* 3 U.N.R.I.A.A. 1371 (1933); 7 Annual Digest and Reports of International Law Cases 91. For the action of the Council of the League, *see* League of Nations, Official Journal, 15th year 1432, at 1477 (1934).

In recent years there have occurred two unusual incidents regarding the enforcement of arbitral awards rendered by the Iran-US Claims Tribunal, deserving of notice although they are not on all fours with inter-state arbitrations. These incidents are mentioned as they indicate some unease at a possible gap if not flaw in the law.

The first is the decision of a US Court of Appeals that an award against an American corporation rendered by the Iran-US Claims Tribunal was enforceable in the United States under the Convention on Recognition and Enforcement of Foreign Arbitral Awards signed in New York in 1958.[39] The second was the attempt to bring an award of that same Tribunal within the framework of the Dutch internal law regarding commercial arbitration.[40]

These incidents are curious. The fact that attempts such as these were made to secure enforcement with awards rendered by an international tribunal gives food for thought.

6. CONCLUSION

This survey leads to several conclusions.

It is, in the first place, to be noted that in no case has either the Permanent Court, in relation to decisions of the Mixed Arbitral Tribunals, or the present Court in relation to formal appeals, done anything other than to uphold the impugned decision. Indeed, one can see a strong reluctance to upset the impugned decision even in face of alleged procedural irregularities.[41] This is not to imply that in no circumstances would the Court not accept an appeal: the very fact that in appeals it regards its task as requiring it to examine the case *de novo* mitigates against any categorical conclusion on this aspect.

Secondly, the Court has been meticulous in interpreting the interrelationship between the title of jurisdiction under which it itself had been seised of the case and the compromissory clauses relating to the other international bodies. This is brought out above all in the second phase of the *Peace Treaties case* which, given the known

---

39. Ministry of Defense of the Islamic Republic of Iran *v.* Gould, Inc., 887 F.2d 1357 (9th Circuit, 1989); *certiorari* denied, 110 S.Ct. 1319 (1990); 969 F.2d 764 (9th Circuit 1992). On the New York Convention, *see* 330 U.N.T.S. 3. This is to be contrasted with the attempt to enforce judgment in the Military and Paramilitary Activities in and against Nicaragua case through the United States Courts. *See* Committee of United States Citizens living in Nicaragua *v.* Reagan, 859 F.2d 929 (D.C. Circuit, 1988).
40. On this, *see* 4 Iran-U.S. Claims Tribunal Reports 299; 5 *id.*, 405; further in Iran-US Claims Tribunal, Annual Report for the Period Ending June 30, 1992 (1992), at 11.
41. The same approach is seen in the advisory opinions of the present Court in the Applications to review judgments of the United Nations Administrative Tribunal. In no case has a decision of that Tribunal been found to be defective.

attitude of the former Soviet Union to any form of judicial or quasi-judicial activity without the consent of all parties, seems to have correctly interpreted the intentions of an admittedly ambiguously drafted compromissory clause.

Thirdly, the Court has been scrupulous in maintaining a sharp distinction between its own functions in the concrete case brought before it, and those of the organ in question. This is seen both where the Court has to decide the previous question of the obligation to arbitrate or the derivative questions of the validity or nullity of an existing award (and objections to its deciding that question) or an appeal from some other adjudicatory body, whether 'legal' or not. In particular, what is to be stressed is the repeated unwillingness and refusal of the Court to trespass on the duties and functions of that other body, or interfere in its procedure duly applied. At the same time, however, the Court has emphasized that the competence of that other body itself is strictly defined by the constituent instrument and the compromissory clause on the basis of which that other body works.

In that connection the Court has made an important statement on the function of judicial control by the Court in the context of the more general régime in which that control is embedded. In the *ICAO Council Appeal case* the Court said:

> [S]ince this is the first time any matter has come to it on appeal, the Court thinks it useful to make a few observations of a general character on the subject. The case is presented to the Court in the guise of an ordinary dispute between States (and such a dispute underlies it). Yet in the proceedings before the Court, it is the act of a third entity -the Council of ICAO- which one of the Parties is impugning and the other defending. In that aspect of the matter, the appeal to the Court contemplated by the Chicago Convention [...] must be regarded as an element of the general régime established in respect of ICAO. In thus providing for judicial recourse by way of appeal to the Court against decisions of the Council concerning interpretation and application- a type of recourse already figuring in earlier conventions in the sphere of communications- the Chicago Treaties gave member states, and through them the Council, the possibility of ensuring a certain measure of supervision by the Court over those decisions. To this extent, these Treaties enlist the support of the Court for the good functioning of the Organization, and therefore the first reassurance for the Council lies in the knowledge that means exist for determining whether a decision as to its own competence is in conformity or not with the provisions of the treaties governing its action. If nothing in the text requires a different conclusion, an appeal against a decision of the Council as to its own jurisdiction must therefore be receivable since, from the standpoint of the supervision by the Court of the validity of the Council's acts, there is no ground for distinguishing between supervision as to jurisdiction, and supervision as to merits (Para. 26). [42]

---

42. The view that control is a necessary component of the arbitral process has been forcefully expounded *in* W.M. Reisman, Systems of Control in International Adjudication and Arbitration (1992).

In fine: the approach of the Court to these questions, taken in its ensemble, shows concern to maintain the integrity of the international arbitration process no less than in its judicial work the Court has shown concern to maintain the integrity of the judicial process itself.[43] Perhaps an unexpected illustration of this can be seen in the order of the President (Waldock) regarding the discontinuance of the proceedings in the *US Diplomatic and Consular Staff in Tehran case*. Here the initial letter of discontinuance referred to certain provisions of the Declaration of Algeria of January 19, 1981 resolving the crisis, and sought to reserve the right to 'reinstitute' the proceedings if the Government of Iran failed to "live up to its commitments under the foregoing declarations". Those declarations inter alia dealt with the establishment and working of the Iran/U.S. Claims Tribunal. The President refused to accept a discontinuance in these terms and required an unconditional discontinuance. In the order of discontinuance the President recited "the adherence by the Parties to the two Declarations of the Government of Algeria dated January 19, 1981" and placed on record the discontinuance of the case "following upon an agreement between the

---

43. For this reason, concern must be expressed at the attitude adopted by the Chamber of the International Court deciding the Land, Island and Maritime Delimitation Dispute between El Salvador and Honduras, Nicaragua intervening, with regard to the 1917 judgment of the Central American Court of Justice in the case of El Salvador *v.* Nicaragua regarding the Gulf of Fonseca. While it is a fact that one of the parties to that litigation rejected the judgment, nevertheless it remains that the judgment is equally in fact *res judicata* as between its parties. Nevertheless, the Chamber included in its judgment the statement that "It does not appear [...] that this Chamber is required now to pronounce upon whether the 1917 Judgement is *res judicata* between the parties to it [...]". 1992 I.C.J. Rep. 351, 600 (Para 402). The Chamber saw that judgment as a 'subsidiary' source of the law within the meaning of Article 38, Paragraph 1(d), of the Statute of the Court. This can be taken as throwing doubt on the force of the *res judicata* of a judgment of a competent judicial organ delivered in 1917. For that case, *see* VI *Anales de la Corte de Justicia Centroamericana*, Nos. 16-18, 96 (1917). For an English translation, accepted by all concerned in the 1992 case, *see* 11 AJIL 674 (1917).

Parties".[44] The case-law shows no sign of competition between arbitration and judicial settlement, both of which are, indeed, placed alongside and on the same footing in Article 33 of the Charter. Furthermore, although never cited, this is also in conformity with the letter and the spirit of Article 95 of the Charter, according to which nothing in the Charter prevents Members of the United Nations from entrusting the solution of their differences to other tribunals by virtue of agreements already in existence or which may be concluded in the future.[45]

No other position would be compatible with the standing of the International Court of Justice as the principal judicial organ of the United Nations.

44. 1981 I.C.J. Rep. 45. For the Algiers Declarations, *see* 1 Iran-US Claims Tribunal Reports 3.
45. It is thus significant, and healthy, that in appropriate cases Members of the Court have agreed and have been permitted by the Court to act as arbitrators. This practice is as old as the Permanent Court: Judges Viscount Finlay, Guerrero and Huber and Deputy Judge Beichmann at one time or another served as arbitrator. In the present Court all the arbitrators in the Guinea-Guinea-Bissau Maritime Delimitation arbitration were Members of the Court of Arbitration. 89 RGDIP 484 (1985); 77 I.L.R. 635. In the later Guinea-Bissau *v.* Senegal Maritime Delimitation arbitration, among the arbitrators was one Member of the Court (94 RGDIP 204 (1990); 83 I.L.R. 1). There are, however, disadvantages in view of the development in recent years of the invocation of the International Court through some surprise acceptance of its jurisdiction, to control an arbitration process. The Member of the Court who was an arbitrator in the Guinea-Bissau *v.* Senegal arbitration had to recuse himself when the question of the validity of that award was unexpectedly brought before the Court in this manner. According to the latest Report of the Permanent Court of Arbitration, the following present Members of the Court are also Members of the Permanent Court of Arbitration: Judges Ago, Aguilar, Ajibola, Evensen, Guillaume, and Sir Robert Jennings. The late Judge Lachs was also a member of the PCA. *See* Permanent Court of Arbitration, 91st Annual Report 1991, 22-42 (1992). The participation of former Members of the Court in international arbitration proceedings is also a healthy development.

EQUITY IN ARBITRATION AND IN JUDICIAL SETTLEMENT OF DISPUTES

Judge Manfred Lachs[*][†]

Much has been written on the similarities and differences between arbitration tribunals and international courts; much more could and will certainly be written in the future. The purpose of my comments is to define similarities and differences in regard to the role of equity in both. However, I hope to enter the caveat at the very outset that in this paper I will focus solely on the role of equity in cases where the decision is to be based on international law. Accordingly, I will not here discuss cases of the type I had in mind when I pointed out in a speech delivered 34 years ago to the Legal Committee of the UN General Assembly that "[t]he arbitral solution has been applied in the past to a variety of problems, some of which were not judicial in character and did not raise issues of law".[1] Nor will I now discuss arbitrations in which the parties have agreed that the arbitrators need not be guided by law, or where the arbitral tribunal is expressly authorized by the parties to decide *ex aequo et bono*[2] and thereby to settle the matter in a liberal spirit without regard to legal requirements and technicalities. Thus, cases in which the arbitrators have been empowered to seek mutual accommodations that would give offense to neither party are outside the scope of this discussion, as are cases where arbitrators recommended action by one of the parties as an act of grace.

It becomes ever more evident that the complexity of contemporary international relations calls for a variety of means and methods in the settlement of disputes. Thus, there are many cases which could be easily submitted to an international court but are being submitted to arbitration. As examples, one can recall the recent arbitrations between France and the United Kingdom, between Canada and France, and the dispute of Guinea Bissau and Guinea, all of which could have easily been dealt with by the International Court of Justice. In those cases the will of the parties, their insistence of having a say in the composition of the tribunal and other factors, may have been decisive in the choice of forum.

---

[*] Chairman of the Working Group on the revision of the Permanent Court of Arbitration (PCA), member of the Expert Group on the revision of the PCA, member of the PCA, member and former President of the International Court of Justice.

1. U.N. GAOR, Sixth Comm., 563rd Meeting, at 65-66. *See also* my report on Arbitration and International Adjudication *in* A.H.A. Soons (ed.), International Arbitration: Past and Prospects, 37 *et seq.* (1990).

2. *See* Article 38(2), Statute of the International Court of Justice. *Cf.* UNCITRAL Arbitration Rules, Article 33(2); *see also* Permanent Court of Arbitration Optional Rules for Arbitrating Disputes Between Two States, Article 33(2).

S. Muller and W. Mijs (eds.), The Flame Rekindled, 125–131.

Law having expanded its reign is becoming an ever more powerful factor. Hence the need to give some thought to the ways and means of its application. This is paramount in the administration of justice. Need I recall that for centuries it has been the subject of study and reflection of philosophers, jurists and social scientists. The Magna Carta proclaimed the principle "For no man will we sell, to no man deny, to no man delay, justice or right". But that witty jurist, A.P. Herbert, 'reported' a judge to have said: "But we in this court are well aware that these undertakings have very little relation to the hard facts of experience".[3] Without engaging in philosophical speculations I think it would be right to simply say that in a dispute between two or more states, whether in an international arbitration or in an international court, justice implies a series of elements common to a specific situation and calling for a specific decision. In this context the application of law calls for a special consideration. "Judicial justice" calls for a judge not to resort to theoretical fictions nor to myths, but to apply the law in such a way that justice be done. This is far from claiming that parties are at the mercy of the subjective caprice of a man, or several men, who may resort to theoretical speculations. As it has been said by some judges, "It is not us, but the law that judges you". Then the question arises what does the law say and how do we interpret or apply it?

The concept of equity has been subjected to very close scrutiny and analysis. Its history is well known and there is no need for me to go into details of its development in the common law where it is so strongly anchored, nor to recall the frequent attacks launched against it. Those criticizing equity have claimed that it is too subjective, linked with intuition, devoid of objective criteria, abstract and in some respects too general. These objections have led to the well known metaphor that when equity is applied justice may be measured merely by "the length of the chancellor's foot". Hence also the suggestion that equity amounts to a kind of '*technique juridique*' or '*politique juridique*'.[4]

Moreover, some have argued that equity should only be invoked if the application of law would "produce [...] extraordinary, unnatural or unreasonable results".[5] It has also been suggested that equity should be "contrasted with the rigid rules of positive law, the severity of which had to be mitigated in order to do justice".[6] Another approach calls for equity to be considered in the context of the principle *ex aequo et bono* and maintains that this principle has never gained acceptance by any state whatsoever. Yet another theory suggests that "equity is, indeed the absence of law;

---

3. A.P. Herbert, Misleading Cases in the Common Law 77 (1927).
4. *See, e.g.*, Michel Virally, 2 *L'Equite dans le Droit; Le Droit International à l'Heure de sa Codification, Etudes en l'Honneur de Roberto Ago*, at 30 (1987).
5. *Continental Shelf case* (Tunisia *v.* Libyan Arab Jamahiriya), Dissenting Opinion Judge Gros, 1982 I.C.J. Rep. 149, citing North Sea Continental Shelf case, (The Netherlands and Denmark *v.* Federal Republic of Germany) 1969 I.C.J. Rep. 23 *in fine*.
6. *Id.* (Judgment), at 60 Para. 71.

or that it represents natural justice as opposed to legal justice".[7] These are some of the many manifestations of mistrust and caution in regard to equity and its role within the context of law.

In response to such criticisms, I submit that it is important to bear in mind that the relationship between equity and law is not one between the legal system and a phenomenon exterior to it; equity is built into the legal system.[8] In order to remove every possible misunderstanding and confusion on the issue it is important to emphasize that equity cannot be detached from law; it is inherent in it. Equity aims at proper application of law in a particular case in order to avoid decisions that are a reflection of abstract principles detached from the circumstances that a court or arbitration tribunal may face. Its function is to lead to an interpretation of a rule of law in the context of a concrete situation and to balance all the elements of the relationship between the parties concerned. Thus equity gives law vitality and makes it meet the requirements of the circumstances of each case. Equity provides a means by which rules of law, provisions of treaties or other sources of law may take a needed breath in order to meet the challenge of specific situations arising between two or more states or in international relations in general. In sum, equity is the element to which Frederick William Maitland rightly referred when saying that it comes "not to destroy the law but to fulfil it".

These comments concern equity within the framework of general international law. But it may be of interest that recently equity has come to the forefront in the context of many disputes arising from the application and implementation of the law of the sea. It is there that the recent Law of the Sea Convention defined equity's task, in unequivocal terms: "The delimitation of the continental shelf between states with opposite or adjacent coasts shall be effected by agreement on the basis of international law, as referred to in Article 38 of the Statute of the International Court of Justice, in order to achieve an equitable solution".[9] One could hardly think of a more explicit and more precise definition of the role of equity within the framework of law. For, obviously, this provision recalls the sources of law which the International Court of Justice has to apply pursuant to the well known Article 38 of its Statute, and at the same time articulates the goal of an 'equitable solution'. Is this role limited to the new institution of law of the sea? One could argue that what applies to the continental shelf may have a more general application. In brief, would it be unreasonable to claim that

7. *See* the reports submitted by the Rapporteur of the International Law Commission on the Succession of States. He recognized that "Equity may mean everything and may mean nothing" (8th Special Report, Para. 260).
8. *See, e.g.,* Charles De Visscher, *De l'Equité dans le Règlement Arbitral ou Judiciaire des Litiges de Droit International Public*, (1972). *See also* Paul Reuter, *Quelques Réflexions sur l'Equité en Droit International*, 1980 Revue Belge de Droit International 165.
9. Article 83(1) of the Law of the Sea Convention.

each dispute, whether it concerns the law of the sea or any other subject, should be judged bearing in mind "its own merits" and "having regard to its special circumstances"[10] and with the goal of achieving an "equitable solution"?

Equity may play various roles in the application of the law. In view of the variety of circumstances and what has been called "the unique character of every case and every situation" it is difficult to establish a general guiding principle concerning the ways and means of applying law. No specific method should be given priority.[11] This is equity's task.

Equity is certainly an element '*infra legem*'. It is a link between the specific rule or provision of law and reality. As it has been pointed out, "The error lies precisely in searching general international law for, as it were, a set of rules which are not there".[12] The very function of equity is the application of the law to a particular situation.

It is, as said, an element inherent in law and applies to all its sources. While treaty provisions may be more detailed, they in themselves could hardly meet the multicolored situations which arise in the daily life of nations. Equity enriches the rule of law whatever its source, by requiring that attention be paid to the specific circumstances of each individual case. It performs this function in the relationship between states, as well as between a state, man and nature. It has evolved with the passage of time: as the ICJ held "[i]n the course of the history of legal systems the term 'equity' has been used to define various legal concepts".[13]

Thus it has been rightly pointed out that the notion of 'equity' "*procède directement de l'idée de justice*";[14] principles and rules of law are not equitable in themselves, it is equity that confers upon them that quality.

It has been suggested that equity is not identical with reasonableness as the latter is subject to several criteria. What was reasonable yesterday need not necessarily be so today; and in determining reasonableness, geographical, cultural and religious factors[15] can be of paramount importance.

Equity is viewed as "a legal concept, a direct emanation of the idea of justice".[16] It has been stressed that:

10. 1982 I.C.J. Rep., at 92, Para. 132.
11. 1984 I.C.J. Rep., at 315, Para. 163.
12. 1984 I.C.J. Rep., at 298, Para. 110.
13. 1982 I.C.J. Rep., at 60, Para. 71.
14. J. Charpentier, *L'affaire de la Barcelona Traction* 320 (1970).
15. *See* Michele Sicart-Bozec, *Les Juges du Tiers Monde à la Cour Internationale de Justice*, Economica H, 290-291.
16. 1982 I.C.J. Rep., at 60, Para. 71.

the justice of which equity is an emanation is not abstract justice but justice according to the rule of law: which is to say that its application should display consistency and a degree of predictability; even though it looks with particularity to the peculiar circumstances in an instant case, it also looks beyond it to principles of more general application. This is precisely why the courts have, from the beginning, elaborated equitable principles as being, at the same time, means to an equitable result in a particular case, yet also having a more general validity and hence expressible in general terms.[17]

Thus while equity performs a specific function in a particular case leading to a just judgement or a just resolution of a dispute, its functions go beyond and have a more general character. It is of course clear that in an individual case, the Court or arbitral tribunal selects those 'equitable principles' that are suitable for the resolution of the dispute in question and that lead to a just decision. As the International Court of Justice has said

[i]t is a truism to say that the determination must be equitable; rather is the problem above all one of defining the means whereby the delimitation can be carried out in such a way as to be recognized as equitable.[18]

The ICJ has made it clear that both objective and subjective criteria have to be taken into account. As it was once pointed out: "Equity exists when exactly the right thing is done between the parties. Neither more nor less than this is equity".

In my view, this conclusion leaves little room for doubt. Equity acquires today an ever more important role in international relations and international law. In the many disputes concerning the relationship between states and nature equity leads to solutions which take account of the rights and interests of states concerned: one party is not to take advantage at the expense of the other, each of them will retain equitable parts of the whole area. Gone are the days when equity was shunned: in the times of the *ancien régime* one used to say *"Dieu nous garde de l'équité et du parlement"*. But today it is recognized that equity has become a very important tool in the administration of justice. For justice cannot be achieved without equity playing its part.

There are, as I pointed out in another context, two areas in which equity plays a very important role: the relationship between the parties and the relationship between the parties and nature. I hardly need to recall that nature is not always friendly to man. It creates hardships and sometimes undue difficulties for the life of men and communities. Thus, when some principles of law are to be applied it is necessary for

17. 1985 I.C.J. Rep., at 39, Para. 45.
18. 1969 I.C.J. Rep., at 50, Para. 92.

equity to intervene and to remedy the situation. As I pointed out in my speech addressed to the parties, when delivering the award in the Guinea *v.* Guinea Bissau arbitration:

> our principal concern has been to avoid by one means or another, one of the parties finding itself faced with the exercise of rights, opposite to and in the immediate vicinity of the coast, which might interfere with its rights to development or put its security at risk.[19]

I went further because I take the position that:

> Equity serves to make a bridge between nature and the law. We seek to ensure that neither of the two [states] is subject to any significant cut-off to the advantage of the other, and that its coastline, or rather, the effect of its coastline, cannot be unduly reduced away to a whim of nature. However, I would say that this definition is perhaps too narrow. Today it plays a much greater role and I would rather say should dominate law wherever it is to be applied. It introduces and stresses the element of equality but equality in its special sense, one which establishes an equilibrium between different situations. Thus it is of paramount importance as the guiding spirit in the application of the law: it has been our cicerone in the journey through your case. It does not mean that the basis of the decision is the result of intuition taken in the abstract, which has not roots in law at all. This is not true for a legal basis for it does exist. In it and within it, as in other domains of international law, equity plays a most decisive role. Thus, it is neither calculated like the work of a mathematician or physicist, nor is it a work of fiction, but creates a link between the law as a letter and life as a phenomenon of nature. Hence, it has inseparable links with both.[20]

One could amplify this statement by quoting a distinguished jurist:

> This has not been a soft option for the courts since, in each and every case, they have to strike the difficult balance between the safety of respect for nature and the temptation to rewrite geography so as to impose their own idea of justice. The path between blind pursuit of the given and the total freedom of *ex aequo et bono* is not an easy one.[21]

However, it would be wrong to consider equity solely as a product of contemporary courts and arbitral tribunals, or contemporary law. It is worth recalling Grotius, who suggested that law "includes everything, which it is more proper to do than to omit,

---

19. Arbitral Award, 124.
20. *Id.*.
21. Prosper Weil, The Law of Maritime Delimitation - Reflections 88 (1989).

even beyond what is required by the express rules of justice".[22] Thus equity had ancestors in the remote past.

With international law becoming ever more important, covering increasing domains of international relations and deciding issues of major importance to peace and war, to the rights and survival of states, equity is acquiring an ever greater role. It does so in both arbitration and judicial settlement.

Though at first sight it might seem "a squaring of the circle",[23] equity enriches international law and in many domains of life, makes it respond effectively to the needs of the international community in the interest of peaceful cooperation.

22. H. Grotius, *De Jure Belli ac Pacis,* III, Cap. XX, at 47 (New York ed., 1901).
23. Prosper Weil, *op. cit.,* note 21, at 89.

THE PERSPECTIVES OF AFRICAN COUNTRIES ON INTERNATIONAL COMMERCIAL ARBITRATION

Samuel K.B. Asante[*]

1. INTRODUCTION

The participation of developing countries in the international legal system poses a perennial dilemma. On the one hand the brutal facts of international economic and commercial interdependence make such participation inevitable. On the other hand, developing countries, for various reasons and with varying degrees of intensity, have articulated their reservations, or indeed experienced considerable difficulties, with respect to such participation. This article considers this dilemma with special reference to the experience of Sub-Saharan African countries in international commercial arbitration.

It is trite that the attainment of political independence in Africa and elsewhere did not mean insulation from the international economic system. Indeed, independence has highlighted the hard fact of international economic interdependence. The internationalization of production and services is a salient feature of the modern world economy, and international transactions, whether they are of a bilateral or multilateral variety, whether they are with foreign governments, international institutions or transnational enterprises, whether they are for trade, investments, technology, finance, debt rescheduling, or for procurement of goods and services, are now essential aspects of the dynamics of international commercial intercourse. More importantly, African countries, like other developing countries, appreciate that these transactions are inescapable for the implementation of their economic and social programmes. African governments and private parties involved in negotiating international business transactions such as loan agreements, petroleum and mining agreements, industrial joint ventures, management agreements, international procurement contracts, international supply contracts, bilateral or international trade agreements and bilateral investment agreements have come to the realization that foreign parties to these transactions, *i.e.*, foreign governments, transnational corporations, international banks, foreign investors, international suppliers and

[*] Director, Legal Advisory Services for Development, United Nations Department of Economic and Social Development (UNDESD); Formerly Solicitor-General of Ghana. This paper represents the personal views of the author.

133

S. Muller and W. Mijs (eds.), The Flame Rekindled, 133–158.

contractors, all insist on an appropriate dispute settlement mechanism, which is invariably international arbitration.

Parties to international transactions predominantly prefer international arbitration because of the strong perception that an international forum for settling disputes provides some insurance against possible bias by a national judiciary. Thus, African countries caught in the web of a plethora of international transactions recognize the virtual inevitability of international commercial arbitration. Indeed, the acceptance of international arbitration has become an invariable ingredient of the liberalization package which African countries, and developing countries elsewhere, provide as a *sine qua non* of their strategies to attract foreign investment and technology, international finance and foreign trade.

Notwithstanding this realism, which is reflected in the acceptance of international arbitration clauses in numerous international transactions and several international conventions, as well as the stipulation of arbitration provisions in national legislation, African reservations about actual participation in the international arbitration process still persist. The endorsement of the concept of international arbitration has not been matched by enthusiastic practice; nor has actual practice been free of considerable difficulty. What follows is an attempt to examine this apparent gap between theory and practice. The writer will rely primarily on his experience of organizing and lecturing at workshops on international arbitration and international negotiations for middle level and senior professionals and executives in Africa. This article therefore dwells on the practical constraints and perspectives. For a scholarly approach to this problem, the reader is referred to an excellent and up-to-date study by Sampson L. Sempasa.[1]

2.   ATTITUDES TO INTERNATIONAL ARBITRATION

The contemporary attitudes of developing countries to international arbitration present a complex heterogenous picture, depending on the history, culture and legal traditions of the various countries, as well as such factors as geography and level of sophistication in international business.

In a recent paper, Nariman[2] cited the following sombre assessment of the attitudes of developing countries to international arbitration by Judge Keba Mbaye in 1983:

> When, at the 60th Anniversary of the Court of Arbitration of the ICC (in 1983), Howard Holtzmann stressed the idea of Judge and Arbitrator being "partners in a system of international justice", Judge Keba Mbaye (then a Judge of the International

1. S. L. Sempasa, *Obstacles to International Commercial Arbitration*, 41 ICLQ 473 (1992).
2. F.S. Nariman, *International Arbitration and Developed Countries*; Unpublished paper presented to ICSID's Seminar on International Arbitration and Developing Countries in 1991.

Court of Justice and its former President) responded with some home truths; the notion that there is a system of international justice (he said) was not shared by countries in Africa, Asia and Latin America, who still saw arbitration as a foreign judicial institution imposed upon them: developing countries were rarely the venue of an international arbitration, and, even more rarely, produced arbitrators. He spoke of: the African concept of law being favourable to arbitration, though not as we know it, tribal arbitration rendered by an arbitrator known to both sides, and of the hostility of African Courts to arbitrations by foreign tribunals. In addition, he said, "as everybody knows, arbitration is seldom freely agreed to by developing countries. It is often included in contracts of adhesion, the signature of which is essential to the survival of these countries". However, the Judge from Senegal then predicted that International Arbitration would ultimately obtain third world recognition, but only gradually.

This assessment echoes the findings of a study[3] by the Asian-African Legal Consultative Committee on International Commercial Arbitration in the 1970s which concluded:

> These institutions had rules which did not work out particularly favourably for the developing countries in the matter of venue, choice of arbitrators, as also fees and charges leviable by the institutions concerned. Since most of these institutions functioned under the auspices of Chambers of Commerce and other associations of trade, it was difficult to visualize the manner or the means by which practical steps could be taken to effect modification of the rules of such institutions to bring them in conformity with the interests of developing countries.

The primary issue is whether the above strictures are valid today.

The traditional objections of Latin America to international arbitration rooted in the Calvo doctrine are well known to every student of international law. Recent developments however indicate a significant modification of this traditional position. Indeed Horatio A. Grigera Naon asserts that:

> [...] it appears to be no longer true to speak of Latin American hostility *vis-à-vis* arbitration and it would be more accurate to say that Latin America is considering arbitration with growing sympathy, although many of the present rules applicable to arbitration in a number of Latin American countries still need to be adapted to this new trend.[4]

---

3. AALCC Report of The Seventeenth, Eighteenth and Nineteenth Sessions held in Kuala Lumpur (1976), Baghdad (1977) and Doha (1978), at 131-138.
4. H. A. Grigera Naon, *Arbitration in Latin America: Overcoming Traditional Hostility*, 5 Arbitration International 137 (No. 2, 1989).

As evidence of this trend, the author cites the ratification by many Latin American countries of the New York Convention, 1958, on the Recognition and Enforcement of Foreign Arbitration Awards and of the Inter-American Convention on International Commercial Arbitration 1975, several legislative developments favourable to international arbitration in the Andean Pact, Colombia, Brazil, Peru and Venezuela, and the widespread acceptance of arbitration clauses in transactions conducted with foreign entities by Latin American private and public parties.[5] To this evidence should be added the accession of many Latin American countries to the 1965 Convention on the Settlement of Investment Disputes between states and nationals of other states.

Other developing countries, in particular, Asian and African countries, that attained independence after World War II, had their own reservations about international arbitration although these emanated from doctrinal grounds other than Calvo. As the Working Group on the Permanent Court of Arbitration observed, the main difficulty developing countries have in participating in international arbitration derives from "a perception that they have neither participated in the creation of international law to be applied by the Tribunal in arriving at its decision, nor recognised or endorsed them".[6]

Various writers have contended that the attitudes in other developing countries towards international arbitration have changed significantly. Nariman has confidently asserted that Judge Keba Mbaye's criticism voiced in Paris in 1983 "is now an echo of the historical past".[7] While Nariman recognizes the traditional cultural bias in Asia against the type of adversarial confrontation associated with modern international arbitration, he presents an optimistic picture of the growing acceptance of international arbitration in key Asian countries like Japan, People's Republic of China, India, South Korea, Singapore and Hong Kong.

An even more sanguine account of the embrace of international arbitration by developing countries generally is provided by Jan Paulsson:

> As we approach the last decade of the 20th century, parties from developing countries may face the prospect of international arbitration with an entirely new attitude. By and large, they have learned how to ensure that their interests are defended completely, and have come to view the mechanism of international arbitration as it is: a neutral means for the resolution of conflicts arising in trade and economic development, to be mastered rather than complained about.[8]

---

5. *Id.*.
6. *The Permanent Court of Arbitration - New Directions*, Report by the Working Group on Improving the Functioning of the Court, May 13 1991, at 9.
7. F.S. Nariman, *supra* note 2.
8. J. Paulsson, *Third World Participation in International Investment Arbitration*, 2 ICSID Review-Foreign Investment Law Journal 19 (1987).

The question which may be raised is whether this evaluation is valid with respect to Sub-Saharan Africa, or whether Judge Keba Mbaye's characterization of international arbitration as a foreign judicial institution imposed upon Africa is still true.

3.   ASSESSING CONTEMPORARY ACCEPTANCE OF INTERNATIONAL ARBITRATION IN SUB-SAHARAN AFRICA

3.1.   Participation in the establishment of arbitral institutions

Although African states have participated in the creation of a number of arbitral systems, it cannot be seriously disputed that the main sinews of international arbitration were in fact established before these states attained independence. True, African states participated in the preparatory meetings organised by the World Bank for the negotiation and drafting of the ICSID Convention of 1965; and as many as 42 such states are signatories to the Convention, accounting for about a third of all signatories to the Convention. To a limited extent, African states participated in the formulation of the UNCITRAL Arbitration and Conciliation Rules and the UNCITRAL Model Law. However there was hardly any African participation in the establishment of the ICC arbitral system, the PCA, London Court of Arbitration, the AAA or any major European Arbitration Institutions; and the proposition that international commercial arbitration is essentially Western in origin is trite. The New York Convention on the Recognition and Enforcement of Arbitration Awards of 1958 antedated the birth of most African states.

It should be further pointed out that even the historical fact of African participation in the establishment of the ICSID and UNCITRAL arbitration systems provides little assurance that these systems have been fully absorbed into African legal or commercial culture. This writer's experience of organising seminars on international arbitration in African counties for middle level lawyers demonstrates that a number of factors -paucity of training facilities in international arbitration, political instability, rapid turnover of public servants, bureaucratic barriers to transmitting or utilizing valuable international experience- have combined to limit the exposure of African lawyers in the public and private sectors to the intricacies of international arbitration. As discussed below, it is not insignificant that African parties to international commercial arbitration have predominantly retained counsel outside of the African continent.

The familiar contention that African states, like other developing countries, cannot be expected to subscribe wholeheartedly to international institutions and rules established without their participation may strike some commentators as somewhat hackneyed. It may be pointed out, with some justification, that the non-participation argument has not prevented developing countries from accepting and participating vigorously in the UN system, which was of course established prior to the emergence of the overwhelming majority of Asian and African states. However, the critical criterion for acceptance is not so much the historical fact of participation in the establishment of institutions and rules, as whether the contemporary structure and operation of these institutions and rules fully address the concerns of an expanded international community, in particular, those of the developing countries. It is against this criterion that the international arbitration systems have to be evaluated *vis-à-vis* sub-Saharan Africa.

3.2.   Endorsement of an international arbitration system

As intimated above, the compelling requirements of international trade, investment and finance have induced many African countries to subscribe to international arbitration through various mechanisms. The overwhelming accession to the ICSID Convention, alluded to above, is clearly a reflection of African strategies to attract international investment. It is regarded realistically by many African governments as an appropriate signal to give to the World Bank, the sponsor of the Convention, and to prospective investors. Indeed, the French Export Credit Guarantee Agency COFACE insists on the inclusion of arbitration clauses in operating contracts as a precondition for issuing a guarantee for overseas operations. A fair number of African states have acceded to the New York Convention, although only a limited number of them have actually enacted the UNCITRAL Model Arbitration Law.

As far as international transactions are concerned, it would be no exaggeration to assert that the invariable African practice is to accept international arbitration. Contractual provisions for recourse to the ICSID, UNCITRAL, ICC, London Court of Arbitration, etc. or *ad hoc* international arbitration are an established feature of such transactions as bilateral investment or trade treaties between African states and capital exporting countries, or various international business transactions between African parties (both public and private entities) and foreign parties. Whether these arbitration clauses are accepted as contracts of adhesion or out of a shrewd appreciation of commercial realities, there can be no denying that they are part of the development strategies of African states.

Although in diplomatic conferences, African states have sometimes supported Latin American states in adopting resolutions asserting national jurisdiction over disputes relating to international investments, African states have, on the whole, not manifested a strident, doctrinaire opposition to international arbitration within the context of particular international business agreements. African states have been markedly more receptive to ICSID arbitration than their Latin-American counterparts. However, acceptance of international arbitration provisions does not necessarily mean a full appreciation of the implications of such arrangements. Pragmatism and, in some cases, ignorance, may have triumphed over ideology, without erasing the pervasive reservations and the formidable practical difficulties with respect to the practice of international arbitration, which still retains its character as a foreign system of adjudication in Sub-Saharan Africa.

3.3.   Participation in international arbitration

Participation in particular cases of international arbitration has sometimes been cited as evidence of a more congenial attitude to international arbitration in Third World countries. However, apart from the question of the statistical evidence of actual participation, it is submitted that in view of the factors recounted above, there is no logical linkage between empirical data as to the number of African states that have been involved in arbitration proceedings, particularly as respondents or defendants, and African attitudes to international arbitration.

As to the data on participation, it would be meaningful to examine not only the data on African parties to international arbitration, but also the data on African arbitrators and African counsel in arbitration proceedings. In this respect, a clear distinction should be drawn between the data on Sub-Saharan African and North Africa. It would appear that by reason of their proximity to Europe, their long history of close commercial relations with Europe and the development of a comparatively more sophisticated level of international commercial discourse, North African states have been more involved in international commercial arbitration than Sub-Saharan African states.

With respect to parties to international commercial arbitration proceedings, the data on African participation in ICC arbitration for the period 1980-1988 show fairly modest figures.[9] There were 64 African claimants and 149 African defendants. The corresponding figures for North African countries are 94 and 212 respectively. Middle Eastern/Asian countries, excluding North Africa, accounted for 183 claimants and 249 defendants. There were as many as 1610 claimants and 1475 defendants from Western Europe. The only region which was comparable to Sub-Saharan Africa was Latin America, including the Caribbean, which accounted for 89 claimants and 71 defendants.

The data on African participation in ICSID arbitration show a higher profile for African states, though predominantly as respondents.[10] Of the 28 ICSID cases so far, 17 African states account for 17 of the parties, of which 13 are Sub-Saharan African states. Except in one case, all the African parties, both North and Sub-Saharan, are respondents. This would seem to indicate a high incidence of investors presenting their claims against African respondents. It is interesting to note that there has been no definitive ICSID award in favour of any respondent state.

As far as the number of Africans serving as arbitrators is concerned, the ICC data disclose that there were 203 African arbitrators altogether for the period 1980-1988. However, only 25 of these came from Sub-Saharan Africa. North Africa accounted

---

9. *See* Craig. Park and Paulsson, International Chamber of Commerce Arbitration, Table 5, Appendix 1 (2nd ed. 1990).
10. ICSID Cases: Document ICSID/16/Rev.2, November 15, 1991.

for 178. The data for the other regions were: the Middle East and Asia 296, Eastern Europe 155, Western Europe 3106, and Latin America 45.[11] The figures as to African participation are no less dismal with respect to ICSID arbitration. Of the 97 arbitrators appointed for all ICSID cases, there have been no more than five arbitrators from Sub-Saharan Africa, despite the interesting statistic that African states provided the majority of respondents in these cases (*see infra*).[12]

Another factor that is overlooked in the statistical analysis of participation in arbitration is the data on counsel acting for parties in international arbitration. While a compilation of statistics on this aspect does not seem to exist, the writer is not aware of any established practice of retaining Sub-Saharan African lawyers as counsel in international commercial arbitration. The evidence overwhelmingly supports the practice of retaining European or American lawyers as counsel for African parties. It is a practice dictated by the sober realization that African lawyers lack the requisite expertise to handle the intricacies of international arbitration before the various international arbitral institutions. However, this overwhelming reliance on foreign counsel to unravel the mysteries of the international arbitration procedures or the laws of some distant country cannot but reinforce the perception of international arbitration as an alien system.

This perception is not diminished by the high incidence of designating European or American towns as the sites of such proceedings. Although, through the efforts of bodies like the Asian African Legal Consultation Committee, and the Preferential Trade Area of Southern and East African states (PTA), arbitration centres have been established in Cairo, Lagos and Djibouti, the predominant practice is to conduct arbitration proceedings in Western cities. Thus, in the period 1980-1988, 1733 arbitrations (i.e. 88.5% of all ICC arbitrations) were conducted in Europe, while 48 (2.0%) took place in Africa. Out of the 48, only 12 were conducted in Sub-Saharan Africa.[13] The location of 8 out of these 12 arbitrations was fixed by the ICC itself.

3.4. International arbitration in African domestic legislation

In his illuminating essay on International Arbitration in Africa, Sempasa points out that Sub-Saharan African countries, (see for example, Kenya, Malawi, Uganda, Zambia, Tanzania, Zimbabwe, Mauritius, Rwanda, Burundi, Somalia), on the whole, have no modern legislation on international arbitration. Their statute books still reflect a colonial legacy in the form of outdated arbitration laws modelled on metropolitan legislation of the nineteenth or early twentieth century. This legacy has not been revised in Africa although the original legislation in the metropolitan

---

11. *See supra* note 9.
12. *Source* Conversation with ICSID Secretariat, Washington D.C..
13. *See supra* note 9, Table 7.

countries has long been reformed. Among the notable exceptions to this is Nigeria, which promulgated a modern regime on international commercial arbitration with its Arbitration and Conciliation Decree 1988.[14] This legislation incorporated some of the provisions of the UNCITRAL Arbitration Rules 1976 and the Model Law of 1985. Nigeria is also a party to the New York Convention on the Recognition and Enforcement of Arbitral Awards and the Washington Convention on the Settlement of International Investment Disputes, 1965. The above-mentioned Arbitration and Conciliation Decree, in fact, implements the New York Convention in Nigeria.

In Ghana also, the New York Convention was applied as early as 1965 when the local High Court allowed the enforcement of an international arbitral award against a Ghanaian party. Djibouti is perhaps the best example of an African Country that has enacted a comprehensive law on international arbitration as part of its efforts to establish itself as an arbitration centre.

Although comprehensive legislation on international arbitration may not be widespread in Sub-Saharan Africa, several African states have made adequate provisions for international arbitration in respect of investment disputes under their Investment Codes, *e.g.* Uganda, Namibia and Ghana.

4.   AFRICAN RESERVATIONS AND DIFFICULTIES

While the empirical evidence examined above points to a mild flirtation with international commercial arbitration in Sub-Saharan Africa, it is not enough to sustain the sanguine prognosis of a consummated marriage. No sweeping or optimistic declaration about the reception of international arbitration in developing countries can obscure the persistent reservations and the practical constraints that one encounters in any dealings with African authorities in this area.

The feeling still persists among African officials, lawyers and businessmen that international arbitration is essentially a distant and alien system, located in a foreign country, administered by foreign experts and applying foreign law, with little appreciation of the conditions in African countries. In short, it is essentially a proceeding whose outcome African parties are powerless to affect. Some of these reservations are shared by other developing countries,[15] but there are constraints that are peculiarly characteristic of Sub-Saharan Africa.

The factors that account for this persistent perception will be discussed in the following paragraphs. They pertain to the substantive rules, the appropriateness of arbitration, the legal environment of the arbitral proceedings, the procedural rules, the outcome of the arbitration and limited experience of African lawyers.

14. Y. Osinbajo, *Sovereign Immunity in International Commercial Arbitration: the Nigerian Experience and Emerging State Practice*, 4 African Journal of Int. and Comp. Law Quarterly 1 (1992).
15. M. Sornarajah, *UNCITRAL Model Law: a Third World Viewpoint*, 6 Journal of International Arbitration 7 (1989).

4.1.   The substantive rules

We have already alluded to the historical factor of limited African participation in the creation of the main institutions of international arbitration. However, the non-participation factor is much more fundamental, and applies to the entire fabric of substantive international legal rules applied by most arbitral institutions. Thus African reservations about international commercial arbitration are but an aspect of the larger issue of the need to reform the general rules governing international business transactions to address the concerns of the developing countries. What this writer said a few years ago, with respect to international law and foreign investment applies with equal force to international commercial arbitration:

> The persistent contention of developing countries that the traditional principles of state responsibility were established without their participation and consent and indeed prior to their attainment of independence cannot be dismissed by merely asserting the validity of the traditional principles. Whatever the legal merits of this contention, the viability or functional efficacy of any international legal system depends on the extent to which it enjoys wide international support. The formulation of a new set of norms with respect to foreign companies does provide the developing countries with an opportunity of meaningful participation that can only enhance the viability if not the validity of the principles.
>
> [...]
>
> The traditional concept of state responsibility will be perceived as inequitable so long as it remains primarily preoccupied with the protection of foreign investment against the legitimate sovereign interests of the host state. An international system which exclusively addresses the concerns of one party to an investment relationship cannot inspire confidence as a fair, international regime. Such a system should also protect the interests of host states by imposing appropriate restraints and obligations upon foreign companies and TNCs.[16]

4.2.   The appropriateness of arbitration

The perception that the underlying substantive rules are inequitable raises the whole question of the suitability of arbitration as a mechanism for settling certain categories of disputes arising from an international business transaction between an African Government and a foreign company or a transnational corporation. If the concern of the African party is to readjust the entire transaction, which is regarded as inequitable, or to reform the underlying substantive rules, a reference to an arbitral tribunal

---

16. S.K.B. Asante, *International Law and Foreign Investment: A Reappraisal*, 37 ICLQ at 588-627 (1988).

relying on traditional doctrines for the application of legal rules would not seem particularly meaningful. In such circumstances, a renegotiation for the purpose of redressing the inequities of the agreement would seem more profitable. African countries consider the traditional format of a commercial arbitration, predicated on the adjudication of legal disputes on the basis of legal rules, as unsuitable for such a purpose.[17] The more strategic disputes between African governments and transnational corporations have in fact been settled by negotiation and other amicable means, (*e.g.* the renegotiation of the Valco Agreement in Ghana, renegotiation of the Rutile Mining Agreement in Sierra Leone, the renegotiation of the Shashi Project in Botswana, the negotiation of the Gambia Telecommunications Project, and the restructuring of the Zambian Copper Agreement). It is also significant that several arbitrations with African parties that were initially instituted before arbitral tribunals have been settled by negotiation, for example, *Gabon v Société Serete S.A.*,[18] *Guadalupe Gas Products Corporation v. Federal Military Government of Nigeria*,[19] and *Seditex Engineering v. Madagascar.*[20]

A discussion of the appropriateness of international commercial arbitration raises the issue of the African concept of arbitration. African traditional legal and social systems are replete with informal mechanisms for settling disputes which have "been characterized as arbitration". African customary arbitration in Ghana, for example, has the following basic ingredients:

(a) a voluntary submission of the dispute by the parties to a third party for the purpose of having the dispute decided informally, but on the merits;
(b) prior agreement by both parties to accept the award of the arbitrators;
(c) publication of the award.[21]

The accent here is on the informality of the traditional proceeding. This ingrained idea of the essentially informal character of traditional African arbitration collides sharply with the modern concept of international arbitration. It comes as a surprise to many African lawyers and executives to realize that a party to international commercial arbitration has to navigate through a bewildering and complex maze of arbitration institutions, rules and procedures, with rigid formalities and set deadlines,

---

17. *See* S.K.B. Asante, *Commentary, in* Rubin and Nelson (eds.), International Investment Disputes: Avoidance and Settlement (American Society of International Law 1984); Asante & Agyemang, *The Suitability of Arbitration for Settling 'Political' Investment Disputes Involving African States*, 22 Journal of World Trade 123-127 (6th Issue, 1988).
18. ICSID Case No. ARB/76/1. *Source* ICSID Cases 4.
19. ICSID Case No. ARB/78/1. *Source* ICSID Cases 6.
20. ICSID Case No. CONC/82/1. *Source* ICSID Cases 11.
21. L.K. Agbosu, *Arbitration Under Customary Law*, XV Review of Ghana Law 204 (1983-1989).

which can only be breached to the great detriment of the unwary party. Modern international commercial arbitration has all the characteristics of a formal adjudication, a far cry from the informality associated with traditional customary arbitration. The highly technical nature of this process again reinforces the idea of an alien system. It is indeed disconcerting for African officials to realize that failure to comply with technical procedures does not arrest the inexorable progression of the arbitral process to a definitive award against the delinquent party.

4.3.   The legal environment of the arbitral proceedings

African reservations about modern arbitral proceedings also stem from the legal environment of arbitral proceedings. This has three aspects, namely: (a) the fundamental concept of the underlying transaction, which is the subject of adjudication; (b) the admissibility of certain substantive rules that have been invoked by arbitral tribunals as universal postulates; and (c) the suitability of the rules and procedures governing the arbitration.

Western arbitrators tend to treat international commercial arbitration as essentially the resolution of a dispute arising from a private commercial transaction to be decided by invoking general legal principles without reference to considerations of public policy of the African countries. Such an approach, which focuses exclusively and mechanically on the culture of private commercial transactions and traditional legal principles is invariably favourable to transnational corporations. However, as this writer has said elsewhere:

> A long-term investment agreement spelling out comprehensively the relations between the government and the corporation in respect of the development and marketing of a natural resource and specifying all relevant fiscal arrangements is anything but a private contract or an institution of the market place. Governments of less developed countries quite properly regard these agreements as major instruments of public policy and a prominent feature of their development strategies, hardly distinguishable from a development plan. These transactions are a framework for a joint public enterprise in which the government and the foreign partner are engaged in the development of a strategic public resource or the operation of a vital public utility. In short, they lie more in the domain of public law than in the province of private contract. It follows that these transactions cannot be insulated from the pressures which impinge on public institutions such as political changes in the country, changed economic conditions and the general expectations of the public.[22]

The classification of the underlying transaction as essentially a private commercial arrangement uncomplicated by public policy considerations in a developing country

---

22. S.K.B. Asante, Stability of Contractual Relations in the Transnational Investment Process, 28 ICLQ 401-404 (1979).

is fortified by the concept of arbitral autonomy, which is strenuously canvassed in Western legal and commercial circles. While the autonomy of arbitral tribunals from local courts or authorities is indeed an essential ingredient of the integrity of the arbitral process, it also serves to insulate the panel, invariably composed of non-Africans, from the economic and political realities of an African country. Thus, for example, while an African country faced with a chronic shortage of foreign exchange may initiate stern regulatory measures which it considers crucial for controlling or eliminating financial malpractices, such measures may strike a distant panel as constructive or creeping expropriation. The very concept of an economic crime or offense may vary according to the perspectives of the members of the tribunal. An African country which considers that its public interest has been ignored in an arbitration is virtually without a remedy. Most arbitral systems have no international mechanism for review (ICSID is an important exception) and the public policy grounds enunciated in the New York Convention are not likely to be particularly helpful if the forum for the recognition or enforcement proceedings lies outside Africa.

African lawyers who have observed particular instances of international commercial arbitration have come away with an uneasy feeling that the substantive laws of their respective countries have virtually been ignored by international arbitrators even where such laws have been designated as the applicable law of the transaction. This trend is by no means peculiar to cases involving African countries. Indeed there is a discernible trend among the community of international arbitrators to give little weight to the substantive laws of non-industrialized countries. Several ICSID cases have been challenged in annulment proceedings, specifically on the ground of failure to apply the governing national law of a host developing country. Similarly, a recent study of the decisions of the Iran-US Claims Tribunal concludes that Iranian law was hardly applied even when it was expressly stipulated in the transaction as the applicable law.[23]

An obvious factor accounting for this practice is the unfamiliarity of the foreign arbitral panel with nuances of the national law of distant countries. However, a more disturbing phenomenon is the inclination of some western arbitrators to invoke what they conceive as universal principles of commercial law in the form of *lex mercatoria*. Inasmuch as this practice purports to consolidate and apply principles developed out of a commercial or legal culture, which was fashioned by the industrialized world without participation of developing countries, it raises the sensitive issue of equity *vis-à-vis* developing countries generally, and African countries, in particular. A major doctrinal premise of these principles is primacy accorded to the will of the

---

23. *See* John A. Westberg, *The Applicable Law Issue in International Business Transactions with Government Parties - Rulings of the Iran-United States Claims Tribunal*, 2 Foreign Investment Law Journal-ICSID Review 473 (1987).

parties; the individualistic concept that a commercial arrangement shaped by the will of the parties should prevail without reference to the dictates of the public interest. This exaltation of party autonomy may sometimes collide with the exacting demands of development or the impelling requirements of equitable redress.

4.4.   Procedural rules

African parties to arbitration derive little comfort from the operation of the procedural rules governing the arbitration. Where the arbitral system does not specify or stipulate the rules governing the procedure, the tendency of many international arbitrators is to apply the law of the forum which is often located in a developed country. This invariably compels African parties to retain counsel from developed countries for the purpose of the arbitration proceedings. However, it is not often realized that the seemingly innocuous procedural rules of some of the major arbitration systems can be burdensome to African parties. A few examples may be cited.

The requirement of advance payment of arbitration costs in modest amounts of $50,000 to $200,000 may be a heavy imposition on an African country or party which suffers from an acute shortage of foreign exchange resources, and has made no provision for such a contingency. A private party which may be obliged by the exchange control law of its country to seek formal governmental approval for the payment of such costs in foreign exchange may well be unable to meet the deadline for such payment, with dire consequences. An African Minister of Finance is not likely to release $100,000 for such costs when confronted with a critical decision to procure medication or equipment for a needy hospital. Arbitration costs are indeed regarded as prohibitive. African Governments recoil at the thought of spending anything between US $400,000 to US $1 million on one arbitration, in respect of administrative costs, arbitrator's fees and counsel's fees.

African officials have also complained bitterly about the unrealistic deadlines imposed by arbitral systems. They contend, with some justification, that deadlines of 30 days or thereabouts stipulated by several arbitral systems for the payment of costs, appointment of arbitrators, the filing of pleadings or taking various procedural steps are woefully unrealistic having regard to the constraints of time, distance and the normal bureaucratic delays in Africa. It would be instructive to consider the steps involved in complying with the requirement of advance payment of costs.

In a typical scenario, the process is initiated by a memo from the Attorney General or Minister of Justice to the Minister of Finance for his concurrence. This is then followed by a second memo to the Cabinet for its approval, a decision by the Cabinet, an authorization to the Central Bank from the Cabinet to release the funds from the country's foreign exchange resources, and an instruction from the Central Bank to its correspondent bank overseas to pay the costs.

As intimated above, the choice of a developed country as the forum is detrimental to African parties for several reasons. The obvious consequence is the high cost of travel which must necessarily be incurred in foreign exchange. A protracted arbitration may impose a heavy burden on the slim foreign exchange resources of an African country. Another consequence of such a choice is the tendency of arbitral panels to rely on the law of the forum as the procedural law of the arbitration, even where the parties have selected another law as the applicable law of the transaction. The choice of a developed country forum carries with it the requirement that counsel chosen must be well-versed in the law and practice of the forum. This inevitably leads to the appointment of a European or American counsel to represent African parties, which further raises the question as to whether the African party is well-equipped to monitor the work of its foreign counsel.

The difficulties posed by the arbitral rules of various arbitration systems are aggravated, in the African perception, by the sombre realization that the consent of the parties is not a prerequisite to the progression of the arbitral proceedings once the arbitration tribunal is properly seized of the case. Unwary African parties have discovered, to their dismay, that after the initial provision in a treaty, agreement or legislation accepting the jurisdiction of a particular arbitral system, the entire arbitral process can be triggered into full operation up to a definitive award even in the absence of any explicit manifestation of the respondent's consent to the various consequential steps in the process. Thus, neither delay, default nor non-participation by the respondent or defendant will prevent most arbitration systems from appointing an arbitrator for the erring party, from constituting the full tribunal, from admitting the pleadings of the claimant or plaintiff, from hearing the case or from issuing the final award against the respondent. Furthermore, by virtue of this involuntary process, such an award could be enforced against the respondent in a foreign country whether he contests the proceedings or not. An African party, in these circumstances, feels victimized by the inexorable progression of an alien process culminating in an arbitrary imposition.

While a certain measure of this involuntary process is essential for the viability of the arbitral system, there is considerable unhappiness with the automatic character of some aspects, in particular, procedures for the appointment of the arbitrators. For example, under the UNCITRAL rules, the non-consensual aspect is highlighted by the fact that failure by one party to appoint an arbitrator does not result in the direct appointment of arbitrators by the Secretary General of the Permanent Court of Arbitration, an office formally mentioned in the Rules. Although an appointment by the Secretary General would still constitute an involuntary process, at least he has been explicitly designated in the UNCITRAL rules, a fact which should be known to all parties to UNCITRAL arbitration. It should be pointed out in all fairness to the Secretary General that this provision enables him to designate an appointing authority who is better placed to appoint arbitrators who are closer to the subject matter of the arbitration or the relevant geographical area. Furthermore, the Secretary

General invariably informs the parties of his intention to designate a particular appointing authority before doing so.

4.5.   The outcome of arbitral proceedings

The various factors discussed above as inhibiting African enthusiasm for international commercial arbitration could have been conceivably tempered by success in these proceedings. Unfortunately the indications are that African parties have not been markedly successful as litigants. ICSID awards, for instance, have been predominantly favourable to foreign investors. It is to be noted that African states have featured in 17 ICSID cases as respondents. As to the arbitrators in other arbitral systems, Andrew Armfelt has observed:

> There are no authoritative statistics on international arbitration results, owing to the confidential nature of arbitration. Nonetheless, anecdotal evidence indicates that international arbitrators have tended to decide in favour of transnational corporations.[24]

4.6.   Limited experience

The burden of the above discussion is that international commercial arbitration has not been sufficiently internationalized. It still remains a predominantly Western institution located in developed countries. As discussed below, the institution of arbitration is unlikely to become more congenial to Africans unless it is truly internationalized.

Nevertheless, there can be no realistic discussion of this subject without recognizing that a contributory cause of African unease about international arbitration is limited experience in this area. Indeed, African expertise in international commercial arbitration is closely related to African experience in the whole area of international business transactions.

Since independence, African governments have grappled with the negotiation and administration of many kinds of international transactions; loan agreements with international and foreign banks, international procurement contracts, supply contracts, joint ventures, international construction contracts, management agreements, technical assistance agreements, mining and petroleum agreements, licensing agreements and the like. Some countries have made impressive strides in handling such transactions which require multi-disciplinary teams. Throughout the past fifteen years, this writer has organized numerous workshops and seminars on such transactions for developing country personnel under the auspices of the United Nations. The negotiation and drafting of arbitration clauses are covered in these sessions. However, it was realized

---

24. A. Armfelt, *Avoiding the Arbitration Trap*, Financial Times, October 27, 1992, at 17.

that the dearth of experience was such that special seminars had to be organized, focusing exclusively on international commercial arbitration. It is evident from these seminars that there is no equivalent of an 'Arbitration Bar' in the overwhelming majority of Sub-Saharan African countries.[25] The normal law school curriculum does not address international commercial arbitration, and most African lawyers have not specialized in international business transactions, still less, the intricacies of the various arbitral systems. Apart from the UN efforts referred to above, it does not appear that any concerted efforts have been made by the various arbitral institutions to provide training for African lawyers in international arbitration, although the ICC's Institute of International Business Law and Practice provides training facilities in this area. The result is that African parties to international arbitration are compelled to hire overseas counsel.

5.   FUTURE PROSPECTS: SOME REMEDIAL ACTION

It will be evident from our earlier reference to the African experience of international business transactions, that a discussion of the prospects of international commercial arbitration in Africa should proceed from the inescapable premise that African states cannot insulate themselves from international commercial arbitration, so long as they participate in the international economic or commercial system. The issue then is: what can be done realistically and meaningfully to address African concerns and misgivings about international commercial arbitration?

As discussed above, the pervasive feeling that characterizes African attitudes to international commercial arbitration is that, while it is necessary and inevitable, it is, nonetheless, essentially an alien system, devised and practised in distant lands, substantially to the detriment of African interests. The perception is one of alienation and exclusion. While it is conceded that some aspects of this perception may well be ill-founded or are in any case traceable to African inadequacies, it is submitted that all aspects of this perception have to be addressed by both internal and external action if international commercial arbitration is to play a meaningful role in sub-Saharan Africa. Such action resolves itself into three main categories, *viz.*

(a) effective internationalization - making African participation effective;
(b) education;
(c) reform of the basic substantive rules and legal culture underpinning international arbitration.

The Permanent Court of Arbitration (PCA) could, as discussed below, play a critical role with respect to some or all of the above recommendations.

25. The beginnings of such expertise and practice are to be found in Nigeria.

5.1.   Effective internationalization

The challenge before the international arbitration system, as well as the international legal system generally, is to grapple with the full implications of the major expansion of the international community since the end of World War II. While the propagation of international commercial arbitration in the developing world seems to be a major preoccupation of the capital-exporting countries, no serious effort has been made to modify the rules, the personnel, location, practice, and indeed the entire culture of international commercial arbitration to accommodate the peculiar needs and concerns of African countries. Effective internationalization, that is, the conversion of an essentially Western system to a truly cosmopolitan or international system is necessary to inspire the confidence of African states.

In this respect, as discussed above, non-participation by African states in the establishment of the arbitral system need not be an impediment to genuine internationalization of the system, provided the operation of the system is realistically and meaningfully modified to accommodate the interests of new adherents to the system. The International Court of Justice (ICJ), for instance, now passes the test of internationalization despite the fact that, historically, virtually all Sub-Saharan African states came into existence after the establishment of the Court. The Membership of the ICJ has been expanded to include judges from all regions, with the salutary effect that the principal legal systems of the world are represented in the Court. Elections to the Court attract the enthusiastic participation of all countries. The caseload of the Court is at an all-time high, and parties from developing countries are active litigants before the Court, uninhibited by any perception that the ICJ is an exclusive alien club. The United Nations has established a Trust Fund to assist countries in overcoming any financial difficulties in participating in the proceedings of the Court. The rules of the Court, and indeed the entire Statute of the Court are perceived as eminently fair, and the decisions of the Court cannot be fairly characterized as reflecting any particular regional or cultural bias. In short, the term 'World Court', which is used interchangeably with the ICJ, is appropriate and well-merited.

It is, of course, recognized that the ideal of true internationalization is more easily achieved in the context of a system of inter-state adjudication, applying public international law at a fixed forum, than in the framework of an international commercial arbitration system, dealing with both public and private parties and administering a myriad of legal systems, rules and procedures in a multiplicity of capitals. Furthermore, it may be a pious hope to procure the modification of rules and procedures established over decades as the essential underpinning of an entire tradition of international commercial arbitration. Nevertheless, the conclusion is inescapable that if international commercial arbitration is to be fully accepted and meaningfully practised in Africa, an objective which is actively canvassed in capital-exporting countries, then some modification of the rules of the game to ensure a genuine internationalization of the arbitral process is imperative.

There are several aspects of this process of internationalization or making international commercial arbitration truly universal.

(a) Modifying the rules and procedures

Without launching a major or radical overhaul of the arbitral rules and procedures, it should be feasible to effect such modifications that take due account of the constraints of time, distance, communication, as well as the administrative and logistical inadequacies that pose considerable difficulties to African parties to international commercial arbitration. Thus, the time limits prescribed for compliance with the various stages of the arbitral process, the consequences flowing from delay in such compliance, the involuntary component of such process, the costs of arbitration, including the requirements as to advance payments and the consequences of delinquency in this regard, should be realistically revised to address the genuine concerns of African parties, particularly when these parties are public authorities or governmental agencies hidebound by bureaucratic requirements. Apart from the obvious complications of geography and communication and limited foreign exchange resources, African parties are often unable to proceed as expeditiously as their European and American counterparts because they have to overcome the first hurdle of retaining and briefing European and American counsel before addressing each step of the arbitral process. The added complication of selecting a law firm, having the law firm approved by the relevant governmental authorities, negotiating legal fees, briefing the foreign law firm on the law and background to the case and settling pleadings across continents inevitably causes delay, which should not be objectively characterized as delinquent conduct.

With regard to the costs of arbitration, it is suggested that the major arbitral institutions seriously consider ways of alleviating this burden for African parties. The UN Trust Fund for assisting needy developing countries in financing their costs of litigation before the ICJ is instructive. A recommendation on these lines has already been made by the Group of Experts with respect to the revitalization of the PCA. A similar fund could be established to assist in alleviating the costs of arbitration for African countries.

Such financial assistance should be feasible in view of the obvious interest of international and national arbitral institutions of the industrialized countries in promoting international commercial arbitration in Africa and the developing world generally. Such assistance should, in particular, accommodate the foreign exchange costs of arbitration.

Perhaps another way of addressing this problem is to permit the payment of a substantial part of the costs in local currency, with lenient provision for the repatriation of the amounts in question. Such a measure could, of course, be combined with the practice of conducting the arbitration in developing country fora.

(b) Internationalizing the fora

Arbitral institutions, to the extent that they are competent, and arbitral parties from outside of Africa, should be amenable to conducting arbitrations in African cities. The perceived logistical and infrastructural difficulties in Africa are grossly exaggerated. Africa has been able to host some of the most elaborate international conferences, and servicing an arbitration should not pose a serious problem. Any misgivings as to the suitability of the local law for purposes of arbitration could be disposed of by prior agreement as to the governing law. However, where the law of the forum is the designated governing law for the purposes of the arbitral proceedings, it should be adhered to faithfully. Conducting international arbitration in Africa would not only substantially reduce costs, but also help to overcome the perception of alien system. It would also have the additional effect of exposing local lawyers to some aspects of the process, thus paving the way for development of local expertise in this area. This recommendation complements the idea of establishing arbitration centres in Africa; particularly, as these centres are not sponsored by the major arbitration systems of Europe and America.

(c) Diversifying the personnel

Although it is conceded that African experts in international business transactions and international commercial arbitration are limited in number, it is submitted that a more determined effort could be made to identify and appoint more African jurists as arbitrators, particularly when the applicable law of the transaction in question is the law of an African state.

African exposure to international legal matters is steadily increasing. Within the past 10 years, African lawyers have participated actively in the annual meetings of the International Bar Association,[26] the American Society of International Law and numerous seminars where international legal issues, such as international arbitration, are discussed. African jurists have dealt with cases raising both local and external arbitrational issues. Lawyers practising in countries such as Nigeria, Ghana, Zimbabwe and Kenya, which have considerable foreign investment activity, have represented overseas clients. This experience is reinforced by the expertise of government lawyers who have represented their respective governments in numerous international negotiations and transactions. Finally, there is the expertise of Africans who have been exposed to international legal practice in international institutions.

26. The Section on Business Law of the IBA recently awarded 31 scholarships to enable young lawyers from Europe and French-speaking African countries to attend the IBA's 24th Biennial Conference in Cannes (International Bar News, November/December 1992, at 11).

This appeal is addressed both to arbitral institutions and African parties themselves. The appointment of more African arbitrators would be a major step towards the inauguration of a universal and universally accepted arbitral system.

(d) Paying more attention to African legal systems as the applicable law

One important aspect of internationalizing commercial arbitration is to take the legal systems of developing countries and African countries, in particular, more seriously where these are designated as the applicable laws of the transactions giving rise to the disputes. The international community no longer entertains the anachronistic notion of classifying some laws as the laws of 'civilized nations'. Where parties to an international business transaction, say, a turnkey construction contract, to be carried out in an African country, have, after due deliberation, designated the law of that country (including its tax laws, procurement laws, labour laws and laws governing civil and engineering works) as the law governing the transaction, arbitrators handling the dispute arising from the contract must not brush aside such law in favour of some supposedly universal principles or rules, such as *lex mercatoria* or other system with which they are more familiar. Nothing raises the spectre of arrogant exclusivity more than such cavalier treatment of the laws of the various members of the international community. With regard to the law governing the procedure, arbitrators should resist the tendency to apply the law of the developed country forum even where the parties have settled for another legal system.

(e) Recognizing the public interest in transactions involving governmental entities

Most of the international commercial arbitrations affecting Africa involve governmental parties. As mentioned above, this raises a serious question as to the extent to which transactions with public authorities can be treated as ordinary commercial transactions between private parties. In a developing region, where public agencies were obliged to take the initiative in undertaking transactions which would normally fall within the province of private parties in the developed world, mainly by reason of the paucity of viable private entities, the public interest in such transactions simply cannot be ignored. A panel exclusively composed of developed country jurists is unlikely to appreciate and be sensitive to the compelling demands of the public interest in such transactions. African countries are unlikely to embrace international commercial arbitration wholeheartedly unless the implications of this public interest are fully recognized even at a time when privatization is proclaimed as an eminently desirable goal.

5.2. Education

Nothing suggested above detracts from the critical importance of national as well international educational programmes to equip African lawyers and businessmen with knowledge and expertise in the handling of international commercial arbitration. The need here is indeed compelling. In this regard, it might be instructive to mention the efforts of the former United Nations Centre on Transnational Corporations (UNCTC) and the United Nations Department of Economic and Social Development (UNDESD) in organizing training workshops in Africa in the field of international business transactions generally and international commercial arbitration, in particular.

As part of its technical cooperation programme, the former UNCTC elaborated and organised some 200 workshops and seminars in numerous developing countries and economies in transition on the negotiation, structuring and drafting of international business transactions as well as the legal, financial and technical issues arising from such transactions for the benefit of middle level to senior professionals and executives in the public and private sectors. These transactions included international joint ventures and other types of investment agreements, petroleum and mining agreements, management agreements, international construction contracts, consulting contracts, loan transactions, debt rescheduling agreements, international procurement contracts and licensing agreements and compensation trade agreements. The object of this programme was to enhance the capabilities of these countries in handling international business transactions and to demystify the phenomenon of dealing with transnational corporations.

An important ingredient of this programme is the organization of special workshops and seminars exclusively devoted to international commercial arbitration, which specifically target lawyers from the public service and the private Bar. A number of these have been held in various African countries for the benefit of the lawyers in these countries. A typical workshop consists of a 5-day programme of lectures, case studies and simulation exercises covering the following subjects, *inter alia*:

(a) A description of the main systems of international commercial arbitration, *e.g.*, ICC, London Court of International Arbitration, AAA, UNCITRAL and ICSID: their salient and distinguishing features, their rules and procedures and their areas of concentration. Regional centres of arbitration in Africa.
(b) Negotiating and drafting the arbitration clause in an international business transaction, including arbitrable subjects.
(c) Constituting the arbitral panel.
(d) Evidence in arbitration proceeding.
(e) The law governing the arbitration.
(f) The arbitral award, including enforcement, nullity and challenge.
(g) Special types of arbitration such as arbitration of disputes in construction contracts or investment disputes.

(h)   The host country's experience of international commercial arbitration and the problems encountered.

(i)   Specific case studies of arbitrations considered instructive.

(j)   An evaluation of the workshop by the participants.

Lectures are provided by an international faculty consisting of experts from UNCTC, and later UNDESD, and eminent lawyers retained *ad hoc* for the workshop.[27]

Our programmes have been enthusiastically received by the participants and have demonstrated that there is a yawning gap in the knowledge and expertise of Africans in this area. There is an overwhelming need for more intensified efforts in this connection by national authorities and institutions of professional training in Africa, by the main arbitral institutions of the world, by various international organizations and by international professional associations, such as IBA or ILA.[28] Whatever the imperfections of the present international arbitral systems may be, African countries cannot afford the luxury of disengagement. The dynamics of international commercial intercourse dictate active African participation in the arbitral process. African governments and legal professions have the responsibility to take appropriate initiatives in this field. In short, the realities of the international economic system make it compelling for officials and other personnel of developing countries to familiarize themselves thoroughly with the institutions, concepts and techniques of international arbitration, whatever their reservations may be about the system.

5.3.   The substantive underpinnings of international commercial arbitration

It is a daunting task to call for the reform of the substantive law applied in international commercial arbitration. The first difficulty derives from the fact that analytically one cannot identify a single or uniform body of such substantive law. The applicable substantive law in a particular arbitration could be the national law of a particular country that is designated in the transaction as the applicable law or adjudged by the arbitrators as the governing law. It could also consist of certain relevant principles and rules of public international law that have been designated in the relevant transactions or otherwise adjudged by the tribunal to be the applicable law, particularly in the case of investment disputes. However, as pointed out above, experience has shown that some arbitrators do not feel necessarily compelled to

27. In a workshop held in Accra, Ghana in May 1992, the faculty consisted of Sir Ian Percival, former Solicitor-General of the U.K., Dr. Biswanath Sen, former Secretary-General of the Asian-African Legal Consultative Committee and Senior Advocate in India, Mr. Robert Layton, Senior Partner, Jones, Day, Reavis & Pogue of New York and the author. There were some 50 participants - lawyers from the public service and private Bar in Ghana.

28. The ICC's Institute of International Business Law and Practice and The Institute for Transnational Arbitration of the South Western Legal Foundation could play a critical role in directing special training programmes to Africa.

adhere to the designated national law, while others indeed consider themselves at liberty to invoke and apply principles and rules which cannot be classified as belonging to a particular national legal system or indeed to public international law, *i.e.* the invocation of *lex mercatoria* or its equivalent.

The plea for reform in this section targets the principles and rules of public international law and the emerging *lex mercatoria*. As far as the latter is concerned, the objection is fundamental. Many jurists from the developed and the developing world have challenged the doctrinal validity of a system which does not derive from a particular municipal legal system or from international law. But beyond the doctrinal argument, African countries and other developing countries reject the imposition of a body of rules that was fashioned in Europe without their participation and which makes no attempt to accommodate their interests.

With respect to international law governing investment issues, jurists[29] from the developing world have pressed for an appropriate modification to reflect the interests of an expanded international community and to ensure a more equitable system that comprehensively addresses the obligations and rights of all actors in the international investment process.

Within the past decade there has been a marked liberalization of foreign investment regimes in most countries, especially in developing countries and economies in transition. Foreign investment is now avidly sought in virtually all countries and appropriate measures have been instituted to provide protection for investments and transnational corporations.

These measures at the national level have been reinforced by a plethora of bilateral investment treaties between capital exporting and capital importing countries. At the multilateral and regional levels, instruments and declarations have been issued to ensure fair and equitable treatment of foreign investment. The World Bank, for instance, has formulated Guidelines on the Legal Framework for the Treatment of Foreign Investment.[30] In short, the international legal system is fully equipped with various devices for the protection of foreign investment. However, it can hardly be denied that the international legal system would profit from the formulation of appropriate restraints on corporate conduct, so that the basic ground rules of investment activity would be clarified.

The undoubted virtues of foreign investment and other forms of transnational corporate activity do not detract from the need to make the international legal system more responsive to the concerns of all parties to the investment process, including the host countries. The incidence in Africa of cases where the implementation of

---

29. *See* S.K.B. Asante, Transnational Investment Law and National Development (1981). *See also* by the same author, *supra* note 16 and M. Sornarajah, *The Climate of International Arbitration*, 8 Journal of International Arbitration 69 (2nd Issue 1991).
30. *See* World Bank Group, *Legal Framework for the Treatment of Foreign Investment*, II Report to the Development Committee and Guidelines on the Treatment of Foreign Direct Investment (1992).

numerous investment projects or the execution of industrial plants or civil works has been vitiated by corporate delinquency or corruption or other forms of misconduct argues for a fair and equitable international regime which does not operate on the simplistic premise that misconduct or default is the exclusive preserve of governmental authorities in Africa. In this connection, it is refreshing to note that the World Bank's Guidelines on the Legal Framework for the Treatment of Foreign Investment explicitly condemn corrupt practices.

5.4. The possible role of a revitalized PCA

Since the PCA is in the process of devising rules to revitalize arbitration under its auspices, it may well be better placed to address the concerns recounted above rather than other arbitral institutions which may not be disposed to reform at present. In particular, the new rules being devised for state/non-state arbitration under the PCA could well provide a framework for accommodating the changes recommended above to enhance African participation in international commercial arbitration.

The PCA has several advantages that could make it a congenial forum for international commercial arbitration and an attractive alternative to existing arbitral institutions in this field. First, its location at The Hague, with its tradition as an international centre for the settlement of international disputes, which is not tainted with local or regional bias, would make it an ideal international forum. African states, like other developing countries, do not consider litigation in the ICJ as a proceeding in a European or regional setting, and the same aura of a delocalized, international forum could negate any perception of an alien or exclusive institution as far as the PCA is concerned. A necessary consequence of the choice of The Hague as the forum is that it would arrest any tendency to apply Dutch law to the arbitral proceedings. Second, the PCA is not the creation of any particular trade association. Its status as a creation of an international convention, to which all countries may accede, enhances its claim to universality. Third, the system of appointing members of PCA arbitral panels ensures a greater diversity than some of the nationally based arbitration systems. If the proposal to enlist arbitrators with special expertise in particular areas of international business is implemented, it would enhance the effectiveness of the arbitrators. Fourth, a PCA arbitration, being the product of an intergovernmental collaboration, would be more sensitive to the notion of the public interest compared to an arbitration system which is the creation of a purely commercial organization. Fifth, the PCA would enjoy the crucial advantage that, unlike some other arbitral institutions such as ICSID, its jurisdiction in international commercial arbitration between states and non-state parties is not limited to special categories of international business transactions. On the contrary, it would be in a position to embrace new categories of disputes, such as environmental disputes between states and transnational corporations.

Finally, the PCA could employ its impressive facilities in assisting in training programmes for African lawyers in the area of international commercial arbitration.

6.   CONCLUSION

The remedial action recommended in this paper is a pragmatic and modest effort to bring Sub-Saharan Africa within the mainstream of international commercial arbitration. It must be acknowledged that reservations about international arbitration are by no means peculiar to the Sub-Saharan African region. Other regions, outside of Western Europe, have, at some stage or another, manifested either downright hostility or some form of objection to this process. The traditional antipathy of Latin America to international arbitration is well-documented. In Asia, there is a cultural bias against the kind of adversarial confrontation associated with international commercial arbitration, although attitudes are reportedly changing. America is a recent convert to international commercial arbitration, and even in Western Europe, national judicial authorities have not entirely overcome their inclination to scrutinize international arbitration. Attitudes to international arbitration in the Middle East have ranged from outright hostility to resignation. Some countries in this region originally reacted to their disenchantment by attempting to prohibit or restrict international arbitration, but with no enduring success. The evidence now points to active participation by Middle Eastern countries generally in international commercial arbitration by reason of the volume of their international business transactions and the level of their expertise in this field.

Sub-Saharan Africa has chosen a less confrontational path and recognises the inevitability of international commercial arbitration. It only remains for the institutional framework of this process to be appropriately restructured to ensure the effective participation of African states.

ENFORCEMENT OF AN ARBITRAL AWARD AGAINST A STATE: WITH WHOM ARE YOU DEALING?

A. VAN BLANKENSTEIN*

1.   INTRODUCTION

The effort to attract commercial arbitration to the Permanent Court of Arbitration [hereinafter PCA] in 1962 by introducing the Rules of Arbitration and Conciliation for Settlement of International Disputes between Two Parties of Which only One is a State [hereinafter the 1962 Rules], has met with little success.[1] In other articles of this issue of the *Leiden Journal of International Law* the reasons for this failure are discussed. These articles also contain suggestions on how changes in the legal framework and the administration of the PCA may improve this situation.

Both Van den Berg and Sanders are of the opinion that the 1962 Rules should be replaced by new rules for arbitration between a state and a private party. These two authors also suggest that these new rules should contain a waiver of immunity from execution. This article will elaborate on the necessity of a waiver of immunity from execution in new rules on arbitration between a state and a private party. Parties to an arbitration agreement always have to rely on municipal courts for the enforcement of an award. In those courts, the advantages of arbitration as an independent and international mechanism of dispute settlement may be undermined by the unequal position between a state and a private party caused by a rule on state immunity. By including a waiver of immunity from execution in its rules, the PCA would provide states and private parties with an arbitration mechanism in which the equality of the parties will be maintained throughout the procedure, including the enforcement procedure of municipal courts.

The article is divided into two parts. The first part contains an evaluation of the theory of restricted state immunity. The rule of absolute state immunity will not be discussed because its treatment of the subject is simple, in that enforcement of an arbitral award is only possible when the foreign state has expressly waived its immunity from both jurisdiction and execution. The evaluation aims to demonstrate that immunity from jurisdiction and immunity from execution should be treated

* Allaart van Blankenstein has studied international law at the University of Leiden.
1. The Permanent Court of Arbitration - New Directions 10 (1991).

S. Muller and W. Mijs (eds.), The Flame Rekindled, 159–176.

under a single concept of state immunity. Furthermore, the importance of the equal position between a state and a private party in the restricted theory of state immunity is emphasized. In addition it will be argued that the problem of state immunity should not be confused with issues of jurisdiction.

The second part of the article concerns the effect state immunity has on the enforcement of arbitral awards. It will be demonstrated that the lack of unity among municipal rules on state immunity makes the result of an endeavour to enforce an arbitral award against a state very unpredictable.

The elaboration of state immunity is needed to demonstrate that under the concept of restricted state immunity, theoretically, the immunity of a foreign state cannot hamper the enforcement of an arbitral award against that state. When immunity from jurisdiction or immunity from execution does prevent the enforcement of an arbitral award, this is not the result of the legal function of state immunity but of political considerations. It will be argued that when a waiver of immunity from execution is included in the new PCA rules, states do not abandon a right but waive political favours.

2.   STATE IMMUNITY

2.1.   The scope of state immunity

According to the concept of state immunity,[2] local courts cannot exercise jurisdiction over a foreign state. In order to determine the scope of this immunity of a foreign state, it is necessary to examine the source of this immunity. Rights and obligations between states are defined by international law. As a subject of international law, a state possesses rights which may limit the application of the municipal law of another state.

The question is whether state immunity can be derived from principles of international law. If so, the unequal legal position in municipal law between a foreign state and a private person caused by state immunity can be justified by these principles. However, if this immunity is not based on principles of international law, state immunity should be considered to be a favour granted by the forum state. The extent of such a favour will be determined in accordance with political motives.

2. H. Lauterpacht, *The Problem of Jurisdictional Immunities of Foreign States*, 28 BYIL 220 (1951); L.J. Bouchez, *The Nature and Scope of State Immunity from Jurisdiction and Execution*, 10 NYIL 3-33 (1979); I. Sinclair, *The Law of Sovereign Immunity, Some Recent Developments*, 167 Recueil des Cours 113-284 (1980); S. Sucharitkul, *Developments and Prospects of the Doctrine of State Immunity, Some Aspects of Codification and Progressive Development*, 29 NILR 252-64 (1982); R. Higgins, *Certain Unresolved Aspects of the Law of State Immunity*, 29 NILR 265-276 (1982); G.M. Badr, State Immunity: An Analytical and Prognostic View (1984); P.D. Trooboff, *Foreign State Immunity: Emerging Consensus on Principles*, 200 Recueil des Cours 293-429 (1986); C.H. Scheuer, State Immunity: Some Recent Developments (1988).

2.2.   Source of state immunity

The ILC Working Group on jurisdictional immunities of states and their property says in its 1978 Report that state immunity is the result of an interplay between the principle of territoriality and the principle of state personality, both being aspects of state sovereignty.[3] The application of the principle of state immunity aims to prevent conflicts between a state acting as territorial sovereign by exercising its jurisdiction in a case and another state, involved in that case. The principle is based on the assumption that the exercise of jurisdiction by one state over another state would automatically impair the sovereignty of the latter state. Sovereignty does in fact, by definition exclude the possibility of judgement without consent.[4] However, the function of state immunity to protect the sovereignty of a foreign state also limits the application of a rule of state immunity. It means that jurisdiction is only excluded in cases which concern activities which constitute the exercise of sovereign authority.

The theory of restricted immunity is based on the assumption that not all activities of the state are an exercise of sovereignty. According to the theory of restricted immunity, a foreign state does not enjoy immunity in cases which concern commercial activities of that state. The problem with the application of this theory is the distinction between *acta iure imperii* and *acta iure gestionis*. A simple distinction, achieved by qualifying acts made under public law as *acta iure imperii* and acts governed by private law as *acta iure gestionis* is not always effective.[5]

This method, for instance, is not very practical for lawyers in common law countries for whom the distinction between public and private law is not very familiar.[6] To solve the problem, common law countries have introduced statutes which define the cases in which foreign states do not enjoy immunity. In 1976, the US enacted the Foreign Sovereign Immunity Act [hereinafter FSIA][7] which was followed in 1978 by the state Immunity Act [hereinafter SIA][8] in Britain and similar statutes in several other states.[9] Of these latter statutes only the Australian Foreign States Immunity Act (1985) [hereinafter Australian Act][10] is mentioned additional to the FSIA and the SIA because of some distinguished provisions relevant to the topic

3. [1978] 2 Y.B. Int'l Law Comm'n 153, U.N. Doc. A/CN.4/SER.A/1978/Add.1.
4. This is reflected in the maxim *par in parem imperium non habet*.
5. *See* Badr, *supra* note 2, at 63.
6. *See* Higgins, *supra* note 2, at 268.
7. Foreign Sovereign Immunity Act (1976), 15 I.L.M 1388-1392 (1976), Amendments to the FSIA (1988), 28 I.L.M. 397 (1989).
8. State Immunity Act (1978), 17 I.L.M. 1123-1129 (1978).
9. Singapore; State Immunity Act (1979), UN Legislative Series, Materials on Jurisdictional Immunities of Foreign States and Their Property 28, U.N. Sales No. E/F.81V.10 (1982), Pakistan; State Immunity Ordinance (1981), *id.* at 20, South-Africa; Foreign Sovereign Immunity Act (1982), *id.* at 34, Canada; Act to Provide for State Immunity in Canadian Courts (1982), 21 I.L.M. 798-801 (1982).
10. Foreign States Immunity Act (1985), 25 I.L.M. 715-724 (1986).

of this article. The system used in these statutes, in which state immunity is the rule and the exceptions are listed, is also found in the European Convention on State Immunity (1972) [hereinafter European Convention][11] and the ILC Draft Articles on Jurisdictional Immunities of States and Their Property [hereinafter ILC Draft Articles].[12] In civil law countries, were no codification of rules on state immunity has taken place, the local rules are embodied in the jurisprudence of the courts.

Although the distinction between *acta iure imperii* and *acta iure gestionis* may differ in each legal system where state immunity is restricted, all these systems recognise that not every act of a state is an exercise of its sovereign authority. Therefore, it can be said that the retreat from absolute immunity has been caused by a change in the perception of the personality of the state.

2.3.   The role of equality in the theory of restricted immunity

The change in the perception of the personality of the state has been caused by the increasing participation of states in commercial markets. This trend has induced the restriction of state immunity, the rationale being that a state which acts like a private person should be treated equally by law.[13] This is reflected in the essential role of the comparison between the position in which a state acted to that of a private person in distinguishing *acta iure imperii* from *acta iure gestionis*. The fact that a state performs the same act as a private person means that this act is not in the exercise of sovereign authority, as such acts are the exclusive domain of states.[14]

Although, as has been said, the distinction between public and private acts may vary in each country, there is a principle difference between public and private acts common to all municipal legal systems. A public act of a state is always a unilateral exercise of authority over a party. By contrast, a private act of a state involves a bilateral relationship on a footing of equality between the state and a party.[15]

11. European Convention on State Immunity and Additional Protocol (1972) Europ. T.S. No. 74, in 1987 the following states were party to this Convention: Austria, Belgium, Cyprus, Luxembourg, the Netherlands, Switzerland and the United Kingdom, Chart Showing Signatures and Ratification of Conventions and Agreements Concluded within the Council of Europe (1987).
12. *Report of the International Law Commission on its Work of its Forty-third Session*, 46 U.N. GAOR Supp. 10, at 10.
13. *See* Bouchez, *supra* note 2, at 8; *e.g.* Lord Wilberforce: "It is necessary in the interest of justice to individuals having [...] [commercial, or other private law] transactions with states to allow them to bring such transactions before the court". in I° Congreso del Partido, 1983 A.C. 244, 64 I.L.R. 314 (1984); Alfred Dunhill of London Inc. *v.* Republic of Cuba, 425 U.S. 682 (1976), 66 I.L.R. 66 (1984).
14. *See e.g.* the US Supreme Court: "In their commercial capacities, foreign governments do not exercise powers peculiar to sovereigns [...]" *in* Alfred Dunhill of London *v.* Republic of Cuba, *supra* note 13, at 225; the *Cour de Cassation*: "[...] the foreign state [...] did not carry out any act of public authority [...] but acted, on the contrary, in the same manner as any private individual", *in* Spanish State *v.* SA de L'Hotel George V, judgement of Jan. 17, 1973, Cass., Fr., 65 I.L.R. 62 (1984).
15. *See* Badr, *supra* note 2, at 65.

Therefore it can be said that in cases where a state does not enjoy immunity from jurisdiction its position is characterized by equality to the position of a private person.

2.4.   State immunity and general rules of jurisdiction

Although the question of state immunity is decided by judging the actions of the state, it is the person of the state which is immune and not its actions.[16] The court confronted with a case in which one of the parties is a state, first has to decide whether the case is within its jurisdiction and is competent to judge it according to its usual rules applicable in cases with non-state parties. Only after it has established its jurisdiction and its competence should a court determine whether the state-party is immune from its jurisdiction.[17] It can even be argued that after a court has established its jurisdiction in a case against a foreign state according to regular rules of private international law, the question of state immunity is no longer relevant.[18]

A rule of jurisdiction found in the international law of most legal systems, is the requirement of connection between the case and the territory of the forum state. This territorial connection is frequently linked to the principle of state immunity.[19] The purpose is to limit cases in which local courts have jurisdiction over a foreign state to those that have a close connection with the forum state. I endorse the opinion of those authors who claim that the territorial connection should not be included in a rule of state immunity.[20] The issue of a connection between a case and the territory or the law of the forum state is a matter of jurisdiction. It is difficult to see why in cases in which one of the parties is a foreign state, a closer territorial connection should be demanded in order to fall within the jurisdiction of a local court, than in cases in which none of the parties is a state. Such a requirement cannot be derived from the function of state immunity to protect the sovereignty of the foreign state.

Another concept which should not be confused with state immunity is that of 'Act of State'.[21] According to this concept, a court should refrain from judging governmental acts of a foreign state. In other words, the concept of Act of State limits a court's competence to judge the subject matter of a case. The concept of state immunity, on the other hand, prohibits a court from exercising its jurisdiction over the person of the foreign state. The court only reviews the subject matter of the case to determine whether the foreign state appears in its public or private personality.

16. *But see* I. Brownlie, Principles of Public International Law 323 (1990); Institut de Droit International, 64 Annuaire Tome 2 (1991) at 214-279.
17. *See* Badr, *supra* note 2, at 80.
18. *Id.* at 92; E. Lauterpacht, Aspects of Administration of International Justice 55 (1991).
19. *See* Trooboff, *supra* note 2, at 319.
20. *See* Higgins, *supra* note 2, at 273; *Preliminary Report on Jurisdictional Immunities of States and Their Property, by Mr. Motoo Ogiso, Special Rapporteur*, [1988] 2 Y.B. Int'l Law Comm'n 109, U.N. Doc. A/CN.4/SER.A/1988/Add.1.
21. *See* Higgins, *supra* note 2, at 275.

2.5.   The dual personality of the state

The above mentioned considerations on state immunity justify the conclusion that the theory of restrictive immunity creates the vision of a state with a dual personality. The first personality is immune from jurisdiction of foreign courts while the second personality is not immune. Whether a court is confronted with the immune personality or the non-immune in a case in which one of the parties is a state, is determined by judging the capacity in which that state has acted in that case. Has the state acted in the exercise of its sovereign authority then the foreign court must decide the state is immune from its jurisdiction, because as a sovereign state, it is only subject to international law and can not be judged without its consent. Where the state has acted in a capacity which is equal to that of a private person, then the state is not immune from the jurisdiction of a court competent to judge the case. Once a court has found that it is dealing with such a case, in which the state has, by choice, equalled its position to that of a private person, it may not let the state ascend again to its elevated position as a subject of international law during the settlement of the case.

When speaking of the dual personality of the state no reference is made to any real or legal division in the state. The concept of the dual personality of the state refers to the image of a foreign state which is created by applying the theory of restrictive immunity. This concept will be used to argue that once a court has established that it is dealing with the non-immune personality of the state it should continue to treat that personality in the same way as it would treat a private person.

2.6.   State immunity from execution

The review of state immunity in this article so far, is applicable to the subject of immunity from jurisdiction.[22] Theoretically, execution should not be treated separately from jurisdiction where the issue of state immunity is concerned. Once a court has established it has jurisdiction over a foreign state in a certain case and has also ruled against it, the property of that state should become susceptible to attachment as execution is nothing more than enforcing the law by harmonizing the factual situation with the judgement of the court. It would be senseless if a person over whom a court has jurisdiction would not be liable to measures of enforcement.[23]

Nevertheless most nations distinguish between immunity from jurisdiction and immunity from execution.[24] To a certain extent this distinction can be explained

---

22. J. Crawford, *Execution of Judgments and Foreign Sovereign Immunity*, 75 AJIL 820-869 (1981); Cahiers de CEDIN, L'Immunité d'Execution de l'Etat Etranger (1988); G.R. Delaume, Transnational Contracts, Applicable Law and Settlement of Disputes, Ch. 12 (1990).

23. *See* Scheuer, *supra* note 2, at 125; Delaume, *supra* note 22, at 1; Bouchez, *supra* note 2, at 19.

24. *Second Report on Jurisdictional Immunities of States and Their Property, by Mr. M. Ogiso, Special Rapporteur,* [1989] 2 Y.B. Int'l Law Comm'n 72, U.N. Doc. A/CN.4/SER.A/1989/Add.1.

according to the above mentioned duality of the personality of the state. As has been said, the foreign state has two personalities and the court of the forum state only has jurisdiction over the personality which equals that of a private person. Therefore, the forum state's measures of execution should only be directed against the property which is held by the foreign state in its private capacity.

The function of state immunity which determines the scope of immunity from jurisdiction should also apply in determining the scope of immunity from execution. Just as the immunity from jurisdiction prevents one state from exercising its jurisdiction with injurious consequences to the sovereign rights of another state, the immunity of execution should also be aimed at protecting those sovereign rights. This function of immunity is found in several conventions in which the property that is owned by the state in its sovereign capacity is protected.[25] The conventions relating to state owned ships and aircraft state that ships and aircraft for commercial use should be treated the same as privately owned ships and aircraft.[26]

To maintain the continuity in the concept of state immunity it is necessary that the criterion used to distinguish *acta iure imperii* from *acta iure gestionis* should also apply in the separation between property used for public purposes and property used for private purposes. No measures of execution should be taken by the forum state against property which is used in acts that will provide a state with immunity from jurisdiction. On the other hand, it should be possible to take such measures against property which is used in activities that will result in a denial of immunity from jurisdiction.[27]

Incorporating these considerations into the concept of the dual personality of the state leads to the following result. A foreign state which acts in exercise of sovereign authority will be immune from both jurisdiction and execution. No measures of execution can be taken against property used for these kinds of acts. The foreign state which, by its own acts has made itself equal to private persons will neither have immunity from jurisdiction nor execution. Measures of execution can be taken

---

25. For ships: Brussels Convention for the Unification of Certain Rules relating to the Immunity of State-Owned Vessels, 1926, 176 L.N.T.S. 199, Arts. 1-3; the Geneva Convention on the Territorial Sea and Contiguous Zone, 1958, 516 U.N.T.S. 205, Arts. 18-20; the Geneva Convention on the High Seas, 1958, 450 U.N.T.S. 82, Arts. 8,9; United Nations Convention on the Law of the Sea, 1982, U.N. Doc. A/CONF.62/121; for aircrafts: the Rome Convention for the Unification of Certain Rules relating to the Precautionary Attachment of Aircrafts, 1933, 192 L.N.T.S. 289; for diplomatic and consular property: the Vienna Convention on Diplomatic Relations, 1961, 500 U.N.T.S. 95; the Vienna Convention on Consular Relations, 1963, 596 U.N.T.S. 261; the New York Convention on Special Missions, 1969, 9 I.L.M. 127 (1970); the Vienna Convention on the Representation of States in Their Relations with International Organisations of a Universal Character, 1975, U.N. Doc. A/CONF. 67/16.
26. *See* Crawford, *supra* note 22, at 821-822; *see also*, ILC Draft Articles, Arts. 16,18,19.
27. *See* Harvard Law Scool Draft Convention on Competence of Courts in Regard to Foreign States, 26 AJIL supp. (1932) at 706.

against property which is used in activities that equate the position of the state with that of a private person.

However, this is not the distinction between immunity from jurisdiction and execution which is found in practice. In many states which restrict the immunity from jurisdiction of a foreign state, the immunity from execution is still either absolute or far less restricted.[28] This distinction is the result of political and economical reasons. Whereas an unfavourable ruling by a court will only cause nominal harm to the interests of a foreign state, the execution of its property will actually be felt. This might have negative consequences for the relations between the state whose court authorised the execution and the state whose property has been attached.[29] To avoid such conflicts, several states reserve a role for the Executive in procedures to execute judgements against a foreign state.[30] Even in the states where the procedures are left to the courts, the political impact of the execution would appear to be incorporated in their legal considerations. These problems with immunity from execution will subsequently be discussed when dealing with the problem of the enforcement of arbitral awards.

3.   ARBITRATION

3.1 .   Arbitration and state immunity

The application of an arbitration agreement between a state and a private party can be frustrated by the immunity of the state.[31] This is especially so in cases where the private party tries to enforce an award rendered against a state. Municipal law provides the only recourse for enforcing an arbitral award. If the state can not be forced by its own courts to comply with the award, the private party is compelled to enforce the award in another country. Here, the enforcement may be hindered by the immunity from both jurisdiction and execution of the foreign state. The concept of the dual personality of the state provides a good basis for resolving problems of state immunity in the enforcement of arbitral awards.

3.2.   Advantages of arbitration in legal relations between states and private persons

Arbitration provides parties in a legal relationship with a means to settle disputes outside the normal judicial process. It gives parties great freedom in choosing

28. Crawford, *supra* note 22, at 820; Schreuer, *supra* note 2, at 126.
29. *See* Bouchez, *supra* note 2, at 19; G. Bernini and A.J. van den Berg, *The Enforcement of Arbitral Awards Against a State: The Problem of Immunity from Execution, in* J.D.M. Lew (ed.), Contemporary Problems in International Arbitration 360 (1986).
30. *See* Delaume , *supra* note 22, at 1.
31. *See* Scheuer, *supra* note 2, at 63-91.

arbitrators, applicable law and rules of procedure. Furthermore, conventions for the recognition and enforcement of arbitral awards have increased the effectiveness of international arbitration.[32]

Arbitration is often used in contracts between private persons and states. It provides flexibility suitable to solve problems that arise from the inclusion of provisions of dispute settlement in these contracts. The private party will be reluctant to be subjected to the law and jurisdiction of its state counterpart. The state can change the law and leave the private party with no legal protection. The state-party will object to being subject to the laws and jurisdiction of another state. By using arbitration, the parties are able to formulate the applicable law in such a way that it will not enable a party to alter the content of that law unilaterally. It is also possible to 'internationalize' the procedure so that the arbitration takes place outside the jurisdiction of any municipal court.[33] However for the enforcement of an award, parties still have to depend on municipal courts.[34] Whether a private party can enforce an arbitral award against a state depends on the state's immunity rules.

3.3.   Enforcement of arbitral awards

The enforcement of an arbitral award can be divided into two phases.[35] In the first phase, the arbitral award has to be recognised as a legally binding decision under the law of the forum state. This recognition will take the form of a confirmation, an exequatur or a similar proceeding. During these proceedings, the defendant state can raise a plea of immunity from jurisdiction in order to prevent the recognition of the award.

The second phase consists of measures of execution against the property of the defendant state. In this phase, the state can try to prevent the enforcement of the award

---

32. The New York Convention on the Recognition and Enforcement of Foreign Arbitral Awards of 1958 [hereinafter New York Concention], 330 U.N.T.S. 38; The European Convention on International Commercial Arbitration of 1961, 484 U.N.T.S. 349; The Inter-American Convention on International Commercial Arbitration of 1975, 14 I.L.M. 336 (1975).

33. 'Internationalized' arbitration can take place under auspices of the International Centre for the Settlement of Investment Disputes (hereinafter ICSID) according to the Convention for the Settlement of Disputes Between States and Nationals of Other States of 1965, 575 U.N.T.S. 160, the International Chamber of Commerce or national law, S. Ward Attenbury, *Enforcement of A-National Arbitral Awards Under the New York Convention of 1958*, 32 VJIL 471-515 (1992); *see also* A.J. van den Berg, The New York Arbitration Convention of 1958, 34-43 (1981).

34. Scheuer, *supra* note 2, at 63.

35. This separation is also applied in the ICSID Convention: Art. 54 obliges each Contracting State to recognize an ICSID award and treat the award as if it were a final judgement of its court while Art. 55 provides that Art. 54 shall not be construed as derogating from the law on immunity from execution in any Contracting State, A. Broches, *Awards Rendered Pursuant to the ICSID Convention*, 2 ICSID Rev. 287-334 (1987).

by claiming immunity from execution.

According to the concept of the dual personality of the state, a state is not entitled to immunity in procedures relating to arbitration. By agreeing to arbitrate, a state submits itself to a procedure in which the parties are equal. After the state has consented in assuming a procedural position which is equal to a private party, it should maintain that position not only throughout the arbitration procedure but also during the proceedings relating to the enforcement of the award. As a result the state ought to be subject to the same measures of enforcement as a private party.

3.4.   Recognition of an arbitral award and state immunity from jurisdiction

An agreement to arbitrate is often seen as a waiver of immunity from jurisdiction in, or implied consent to, judicial procedures relating to the arbitration.[36] In some countries this waiver is also considered to apply to proceedings for recognition of an award,[37] the reasoning being that the recognition is part of the arbitration process.[38] By submitting to arbitration the state has accepted that a municipal court may recognize the award. This view was expressed by the French *Cour de Cassation* in the *SOABI v. Senegal case*:

> Whereas [...] a foreign state that has submitted to arbitration, in doing so, has accepted that the award may be granted *exequatur* [...].[39]

The same position was taken by the US Congress when enacting the FSIA. It was expected that an action for recognition and enforcement of an award could be brought under Section 1605(a)(1) FSIA.[40] According to this subsection, a foreign state has no immunity from jurisdiction when it has "waived its immunity either explicitly or by implication".

This provision was considered too ambiguous to provide guidance in cases relating to the role of US courts in arbitration outside the US.[41] In 1988 therefore, the

---

36. *Cf.* European Convention Art. 12; ILC Draft Articles, Art. 17; FSIA Sec. 1605(a)(6); SIA Sec. 9; Australian Act Sec. 17(c).
37. Sweden, Libyan American Oil Company *v.* Socialist People's Arab Republic of Libya, judgement of June 18, 1980, Svea Court of Appeals, Swed., 62 I.L.R. 225 (1982); France, Société Européenne et d'Entreprises *v.* Yugoslvia, judgement of Nov. 18, 1986, Cass., Fr, 26 I.L.M. 373 (1987).
38. G.R. Delaume, *State Contracts and Transnational Arbitration*, 75 AJIL 816 (1981): "[Recognition] is the natural complement of the binding character of any agreement to submit to arbitration and should not be impaired by considerations of immunity, which are proper to matters of execution".
39. Judgement of June 11, 1991, Cass., Fr., 30 I.L.M. 1167 (1991).
40. M.B. Feldman, *Foreign Sovereign Immunity in the US*, 19 Vand. J. Transnat'l L. 37 (1986); A.L. Rothstein, *Recognizing and Enforcing Arbitral Agreements and Awards against Foreign States: The Mathias Amendments to the Foreign State Immunities Act and Title 9*, 1 Emory J.Int'l.Dispute Resolution 108 (1986).
41. *See* Feldman, *supra* note 40, at 37; Rothstein, *supra* note 40, at 108.

FSIA was amended by adding subsection 1605(a)(6),[42] which explicitly deals with arbitration. Under the current FSIA, a foreign state is not immune in a case in which an action is brought to confirm an arbitration award. However, there are two requirements to be fulfilled in order for a court to have jurisdiction. Firstly, the subject matter of the arbitration must be capable of settlement by arbitration under US law.[43] Secondly the arbitration must have a connection with the US.

The first requirement which links recognition to the subject matter of the arbitration seems similar to certain requirements found in the arbitration law of other countries but is different. Under the Australian Act, a foreign state is not immune in a proceeding concerning the recognition of an arbitral award if that state "would not be immune in a proceeding concerning [the] transaction or event" which is the subject matter of the arbitration.[44] This Australian requirement limits a court's power to recognise a foreign arbitral award to cases in which the foreign state would not have been immune in proceedings on the merits, under the Australian Act. According to Australian law, therefore, an agreement to arbitrate does not constitute a waiver of immunity from jurisdiction to recognise an arbitral award.

This position is comparable with the approach of Dutch courts. In proceedings for the recognition of foreign arbitral awards against a foreign state, courts in The Netherlands, in determining whether the foreign state was entitled to immunity from jurisdiction have applied the *acta iure imperii/acta iure gestionis* test on the subject of the arbitration. It is noteworthy that the conclusion of the contract containing the arbitration clause, on an equal footing between the foreign state and its private counterpart, was considered to be an indication that the case comprised *acta iure gestionis.*[45]

The first mentioned FSIA requirement is not concerned with the question whether the foreign state would be immune in proceedings on the subject matter of the arbitration.[46] It merely tests whether the dispute is suitable for settlement through arbitration according to US law. This is not a genuine problem of state immunity and is therefore consistent with the view maintained in the FSIA, that an agreement to arbitrate constitutes a waiver from jurisdiction in proceedings relating to the arbitration including recognition of the award.

The second requirement in Section 1605(a)(6) FSIA is a territorial connection between the arbitration and the US. The Section lists four cases in which a connection is present;

42. Amendments to the FSIA, *supra* note 7.
43. *Cf.* Sweden Court of Appeals, *supra* note 37.
44. Australian Act Sec. 17(2).
45. Société Européenne et d'Entreprises *v.* Socialistische Republiek Joegoslavië, judgement of Oct. 26, 1973, HR, 1974 NJ 361 Neth, 65 I.L.R. 356 (1984); NV Cabolent *v.* National Iranian Oil Company, judgement of Nov. 28, 1968, Ger., 1969 NJ 484, Neth, 47 I.L.R. 138 (1974).
46. *Cf.* Art. V 2(a) New York Convention.

a. the arbitration took place in the US;
b. the award is governed by a treaty calling for the recognition and enforcement of arbitral awards;
c. the underlying claim, save for the agreement to arbitrate, was within the jurisdiction of a US Court;
d. a, b or c are not applicable but the foreign state has otherwise waived its immunity explicitly or by implication.

As has been said, the requirement of a territorial connection is an issue of jurisdiction and should not be included in a rule on state immunity.[47] The requirement of a territorial connection in proceedings for the recognition of international arbitral awards is exceptionally harmful. It may limit the possibility to enforce an award against a state to the courts of the state in which the arbitration took place. The FSIA requirement is not that strict. The provision which allows jurisdiction in cases in which a treaty is applicable provides a private party with practically the same remedies for recognition of an award as its state counterpart.

Other statutes on state immunity do not require a territorial connection in a proceeding for the recognition of an arbitral award. Article 9 of the SIA denies a foreign state immunity in proceedings relating to arbitration and does not mention the requirement of a territorial or other connection.[48] The Australian Act is even more clear and expressly excludes a requirement of a territorial connection. Under Section 17(2), a foreign state is not immune in proceedings concerning the recognition of an award, "wherever the award was made".

The requirement of a territorial connection is among civil law countries only found in the jurisprudence of Switzerland.[49] The Dutch Supreme Court denied that international law demanded the existence of a connection between a dispute and the forum state for a court to assume jurisdiction in cases in which one of the parties is a foreign state.[50] This is not contrary to the position of the Swiss Federal Court which emphasizes that the requirement of a territorial connection in proceedings in which one party is a state, is a rule of domestic law not derived from international law.[51]

3.5.   The New York Convention

In proceedings for the recognition of international arbitral awards against foreign states, issues of state immunity should not be confused with those of general jurisdiction. The question whether any foreign arbitral award can be recognised

---

47. *See* text *supra*, 2.4.
48. *But see,* H. Fox, *States and the Undertaking to Arbitrate,* 37 ICLQ 1-29 (1988).
49. Libya *v.* Libyan American Oil Company, judgement of June 19, 1980, BGE, Switz, 62 I.L.R. 228 (1982).
50. Judgement of Oct. 26, 1973, *supra* note 45.
51. Text *infra* 3.6.

depends on the municipal law of the forum state. The recognition can for instance depend on a territorial connection or whether the subject is capable of settlement by arbitration. A uniform basis for the application of the law is created by the New York Convention on the Recognition and Enforcement of Foreign Arbitral Awards, adopted in 1958.[52]

According to Article 1 of the New York Convention, contracting states will apply the provisions of the Convention in cases of recognition and enforcement of an arbitral award made in the territory of another contracting state. The Convention enables a court of a contracting state to confine itself to testing the applicability of the New York Convention, in cases relating to the recognition of a foreign arbitral award. When the New York Convention is applicable recognition of an award can only be refused on the limited grounds of Article 5. As a result of the large number of contracting states,[53] the New York Convention provides parties to an arbitral agreement, falling within the scope of the Convention, with many fora for the recognition of an award. When the New York Convention, or a similar treaty, can not be applied, recognition may be possible in countries were the arbitration law is favourable to recognition of foreign awards.[54]

The New York Convention does not refer to the problem of state immunity. This is in accordance with the above mentioned opinion that state immunity should not be confused with the issue of jurisdiction. A court has to solve the problem whether the recognition of foreign arbitral awards falls within its jurisdiction separately from the question wether a foreign state is immune from jurisdiction in the proceedings relating to the recognition of the award.

3.6. State immunity from jurisdiction as an obstacle in procedures to recognize an arbitral award

On the issue of state immunity from jurisdiction in proceedings related to the recognition of an award, two schools of thought can be distinguished. In some countries, the arbitration agreement is considered to be a waiver of immunity from jurisdiction in proceedings relating to recognition of an award. In other countries a claim of state immunity is treated according to the general rules on state immunity of the forum state. Such a claim will succeed when the foreign state would have enjoyed immunity, under those rules, in proceedings on the subject matter of the arbitration.

52. *Supra* note 32; Van den Berg, *supra* note 33.
53. 84 in 1991, Multilateral Treaties Deposited with the Secretary General, 1992, UN Doc. ST/LEG/ SER.E/10.
54. *E.g.* Dutch Code of Civil Procedure Art. 1076, P.Sanders and A.J. van den Berg, The Netherlands Arbitration Act 1986 48 (1987); French Code of Civil Procedure Arts. 1501-1507, 20 I.L.M. 920-922 (1981).

The advantage of the first approach is that a local court where recognition is sought will abstain from any judgement on the merits of the arbitration. The function of a court in a proceeding for the recognition of an arbitral award should be limited to the assessment whether the arbitrators acted within their mandate. The court should refrain from any comment on the judgement of the arbitrators. This judgement is after all the result of the consent of the parties to grant the arbitrators a mandate to settle their dispute.[55] The addition of Section 15 to the arbitration law of the US,[56] therefore, has been a valuable part of the codification of the principle to consider an arbitration agreement as waiver of immunity. According to Section 15, the recognition of an arbitral award can not be refused on the basis of the Act of State doctrine.[57]

In practice the second approach leaves little opportunity for a successful claim of state immunity to prevent the recognition of an arbitral award. By far, most arbitration agreements between a state and a private person will relate to commercial matters, so the state will not enjoy immunity in the legal system which adheres to the second school. It is, after all, difficult for a private person to engage in a legal relationship concerning a sovereign or governmental matter. An advantage of the New York Convention in this respect, is that a contracting state can make a declaration that it will only apply the Convention to commercial arbitration.[58] In this way a contracting state which considers an arbitration agreement as a waiver from immunity, can protect itself against unwanted involvement with any non commercial dispute.

This survey of the national law of several countries justifies the conclusion that state immunity from jurisdiction does not prevent the recognition of an arbitral award in legal systems were the state immunity is restricted. In these systems an arbitral award made against a state will be recognized without the explicit waiver of immunity from jurisdiction by that state.

3.7.   Execution of an arbitral award and state immunity from execution

The purpose of the recognition of an award is to obtain a title for measures of execution. Only through forceful measures can a victorious litigant acquire satisfaction of its claim against a noncooperative party. When that party is a state, such measures will be frustrated due to the immunity from execution of that state. As said before the immunity from execution should only be granted to a state which is immune from jurisdiction. Property owned by the state in its non-immune capacity should not be

---

55. *See Cour de Cassation, supra* note 37.
56. 28 I.L.M. 397 (1989).
57. *But cf.* Libyan American Oil Company v. Socialist People's Libyan Arab Jamahiriya, 482 F.Supp. 1175 (D.D.C.1980), 62 I.L.R. 220 (1982).
58. Art. I.

protected by the immunity from execution. If all property of a private party is liable for measures of execution, so should be the property of the non-immune state.

In some countries there is no distinction between immunity from jurisdiction and execution. This view is upheld by courts in Belgium,[59] Switzerland,[60] the Netherlands[61] and Germany.[62] Those courts have decided that a state which, in a particular case, does not enjoy immunity from jurisdiction is also not entitled to immunity from execution. This does not mean that all property of a foreign state is liable for attachment. Property in use for public purposes is not suitable for measures of execution. The problem of execution therefore is limited to the assessment of the function of the property against which measures are sought.[63]

There are also states in which the problem of immunity from execution is treated separately from that of jurisdiction. With regard to the enforcement of arbitral awards the question is whether an arbitration agreement is considered to be an implied waiver from immunity from execution. At the moment, only US law considers an arbitration agreement as an autonomous ground for denial of immunity from execution.[64] As a result of the Amendments to the FSIA of 1988, Section 1610(a)(6) was added. According to Section 1610(a)(6) property of a foreign state used for a commercial activity, shall not be immune from execution upon a judgment based on an order confirming an arbitral award against that state.

In other countries where immunity from jurisdiction and immunity from execution are treated as different concepts the possibilities of executing an arbitral award after it has been recognised, are very limited or completely absent. The distinction between immunity from jurisdiction and execution is, in my opinion, based on political considerations which reflect the sensitivity of inter-state relations for measures of execution. These political motivations for distinguishing between jurisdiction and execution are obvious in countries where Executive authorization is required for

59. Socobel *v.* Greek State, judgement of April 30, 1951, Belg., 18 I.L.R. 3 (1951).

60. République Arabe Unie *v.* Dame *X*, judgement of Feb. 10, 1960, BGE, Switz, 55 AJIL 167 (1961), but Swiss Courts require a territorial connection for jurisdiction in proceedings for authorizing measures of execution, *e.g.* judgement of June 19,1980, *supra* note 49; *see also* J.F. Lalive, *Swiss Law and Practice in Relation to Measures of Execution against the Propertry of a Foreign State*, 10 NYBIL 153 (1979); *infra* p. 24.

61. Judgement of Nov. 28, 1968, *supra* note 45.

62. Philippine Embassy Bank Account, judgement of Dec. 13, 1977, 45 BVerwG 342, W. Ger., 65 I.L.R. 146 (1984).

63. *Cf.* Art. 13(4)(b) SIA; Section 32 Australian Act.

64. *E.g.* Birch Shipping Cor. *v.* Embassy of the United Republic of Tanzania, 507 F.Supp. 311 (D.D.C. 1980), 63 I.L.R. 524 (1982).

measures of execution against the property of a foreign state.[65] But even in countries where that decision is left to the courts, political considerations limit the cases in which attachment of property of a foreign state is possible.

Why should, for instance, the immunity of a foreign state demand that property which has no connection with the object of the claim is immune from execution?[66] The object of such a requirement appears to be to limit the exception to the immunity from execution to cases in which the denial of justice to the private party would amount to greater embarrassment than the injury to the relation with the foreign state. The requirement of a connection between the property and the activity on which the claim is based will, in general, narrow the number of persons who can obtain satisfaction of their claim through execution. Only persons engaged in economic activity with the foreign state within the territory of the forum state will be part of this select group.

The Swiss requirement of a territorial connection in proceedings for authorization of measures of execution against property of a foreign state is also a manifestation of Swiss national interest.[67] In the *LIAMCO case,* the Federal Supreme Court stated:

> [it] does not substantively make any sense, to permit any legal actions against foreign states if a somewhat intensive domestic relationship is lacking. The interests of Switzerland do not require such a procedure; they could, on the contrary, easily cause political and other difficulties.[68]

The question is whether it is the function of a court to serve the interest of the state or the interest of justice. In addition, one might wonder if it is not in the ultimate interest of a state for its courts to do justice.

The requirement in any way creates disadvantages for a private person trying to enforce an arbitral award. While all his property is liable for execution, in all countries which recognise the arbitration award, the same measures can only be taken against the property of the state party if certain requirements are fulfilled. Any requirement that is not intended to protect the exercise of sovereign power of a foreign state should, in my opinion, not be included in a rule of immunity from execution. If political motives are included in the considerations on whether measures of execution can be taken against the property of a foreign state, the outcome will be unpredictable.

65. *See* Delaume, *supra* note 22; in the Netherlands the Minister of Justice can prevent measures of execution against the property of a foreign State if in his opinion such measures would be contrary to international law. However this decision can be reviewed by a court which will apply the rule that measures of execution can be taken against property not in use for public purposes. The court therefore, will make the final decision. Krijgman case, judgement of Nov. 24, 1986, Pr. Afd. Rechtspr., Neth., 19 NYIL 439 (1988).
66. EURODIF Corporation *v.* Islamic Republic of Iran, judgement of March 14, 1984, Cass., Fr. 77 I.L.R. 513 (1988); I.L.C. Draft Articles, Art. 18(1)(c).
67. *See* Trooboff, *supra* note 2, at 388.
68. Judgement of June 19, 1980, *supra* note 49.

4.   CONCLUSION

Why is it essential for the Rules of the PCA to contain a waiver of immunity from execution? It is clear that at the present moment the rules relating to immunity from execution are far from uniform. As a result the outcome of a procedure to enforce an arbitral award against a state is very unpredictable. This greatly reduces the usefulness of arbitration in providing legal protection to the private party. In the words of Scheuer:

> [...] the entire object and usefulness of arbitration depends on the effective implementation of awards against the losing party even if it happens to be a foreign state.[69]

Existing arbitration institutions have been confronted with this problem. Even the ICSID arbitration, which is successful as a self-contained truly international procedure, has in certain cases, left private parties empty handed.[70] Without a waiver of immunity from execution, the PCA will not be able to improve legal protection to private parties.

Additionally, the uncertain status of the law is also a disadvantage for states. They do not know if and, if so, which property is protected by the different rules on immunity from execution. Of course it can be argued that some immunity is better than none, but there is a price to be paid. The lack of legal protection will entail a greater risk for private persons in their transactions with a state. This results in higher prices for goods and services rendered to the state in these transactions. Once these costs were compensated by the certainty that state property was not liable to execution measures. Now this is no longer the case. At present, the state still has to pay risk premiums while it is not certain whether an award rendered against it will result in execution against its property or not.

By including a waiver of immunity from execution in the PCA Rules a new arbitration process can be created. This process should be characterized by the equality of the parties. The parties should not only have the same rights and obligations during the arbitration procedure itself but also in the enforcement process in municipal courts. In this way the parties will bring a greater predictability into their relationship and the function of the arbitration agreement as a legal protection for both parties will increase. Inevitably, this will lead to economical benefits for both sides.

---

69. *See* Scheuer, *supra* note 2, at 75.
70. *See* Broches, *supra* note 35.

Through the concept of the dual personality of the state, it has been demonstrated that a legal relationship between a private person and a state on the basis of an equal position under the law can function without interference with the sovereignty and independence of that state. By including a waiver of immunity from execution in the PCA Rules, states will not waive a right they possess under international law. They will merely contribute to a uniform application of the principle of state immunity. It will be necessary to draft a balanced waiver which will make a clear distinction between property in use for public purposes and property liable for measures of execution. In this way, the interests of both states and private parties will be served.

CONCLUDING OBSERVATIONS

I. Stephen M. Schwebel[*]

The editors of the *Leiden Journal of International Law* -a new and promising addition to burgeoning literature of periodicals in the field, and one to be particularly welcomed in Europe where student-edited journals are unusual- have invited me to comment on the papers of this *Special Issue*, insofar as they were in hand by February, 1993. It is a pleasure to do so.

It is a particular pleasure to find that the Secretary-General of the United Nations has written a graceful introduction to the volume. It is a source of gratification to students of international law and organization the world over that so distinguished an international lawyer, a former professor who has specialized for decades in problems of international organization, and a diplomat with an extraordinary record of courageous accomplishment, should today occupy the summit of the United Nations system. His preparation of the introduction to this volume, as well as his continued active participation in the work of the Curatorium of The Hague Academy of International Law despite the demands of his office, illustrate his abiding academic interest in questions of international law. His concern with the practical impact of international law on the daily life of the Organization he heads is an inevitable element of his work as Secretary-General.

The late Judge Manfred Lachs, in what may be the last of his many writings to be published, and to whom this Special Issue is so rightly dedicated, has provided an essay on the role of equity in arbitration and in judicial settlement of international disputes. In his twenty-six years as a Judge of the International Court of Justice, and in an arbitral career that stretched over some forty-five years, Manfred Lachs was a persistent proponent both of the peaceful settlement of international disputes and the infusion of equitable considerations into the substance of such settlement. His essay does not attempt to isolate the essential qualities of equity, whose content in the abstract, however real, is necessarily elusive. Thus when he characterizes the objective of an 'equitable solution', as referred to in Article 83 of the Third United Nations Convention on the Law of the Sea, as 'explicit' and 'precise', generosity may have overtaken accuracy. In fact the terms of Article 83 leave the evolving law of international maritime delimitation in a state of singular flexibility in which firm principles are hard to find. The treatment by the International Court of Justice and

---

[*] Judge of the International Court of Justice, arbitrator in various international commercial arbitrations, and author of International Arbitration: Three Salient Problems (1987).

S. Muller and W. Mijs (eds.), The Flame Rekindled, 177–185.

by international arbitral tribunals of the equidistance principle, to which Judge Lachs refers, may have merit but such merit as it has is not to be found in the guidance the resultant case law gives to law-makers or interpreters. Some may regret that the law did not develop in the contrary direction of treating equidistance as a rule of law which had been accepted into the body of general international law - as Judge Lachs maintained was the state of the law in his penetrating dissent to the Court's Judgement in the *North Sea Continental Shelf* cases. But that is an aside; his essay as a whole gives a fine sense of the importance of equity both in international judicial and international arbitral practice.

A central theme of the *Special Issue* is reviving and extending the utility of the Permanent Court of Arbitration. That is a worthy and sensible objective, which is furthered by the paper of the able Secretary-General of the International Bureau of the Permanent Court of Arbitration, P.J.H. Jonkman. It neatly summarizes the origins and accomplishments of the Permanent Court of Arbitration, and shows that its contemporary contributions to the peaceful settlement of international disputes are more numerous and varied than is generally appreciated. In the last decade, the Permanent Court of Arbitration has been particularly useful in the assistance it has rendered to the operations of the Iran-United States Claims Tribunal, and to various other arbitrations, in its designation of the appointing authority. Mr. Jonkman's paper rightly stresses two cardinal considerations: first, that under the UNCITRAL Rules and the 1992 Permanent Court of Arbitration Optional Rules for Arbitrating Disputes between two States, parties may exercise their autonomy to modify the Rules; second, that once parties have committed themselves to the legal remedy of arbitration, they are bound to perform their obligations in good faith. The considerable potential of the Permanent Court of Arbitration in a number of diverse respects is economically set out in Mr. Jonkman's valuable contribution.

A second, very solid contribution to the revival of the Permanent Court of Arbitration is found in the essay of Mr. J.L. Bleich. In lucid detail, Mr. Bleich provides an exhaustive survey of the process and product of the revision of the Rules of the Permanent Court of Arbitration for inter-state arbitration. That revision builds upon and adapts the UNCITRAL Rules in ways which Mr. Bleich fully sets out.

Judge Howard M. Holtzmann, a member of the Iran-United States Claims Tribunal, one of the principal draftsmen of the UNCITRAL Model Law, and an expert in international commercial arbitration, has drawn on his great experience in the field to write a perceptive comparative analysis of the processes of adjudication by the International Court of Justice and arbitration under the UNCITRAL Rules. He isolates and appraises similarities and differences in those processes. He finds that they share the vital characteristic that, once their jurisdiction has been accepted and activated, it may not be nullified by one party acting unilaterally. Judge Holtzmann's essay is prefaced by a useful summation of contemporary services of the Permanent Court of Arbitration.

Professor Pieter Sanders, the ever youthful 'grand old man' of international commercial arbitration, whose contributions to the principles and practice of modern arbitration are numberless, has provided a further essay on the Permanent Court of Arbitration which concentrates on arbitration between states and private parties. Arbitration between states and private parties is one of the most significant areas of contemporary arbitral practice. It is an area of special fascination to the lawyer, blending as it may considerations of national law with international law and on occasion adding general principles of law common to the parties or applied in international commerce. Professor Sanders' essay is useful in its provision of a preview of some essential elements of what special rules of the Permanent Court of Arbitration for arbitration between a State and a private party might contain. He particularly recommends waiver by the state of immunity from execution. Once such a set of Rules is agreed upon, based upon the UNCITRAL Rules which themselves enjoy such contemporary and universal provenance, the Permanent Court of Arbitration will be equipped with two sets of modern Rules, one for inter-state arbitrations and another for arbitrations between states and private parties.

The question of state immunity from execution of international arbitral awards is critically pursued in a contribution by A. van Blankenstein. He recommends that the nascent rules of the Permanent Court of Arbitration for arbitrating between a state and a non-state party clarify an uncertain area of the law by including an explicit waiver of state immunity from execution. At this writing, the issue is unsettled, but the current draft of the rules includes a provision for waiver of immunity from jurisdiction but not from execution. At the same time, the draft rules append optional language which the parties may use to provide also for waiver of immunity from execution.

Professor Edward McWhinney has contributed a stimulating essay entitled "The International Court as Constitutional Court and the Blurring of the Arbitral/Judicial Processes". His personal reflections as a former member of the Canadian National Group in the Permanent Court of Arbitration are of particular interest. He concludes that the process of National Groups in the Permanent Court of Arbitration nominating candidates for election as Judges of the International Court of Justice should be changed to provide for nomination by Foreign Ministries, i.e., by governments of the states Parties to the Statute of the Court. (Precisely that change of the Statute of the Permanent Court of International Justice was considered when the Statute was modestly revised in connection with the adoption of the United Nations Charter. It was a plausible proposal of the United States which was successfully opposed by the United Kingdom, whose proposition prevailed on the ground that the statutory system had worked well in the inter-war years). Professor McWhinney describes the workings of the Canadian National Group in support of his conclusion. Yet it appears that the Canadian National Group has functioned as a very model of a National Group. Its experience, far from suggesting stripping National Groups of the function of nominating candidates for the Court, rather suggests that other National Groups would do well to emulate the Canadian.

The problem with the current system of nominations being made by National Groups is, it is believed, precisely the contrary of that perceived by Professor McWhinney. He sees the current process as unduly apolitical: National Groups, he indicates, are sufficiently susceptible to the political considerations to which governments are sensitive and -he also seems to imply- National Groups may consider the qualifications of candidates rather than their electability. However, in fact too many National Groups may act as appendages of their Foreign Ministries, expressing the political judgement of those Foreign Ministries, and too few may act with objectivity about the qualifications of candidates. Nevertheless, in some states fortunate enough to be governed democratically, National Groups may actually enjoy the independence which the Statute of the International Court of Justice seems to contemplate; for example, that is the case not only in Canada, but Sweden, the Netherlands, Luxembourg, Greece, the United Kingdom, and the United States.

To illustrate my disagreement with Professor McWhinney's prescription, I may recall that if the U.S. Department of State, rather than the U.S. National Group, had been entrusted with the authority to nominate candidates for the Court, neither Professor Philip C. Jessup nor Professor Richard R. Baxter would have been nominated. The result would have been that of two of the most distinguished of American Judges who have sat on the Court would never have been elected. Professor Jessup was nominated by the U.S. National Group in the teeth of an Administration which not long before had blocked his casual election to the International Law Commission, essentially because Jessup had become controversial as the victim of slander by Senator McCarthy. Professor Baxter, while not politically objectionable, was decidedly not the choice of the then Legal Adviser of the US Department of State, because the then President of the United States had innocently assured former Supreme Court Justice and former Ambassador Arthur J. Goldberg that the job would be his. In neither case was the US National Group deterred from making nominations which its canvassing of learned societies, members of the U.S. Supreme Court, deans of some law schools and others had shown had predominant support. Would the Court and the cause of international law have been better served by excluding Jessup and Baxter on political grounds?

Rather than amending the Statute of the Court to meet Professor McWhinney's prescription (and amending the Statute of itself is a formidable problem, not to be lightly undertaken), the Statute as written should be more fully implemented. It recommends that, before making nominations, each National Group should "consult its highest court of justice, its legal faculties and schools of law, and its national academies and national sections of international academies devoted to the study of law". Now it may be that, as Professor McWhinney indicates, all of such bodies may not be informed about persons who would be suitable candidates for the Court in their own and other countries. But some of them may be informed; and the very process of consulting them may produce a wider awareness in influential circles of the Court and of international legal ability. The United States National Group embarked upon such a system of consultation in 1960 and it has worked well since.

There are other passages in Professor McWhinney's lively contribution which are open to question. The claim that, prior to 1971, the Court (and the PCIJ) were "essentially legalistic, dominated by classical, 'black-letter-law' theories of legal interpretation and the judicial process generally" whereas thereafter "more consciously activist, policy-making conceptions of the judicial role" have prevailed may be overdrawn. Were the Court's opinions in *Reparations for Injuries Suffered in the Service of the United Nations* (1948) and in *Reservations to the Convention on the Prevention and Punishment of the Crime of Genocide* (1950) legalistic and black-letter? And what if a consciously activist, policy-making conception of the judicial role -not necessarily good or bad of itself- in the particular case leads to a purported statement of the law which is an expression of regressive rather than progressive policy? There is room to debate whether courts should be policy-oriented or not; in some measure, the judge is inevitably policy oriented whether or not he knows it or intends it; but in any event is there ground for the apparent assumption that the purported post-1971 policy is inviariably desirable? Nor is it so clear that the members of the Arbitral Tribunal in the *Beagle Channel* case -all of whom were eminent Judges of the International Court of Justice- were, in Professor McWhinney's term, 'confused'. There is room for more than one view about the merits of the *Beagle Channel* judgement as there is about most judgements, just as there is room for more measured judgement as to where to strike the balance between applying and adjusting the law.

As to Professor McWhinney's criticism of the legality of the action of the Court in constituting the Chamber in the *Gulf of Maine* case, what is clear to him about the letter and intent of the Court's Statute and Rules was not clear to the large majority of the Members of the Court. Counsel in cases before the Court, and the Court itself, as well its Members writing individual opinions, have given no less weight to judgements of Chambers of the Court than to judgements of the full Court. The four Chamber judgements rendered to date are fully on a par with judgements of the Court as a whole; they may be subject to one or another criticism, but that is no less true of judgements of the Court as a whole. Chamber judgements show no sign of regional or ideological or other questionable particularity.

To view the creation of *ad hoc* Chambers as a kind of Cold War manoeuvre of doubtful legality -as apparently does Professor McWhinney-is a misperception. The provision for *ad hoc* Chambers was written into the Statute of the Court when it was revised at the San Francisco Conference, before the outbreak of the Cold War; and the provision of the Rules of Court providing that the President may consult with the Parties on the composition of a Chamber was adopted, at the suggestion of Sweden, Cyprus and the United Kingdom among others, under the leadership of Judge

Manfred Lachs and Judge Eduardo Jiménez de Aréchaga, neither easily cast as 'cold warriors'. The states having recourse to *ad hoc* Chambers have been not only those belonging to NATO, but Burkina Faso and Mali, and El Salvador and Honduras, as well. The practice and prospects of *ad hoc* Chambers surely are open to more than one view, but the picture is not so shadowed and outmoded as that suggested by Professor McWhinney.

The essay on "The International Court of Justice and International Arbitration" by that unmatched scholar of the Court, Shabtai Rosenne, is a characteristically acute consideration of the Court's treatment of aspects of the process of international arbitration. It analyzes how the Court has dealt with disputes over the obligation to submit to arbitration, disputes over the validity of an arbitral award, and appeals to the Court from other bodies - particularly arbitral bodies with a power of dispositive decision. Rosenne describes how the Court has dealt with aspects of what might be called 'classic arbitration' in a half-dozen contentious cases and advisory opinions. He shows how the Court has had a major and predominantly positive influence on aspects of the law of international arbitration. He indicates how the Court has endeavoured to maintain and give effect to the integrity of the system of international arbitration when that is what the compromissory clause requires. He points out how the Court has exerted a measure of control over arbitration procedure without attempting to substitute itself for the arbitral tribunal in adjudging the merits of the underlying dispute. "The case-law shows no sign of competition between arbitration and judicial settlement, both of which are, indeed, placed alongside and on the same footing in Article 33 of the Charter". Dr. Rosenne's article is still another of his many incisive contributions to the analysis of the jurisprudence of the Court. It is reassuring to know that Dr. Rosenne has embarked upon the preparation of a new edition of what is *the* classic learned work on the Court, his two-volume study of *The Law and Practice of the International Court.*

Mr. M.C.W. Pinto, who has been Secretary-General of the Iran-United States Claims Tribunal since its inception, and who is an accomplished international lawyer of wide experience in diplomatic and United Nations fora, has contributed a scholarly essay on "Structure, Process, Outcome: Thoughts on the 'Essence' of International Arbitration". Mr. Pinto places understandable emphasis on the importance of conventions on the peaceful settlement of international disputes being acceptable to all states (as, it may be pointed out -as Samuel K.B. Asante does point out in a subsequent contribution to this volume- is the Statute of the International Court of Justice, an appendix to the Charter of the United Nations). The theme of Mr. Pinto's paper is that the 'judicial' model of international arbitration as it evolved during the twentieth century does not accord with arbitration as it is generally understood among states today, by which he appears to mean mainly non-Western states. Mr. Pinto maintains that certain essential features of arbitration do or should set it apart from judicial determination of a dispute in international law. Among the most important of these distinguishing features in his view is that arbitration accepts the admissibility of decisions *ex aequo et bono*, whereas in the Statute of the International Court of Justice the Court is entitled to decide a case *ex aequo et bono* only if the parties so agree. In fact, as Mr. Pinto himself shows, the difference between those who view international arbitration as akin to a 'judicial' or, once undertaken, a compulsory process, and those who view it as akin to a 'diplomatic' process, in which the participants retain the right to stall or nullify the process, is longstanding, profound, and without regard to North-South, East-West, or developed-developing states considerations.

There is much to be said on both sides of that fundamental divide. Mr. Pinto recalls much of the best that has been said. For this part, he embraces the 'diplomatic' camp, whereas I find myself in the 'judicial'. Mr. Pinto however endeavours to equate the diplomatic view of arbitration with what is the general view of the 'essence' of arbitration, a dubious reading of the history and practice which he himself so elegantly expounds. He appears to believe that judicial arbitration favours the party with greater bargaining power, whereas diplomatic arbitration, preserving as it does a kind of party autonomy, favours the party with lesser bargaining power. That is an analysis to which I do not subscribe. On the contrary, that form of party autonomy may favour the stronger party, the party having the strength to wield in its own interest its freedom from effective legal obligation.

Mr. Pinto's essay treats inter-state arbitration. An important complement to his treatment is provided, in the sphere of international commercial arbitration, by Samuel K.B. Asante, in his paper on "The Perspectives of African Countries on International Commercial Arbitration". A former Solicitor-General of Ghana, and a senior international civil servant with great experience in problems of investment and arbitration in Africa and other developing countries, Mr. Asante sensitively sets out the difficulties which Sub-Saharan African countries have had or believe themselves to have had in international commercial arbitration.

It is reassuring to hear that African countries accept international commercial arbitration as "an invariable ingredient" of the attraction of foreign investment, finance and trade. It is cause for concern to hear that African reservations about actual participation in the process of international commercial arbitration persists. Mr. Asante describes international arbitration "as a foreign system of adjudication in Sub-Saharan Africa". But is not international commercial arbitration, in one degree or another, foreign to every national system? It may be said that its very quality of alienage is its attraction; being 'foreign' to both contending parties, it may be thought to be relatively immune to the particular national perspectives of either. Mr. Asante criticizes the relative rarity of African arbitrators and counsel as participants in arbitrations to which sub-Saharan states are parties, while at the same time observing how little training in international arbitration in Africa has advanced. Surely as that training advances, so will that participation.

Mr. Asante ventures upon deeper waters in suggesting that international commercial arbitration will not attract African states until the rules of international law -the rules of state responsibility- are rewritten so as to take fuller account of the sovereign interests of the host state by imposing restraints and obligations upon foreign companies. This is not the place to debate that large and contentious topic. It is an area in which perspectives differ sharply. Some, unlike Mr. Asante, diagnose the problem differently, finding it to be concentrated as much in the apparently arbitrary impositions of governments upon companies as in the allegedly unrestrained activities of companies. In any event, if the price of wholehearted African governmental participation in international arbitration is the revision in their favour of the law to which they have in large numbers agreed in concluding bilateral investment treaties and other treaties, others may find the price too high. The perception may well exist in Africa that the underlying rules of international law and life are inequitable for developing countries. But there is room for debate about the accuracy and objectivity of that perception, and no less for debate about what precisely can or should be done to amend those rules. The suggestion that arbitration may be unsuitable until the day of such amendment is worrying. Mr. Asante is quite right when he seems to suggest that it is not the function of an international arbitral tribunal to reform the underlying substantive rules; as he says "a renegotiation for the purpose of redressing the inequities of the agreement would seem more profitable". I would observe that it cannot be assumed that inequity is necessarily one-sided, nor should it be overlooked that renegotiation of international investment contracts is frequent. The real power of almost any government to promote renegotiation should not be underestimated, just as the real power of companies to resist governmental directions should not be overestimated.

But while perspectives may differ, the perspective offered so perceptively by Mr. Asante is important and instructive. When he complains of instances in which the substantive law of the host country is designated as the applicable law of the transaction, but nevertheless is not applied by the arbitral tribunal, his complaint is well founded. His exposition of the burdens on African respondents of participation in an arbitration in a far-away city is evocative. But is the cure, as he suggests in this and other respects, to condition the arbitral process upon the respondent's specific assent to the various consequential steps of the parties' agreement to arbitrate? That brings us back to Mr. Pinto's preference for 'diplomatic' as contrasted with 'judicial' arbitration, transposed to the international commercial sphere. The result of such a transposition would be to castrate the process of international commercial arbitration, to imbue it with entrenched uncertainty, to subject it to what might be called 'self-judging' procedures. What would such an innovation do to international trade and investment? Why have provision for and process for international commercial arbitration if one party may lawfully interrupt or nullify the process at will?

In all, this *Special Issue on Arbitration* of the *Leiden Journal of International Law* is a valuable and at times provocative collection, which makes a material contribution to the revival of the Permanent Court of Arbitration and to the jurisprudence both of the International Court of Justice and international arbitration, both inter-state and commercial.

II.   MARCEL BRUS[*]

1.   EQUITY AND THE WORLD LEGAL ORDER

The basic question of this book is about the role of institutionalized arbitration as an effective mechanism for the settlement of disputes in the international legal order. This question not only concerns the specific role of the Permanent Court of Arbitration (PCA), but also has its bearing on wider aspects of the relationships between the various actors in the international community. Steps to enhance the role of one method of dispute settlement or one institution, like the PCA, can only be effective if they are taken against the general background of the changing international environment. It is the assessment of these changes that should form the starting point for such steps. The promotion of a particular method of dispute settlement is of secondary importance. The essential question is, to quote the last sentence of Judge Lachs contribution to this book, how to "respond effectively to the needs of the international community in the interest of peaceful cooperation in many domains of life".

Judge Lachs focused on the role of equity in modern international law. With this he addressed one of the most important aspects in the development of law in the present international community.

As international law is acquiring an ever greater role, equity becomes an indispensable element for the realization of the basic principles that form the foundation of the international legal order. Since the end of the Cold War, the complexity of the relations between the actors in the international community is no longer predominantly reflected in relations of power, but more and more in the framework of principles and rules of international law. This does not mean that power is no longer an important factor in international relations, but it means that the effectuation of the power potential of an actor can be challenged by the international community when the limits of international law are transcended. The recent changes in the world have created the opportunity for the emergence of a true international community, capable of active promotion of the well-being of its members. This however can only be achieved with due respect for the rule of law, because law provides the most objective touchstone for the behaviour of individual actors.

[*] Marcel Brus is lecturer at Leiden University, Department of Public International Law. He is currently finalizing his dissertation on aspects of international dispute settlement.

S. Muller and W. Mijs (eds.), The Flame Rekindled, 187–193.

The international legal order is expanding in scope. Obvious examples are the active engagement of the United Nations in international and internal conflicts, the assistance in processes of democratization, the protection of the environment, and the promotion of sustainable economic development. The engagement of the international community in activities in these areas is no longer purely a matter of compromise between the self-interests of its members, but is becoming an interest of the community itself. In other words, though somewhat exaggerated, coordination is more and more supplemented by communal management. The challenges with which members of the community are faced, simply cannot be resolved unless a common effort is undertaken.

This development is reflected in the rules and principles of international law. New areas of international regulation have emerged (e.g. environmental law), whereas the existing law in other areas is revitalized (e.g. with respect to the active role of the Security Council) or expanded (e.g. in the law of the sea, and in international trade). The consequence of these developments of international law is that an ever larger area of international relations is being governed by international law, thus limiting the individual freedom of the members of the community. Such limitations in the freedom to do as one wishes, can only be acceptable if the rules and principles which are adopted, are based on the conviction of the individual members that they have come into existence in a process in which their legitimate interests have been taken into account, and that the application and interpretation of the rules in concrete cases is safeguarded against a one-sided approach. Within such complex setting it becomes increasingly difficult to predict the effects of the creation of new rules and principles of international law. The legal system becomes an open system, a system in which guidelines for behaviour are laid down, instead of the clear and unequivocal standards which are spelled out in a less sophisticated legal system. The example of the rules concerning the delimitation of the EEZ and the continental shelf as laid down in the 1982 Convention on the Law of the Sea is a case in point.

Furthermore, as the scope of international law is expanding, the chance of conflict between various rules and principles is also increased. Judge Lachs mentioned the decision in the *Guinea v. Guinea Bissau arbitration* in which rules concerning delimitation had to be considered in connection with the rights to development or to security. Another example is offered by the present discussion about the reconcilability of the GATT trade rules with the emerging rules and principles for the protection of the environment. Such conflicts can only be resolved by reference to general principles of the community which outweigh the rules and principles as laid down in a specific legal regime.

In a society in which international law is acquiring a greater role, and in which new principles concerning community interests are added to the existing principles concerning the sovereign interests of states, the function of law is changing. It does not only provide concrete behavioral rules which facilitate the peaceful co-existence and cooperation between the individual members of the community, but it increasingly becomes a central value system in which the individual members participate. The development of the international concern for human rights was one of the first steps in this direction, followed, among others, by the more equivocal right to development, the common heritage principle, and most recently the principles concerning the protection of the natural environment. Developing and accepting such principles requires a continuous balancing of interests between the individual members and the community itself. This requires a legal system with a certain amount of built-in flexibility. The concept of equity is an expression of such flexibility.

Equity and other fundamental principles like solidarity, the basic concern for the well-being of all human beings and democratic equality both within states and between states have an essential role to play in the further development of the international legal system. In today's complex world law cannot perform its proper task without these basic principles. They have become foundations and can no longer be regarded as principles which supplement the existing rules of law. The legitimacy and integrity of the fabric of international law requires the incorporation of these principles in the international legal system, in law-making as well as in the interpretation and application of law, if this system is to respond to the needs of the international community.

2. EQUITY AND INTERNATIONAL DISPUTE SETTLEMENT

The reflections on the role of equity inspired by the article of Judge Lachs, affect the way one looks at the issue of peaceful settlement of international disputes, in particular the role of third party procedures. Judge Lachs limited his comments mainly to the role of equity in the application and interpretation of law by courts or tribunals, but one could go further and extent his views to the role the courts, tribunals or other third party mechanisms have to play in the international legal system of today.

Acceptation of the thesis that equity plays an ever more important role as one of the foundations of international law means that one also has to accept that a higher degree of uncertainty is built into the system. The rights and obligations of the members of the community cannot be determined exactly by looking at the positive rules of law. These rules have to be weighed against each other and against basic principles such as equity in order to determine what conduct is in line with the legitimate expectations of the other members of the community. This means that, in spite of the increased scope of law, the individual freedom of the members of the legal system is not necessarily limited in a manner that is equivalent to the expansion of the rule of law. There will remain ample room for choices in actual behaviour. Such freedom can however only be acceptable if the choices that are made can, in case of conflict, be put to an independent test in order to establish whether the outer limits have been overstepped.

The conclusion seems obvious: a system of compulsory dispute settlement cannot be missed in such a system. Unfortunately, this conclusion will not bring us any further, as such system hardly exists in present day international law. There is no reason to assume that such system will be accepted in the near future.

Changes in the procedures of particular courts or tribunals will, in my view, only have a minor effect on the acceptability of compulsory procedures. This conclusion does not mean that all the efforts to adapt the procedures in order to increase the use of arbitration or litigation, such as the changes described in this book in relation to the PCA, are useless. It however cannot be the answer to the fundamental problem as identified above.

Nevertheless, it seem to provide an answer to some of the new trends in international law, like the changing position of non-state actors. The expansion of possibilities for the settlement of disputes between these non-state actors and states through the use of the PCA, as discussed by Professor Sanders, should be welcomed. Also, the modernization of procedural rules of the PCA as recently undertaken, is a prerequisite for any further development of international dispute settlement systems. In itself it can however not provide an answer to the question why states avoid taking recourse to arbitration at all. Modern rules and procedures, and active promotion of the institutions are important in the competition between the existing fora for dispute settlement, but that does not bring any extra cases. Although from the perspective of, for example, the PCA such policies are understandable, it does not solve the basic problem of lack of confidence in international third party procedures. If we want to address that question we have to adopt a different approach.

The analysis of the Working Group of the reasons for lack of recourse to the PCA, as reported by Bleich, is illustrative for the little attention that is spent on questions concerning the promotion of third party settlement procedures as such (i.e. unrelated to a particular method or institution). The question why cases are not arbitrated is answered mainly with a reference to the insufficient participation by developing countries. But what about the developed countries? Is it sufficient to conclude, as Bleich reports, that they "are not comfortable bringing their disputes to arbitral institutions, generally"? That the Working Group did not spend too much time on these general questions, but instead focused on practical achievements within reach, is understandable, but it means that one of the most crucial questions is left unanswered.

The present day international legal order needs the participation of all states in law-making, in procedures for supervision, dispute settlement and law-enforcement. This participation can only be achieved if, as already said, the international legal order is build on legitimacy and integrity. Third party dispute settlement procedures play an essential role in this as they form the bridge between individual behaviour and community values. Without these procedures, which guarantee the equitable application of the rules of international law, the mistrust of states of the international community cannot be taken away. Most of our attention should therefore be directed at the development of procedures that meet the concerns of individual states with respect to their perceived loss of sovereign freedom or alienation from their value system, while at the same time enabling the further development of the role of the community by upholding the rule of law.

The articles by Asante and Pinto show that there is not one single perspective on what arbitration is or should be. Arbitration can be alien to a certain culture, necessary expertise or financial means can be lacking, or the procedures can have an biased effect. But even if one adopts the definition and practice of arbitration as developed in the Western society as the standard for arbitration, it does not mean that there should not be room for dispute settlement mechanisms which are different from this type of arbitration. To try to force the development of the world community into the strait-jacket of Western legal perspectives does not contribute to the development of a system of international law that is legitimate in the eyes of all members of the community.

Asante concludes that, although there exist strong reservations to international commercial arbitration, its use can (and should) be made acceptable if restructured to meet the needs of Sub-Saharan Africa. Without such restructuring the attitude will remain rejective, and, in my view, commercial arbitration retain its limited legitimacy. This does not only mean that their attitude in concrete cases will be rejective, but also that the whole system of which this is a part will remain something of an external order, and that it will be difficult to identify oneself as a loyal member of such an order.

The contribution by Pinto about the essence of arbitration, in my view, also points in a similar direction. He concludes that there is a need to formulate a "commonly held perception of the essentials of the arbitral process" which "could lead to a better appreciation of the expectations of the parties as to what could be achieved through arbitration, and lay the foundation for a genuine consensus as to the implications of a state's agreement to submit to the process". In my view this is not only relevant for the future of international arbitration, but for third party dispute settlement in general. Whether the development of arbitration should be directed at a less judicial approach, or whether, for example, conciliation procedures should be strengthened in order to meet this aim, is of less importance. The main point is that states and other actors are actively encouraged to develop and use third party procedures by adequately responding to their reservations concerning these procedures.

3.   A NEW ROLE FOR THE PCA ?

Pinto recommends the undertaking of a careful analytical study which should be multi-disciplinary in order to fully account of all aspects that are of importance in the promotion of adequate procedures. I agree with him, but I would go somewhat further than that and not only propose such study, but a coordinated effort to encourage states to include appropriate dispute settlement mechanisms in their international agreements, in particular in multilateral agreements.

For an outside observer like myself, the impression is that provisions on dispute settlement are often of minor importance in the negotiations of multilateral treaties. There are of course exceptions, like in the law of the sea where from the beginning the dispute settlement provisions played a central role in the acceptability of the 1982 Convention as a whole. Here, the dedicated attention of a group of international lawyers to that aspect of the Convention resulted in the most complete set of dispute settlement provisions in international law. It is a perfect example of a process in which the views of all participating states have been taken into account, and therefore has led to a result that has added to the perception of legitimacy of the whole Convention. It is perhaps not the most simple solution, but it does respond to the needs of the participants, and at the same time offers a system that subjects most disputes to third party procedures, albeit in a number of cases in the form of non-binding conciliation. But even in the last cases, the behaviour of the individuals can be assessed against the legitimate interest of other parties and of the community in general. The development of the panel-procedures in GATT, and in particular the proposals in the draft version of the outcome of the present round of negotiations, shows that conciliation can perform a very useful function.

Bleich mentions that the Working Group recommended increased activities of the Secretary-General of the PCA in UN activities. This could be a first step in what I referred to as a co-ordinated effort to enhance the role of third party dispute settlement. However, I would like go further and suggest the establishment of an international task-force of specialists in international dispute settlement. This task-force could initiate studies, such as proposed by Pinto, but it could also play an active role as a facilitator in international negotiations with respect to dispute settlement. Its task should not be the promotion of specific dispute settlement systems, but trying to assist negotiating parties in finding the most appropriate provisions for the solution of disputes arising in the context of the negotiated document. Such facilitating institution is to a certain extent already created with the Mechanism that was established in the CSCE Meeting of Experts on Peaceful Settlement of Disputes in Valetta in 1991, although this is aimed at finding the appropriate method only after a dispute has arisen.

Such a task-force should consist of experts with great authority and diversity as to their professional and cultural background. It should have the confidence of the parties that the proposals put forward are in their interest. A task-force of this nature could be set up by the Secretary-General of the United Nations, but why should the oldest institution in the context of international arbitration not expand its tasks and create a centre for international dispute settlement of which this task-force could be a part? The PCA of course has an interest in revitalizing its role as an arbitral institution, and the proposals of the Working Group and Expert Group certainly will have some positive effects. But should that preclude the adoption of a supplementary and totally different approach, perfectly fitting within the Decade of International Law, in which the study and promotion of all kind of third party dispute settlement procedures is turned into one of the fundamental objectives of the PCA?

III.   ALBERT JAN VAN DEN BERG[*]

The editors of this work on international arbitration have asked me to make some concluding remarks, from the perspective of a practising business lawyer about the articles published in this issue. Initially, this would limit these concluding remarks to arbitration involving a state as a party in which commercial interests are at stake. That type of arbitration will virtually always be between a state and a non-state entity (usually a foreign corporation). However, as a fairly large number of the articles in this Issue deal with the field of inter-state arbitration, I will venture to comment on that type of arbitration as well.

J.L. Bleich provides a thorough article on the efforts of the Expert Group on Revision of Some Aspects of the Permanent Court of Arbitration. The efforts are most laudable and impressive. In the final analysis, however, I believe that it is the international political climate that will determine whether the improved arbitration services of the PCA will be effectively used by the states.

Characteristically for Judge Howard Holtzmann, the title of his article is understated: "Some Reflections on the Nature of Arbitration". In fact, it is an in depth reflection on the arbitral process. The following statement by Judge Holtzmann merits quotation as it confirms the current thinking of many international business lawyers:

> The adoption by the PCA of the UNCITRAL Arbitration Rules as the basis for its new procedures for arbitration of disputes between states is a milestone in the steady decline of the old perception that there are fundamental differences between the procedural aspects of international public law arbitration and international commercial arbitration.

The article by Professor Rosenne on the attitude of the International Court of Justice towards questions concerning different aspects of the international arbitration process should be compulsory reading for members of any *ad hoc* ICSID Committee deciding on an annulment of an ICSID award. Professor Rosenne concludes that:

> [I]n no case has either the Permanent Court, in relation to decisions of the Mixed Arbitral Tribunals, or the present Court in relation to formal appeals, done anything other than to uphold the impugned decision.

[*] Partner, Stibbe Simont Monahan Duhot, Amsterdam Office; Professor of Law, Erasmus University, Rotterdam; Vice-Chairman, Netherlands Arbitration Institute (NAI); member, International Council for Commercial Arbitration (ICCA); General Editor, *Yearbook Commercial Arbiration* and *The International Handbook on Commercial Arbitration*.

S. Muller and W. Mijs (eds.), The Flame Rekindled, 195–197.

That is somewhat different for some of the *ad hoc* ICSID Committees in the past. They undertook, in an extensive fashion, to educate arbitral tribunals constituted under the Washington Convention on the manner in which reasons should be given for their awards.[1]

Mr. Pinto's article on the 'essence' of international arbitration examines whether there is a distinction between arbitration in international law and dispute settlement by a court. I submit that currently there is, basically, no such distinction. Two matters should be distinguished clearly: on the one hand, the procedure to be followed by the arbitrators; and the other, the law to be applied by the arbitrators. In my opinion, it is incorrect to assume that because the proceedings are more flexible in arbitration, the application of the law is also more relaxed.

Judge Lachs addresses a similar question by inquiring about equity in arbitration and in judicial settlement of disputes. He reaches the conclusion that equity is acquiring an even greater role both in arbitral and judicial settlement. In this connection, equity decisions are to be distinguished from *ex aequo et bono* decisions. Equity is an inherent legal notion, whereas *ex aequo et bono* is a yardstick with which the parties can entrust arbitrators or international judges.[2]

Both articles quietly do away with the myth apparently existing among international public lawyers that international arbitration is something akin to 'free justice' as opposed to the legal decision making by international judicial tribunals.

In his article on "The Perspectives of African Countries on International Commercial Arbitration", Mr. Asante addresses the rising awareness of the African states concerning international arbitration. It is true that African states have historically exhibited reservations regarding arbitration as method of settlement of international disputes. Recent practice, however, has shown that African states need not worry so much. I am aware of a number of cases in which African states were rather successful. These cases concerned commercial transactions to which an African state was a party. It appears logical that this success on the international commercial level will, with time, translate into a more positive perception of international public law arbitration.

Mr. van Blankenstein focuses on a subject that is frequently underestimated in practice: immunity of execution. A large number of states are proud of the application by their courts of the doctrine of restrictive immunity. "No immunity for a state in commercial transactions", is the slogan. The stated intention, unfortunately, is not in line with reality in a fairly large number of cases. When it comes to actual execution, the doctrine suddenly disappears and immunity becomes absolute. Why? "Oh, that

---

1. One of the arbitrators even being a former President of the ICJ, *see* Klöckner *v.* Cameroon, decision of May 3, 1985, reported *in* XI Yearbook Commercial Arbitration 162-184 (1986).
2. *See, e.g.*, UNCITRAL Arbitration Rules, Article 33(2); Statute of the International Court of Justice, Article 38(2).

is political", is the answer. Only a few states have taken the logical step that the waiver of immunity from jurisdiction also means a waiver of immunity from execution.

Finally, I believe that one of the most prominent future roles of the PCA is that of an alternative for administered arbitration between states and foreign private parties. There is no need to repeat my views here;[3] suffice it to mention that, once more, I agree with Pieter Sanders' suggestions, put forward in his article on "Private Parties and the Permanent Court of Arbitration", as to how to awaken this "sleeping beauty".

---

3. *See* my article *The Permanent Court of Arbitration at the Peace Palace, The Hague - A New Role for International Commercial Arbitration?, in* Law and Reality - Essays on National and International Procedural Law, Liber Amicorum A. Voskuil 19-25 (1992).

TABLE OF CASES

DECISIONS OF INTERNATIONAL COURTS AND TRIBUNALS

S. Muller and W. Mijs (eds.), The Flame Rekindled, 199–202.
© 1994 *Leiden Journal of International Law. Printed in the Netherlands.*

DECISIONS OF NATIONAL COURTS

France

Sweden

Switzerland

United States of America

Index